Animals in Narrative Film and Television

Animals in Narrative Film and Television

Strange and Familiar Creatures

Edited by
Karin Beeler
and Stan Beeler

LEXINGTON BOOKS
Lanham • Boulder • New York • London

Published by Lexington Books
An imprint of The Rowman & Littlefield Publishing Group, Inc.
4501 Forbes Boulevard, Suite 200, Lanham, Maryland 20706
www.rowman.com

86-90 Paul Street, London EC2A 4NE, United Kingdom

Copyright © 2022 by The Rowman & Littlefield Publishing Group, Inc.

All rights reserved. No part of this book may be reproduced in any form or by any electronic or mechanical means, including information storage and retrieval systems, without written permission from the publisher, except by a reviewer who may quote passages in a review.

British Library Cataloguing in Publication Information Available

Library of Congress Cataloging-in-Publication Data Available

ISBN 978-1-66690-481-9 (cloth) | ISBN 978-1-66690-483-3 (paperback) | ISBN 978-1-66690-482-6 (ebook)

Dedication
In honor of the animals that have been a part of our lives.

Contents

Acknowledgments ix

Introduction 1
Karin Beeler and Stan Beeler

PART I: ANIMAL CHARACTERS: RACIAL, ETHNIC, AND SOCIAL CONTEXTS **11**

1   "Beneath the Surface Lies the Future": Narrative, Characterization, and the Natural World in *seaQuest DSV*'s Darwin 13
    Alissa Burger

2   Ducks, Ducks and More Ducks: Comedy and Social Class in Animated TV 33
    David Hipple

3   "Don't Just Fly, Soar": Reading Disability in Disney's Animation *Dumbo* (1941) and Live-Action Remake *Dumbo* (2019) 57
    Jessica Gibson

4   Making the Invisible Visible: Displaced and Marginalized Animal Characters in Samuel Fuller's *White Dog* and Kornél Mundruczó's *White God* 73
    Heather Rolufs and Karin Beeler

PART II: ANIMALS AND NARRATIVE FUNCTIONS: MONSTERS/VICTIMS/HEROES **95**

5	Worse than Their Bite: Dogs and Horror *Catherine Pugh*	97
6	The Bad Habits of Rabbits: An Ecocritical Examination of Rabbits as Antagonists in Film *MK Pinder*	119
7	Of Animals and Aliens: Identifying with the Nonhuman Other in *Guardians of the Galaxy* *Jessica Bay and Jonathan Osborn*	135

PART III: ANIMAL/HUMAN HYBRIDS AND OTHER CREATURES — 153

8	Hormone Monsters and Animal Antagonists: Animating Teen Horrors and Promoting Eudaimonia in *Big Mouth* (Netflix, 2017–) *Georgia Aitaki*	155
9	The Transcendence of the Borders: The Animal Hero in Hosoda Mamoru's *The Boy and the Beast* *Katsuya Izumi*	173
10	The Esperpento of *Kipo and the Age of Wonderbeasts* *Sumor Ziva Sheppard*	187
11	(Un)learning with "Monsters": Animals, Patriarchal Oppression, and Ethics of Care in Guillermo del Toro's *The Shape of Water* *Monica Sousa*	203

Index	219
About the Contributors	225

Acknowledgments

We would like to thank Lexington Books for publishing this unique collection on animal characters in film and television. We are very grateful to Jessie Tepper (associate acquisitions editor) for her initial interest in this book and for her guidance and flexibility along the way. We also thank all of the contributors who have made this book possible; they shared their fascinating research on animals in narrative film and television, and responded to our editorial comments, emails, and deadlines in a timely fashion.

We particularly appreciate our family for giving us the time to focus on this project and will now try to make up for some of the lost moments! On the professional front, we recognize the importance of the work of our colleagues at the University of Northern British Columbia and elsewhere, who have published and presented on animal topics over the years. We thank Irene Gammel and Jason Wang, editors of *Creative Resilience and Covid-19* (2022), who published our chapter on adapting dog performance events and community theater for online environments during the Covid pandemic. Over the last few years, we have learned much about the art of collaboration during the filming of canine performance activities, and it has been rewarding to see how our respective personal and professional interests in screen art and animals have become more interconnected.

The major reason for our focus on the topic of animals undoubtedly stems from the presence of real animals in our lives. For almost thirty-five years, animals have shared our domestic space and have been part of many other activities such as canine performance events, educational visits to schools, and pet therapy visits at long-term care facilities. Our cats, German Shepherds, Newfoundland dogs, Newfoundland cross, Schipperke, Cavalier King Charles Spaniel, Keeshond, Pug, hedgehog, and ferrets have given us some rare insights into animals but have also taught us that they will always remain, on some level, enigmatic. We hope that this volume will assist others in getting closer to understanding animals and their stories as imagined on screen.

Introduction
Karin Beeler and Stan Beeler

In the last ten years, animal studies has burgeoned as a scholarly field and there has been a concomitant increase in the number of books and articles published on the subject of animals in recent years. This ongoing interest in a relatively new area of academic study may be partially due to increasing concern with global climate change and other kinds of environmental factors affecting animal species. A study published in *Animal Conservation* has identified "a total of 562 lost species (137 amphibians, 257 reptiles, 38 birds and 130 mammals)" that "have not been reliably observed in >50 years."[1] In addition to concerns surrounding the survival of wild animals, there has also been a noticeable increase in interest in animal rights for domestic animals, including calls for more humane approaches to animal care. Cultural anthropologists, historians, literary critics, and media scholars have also added their voices to the discussion of animals in society. Kristen Guest, Monica Mattfeld, Brett Mills, and Margo DeMello, for example, have contributed significantly to the corpus of significant multidisciplinary scholarly investigations of animals and their role in our world.[2]

Although many of the texts listed above deal with the situation of animals in a realistic context, our book approaches these concepts in a somewhat different fashion. *Animals in Narrative Film and Television: Strange and Familiar Creatures* engages primarily with fictional representations of animals and the way these representations intersect with a variety of social issues. Fiction can serve as a powerful way of presenting the uncomfortable truths of the treatment of animals in our society that viewers may find off-putting or tendentious in a documentary format. Animals have long functioned as popular subjects in narrative forms. *Aesop's fables*[3] are probably some of the best known texts and most widely circulated examples of the anthropomorphized animal in narrative fiction. As a narrative form, the fable has cemented the relationship between animal representations and human behavior, combining animal traits (e.g., the speedy hare and the slow moving tortoise) with human characteristics (e.g., human language, along with the characteristics of arrogance/hubris vs. perseverance) in order to tell a story that concludes with a moral. One of *Aesop's fables'* most famous fables, "The Hare and the Tortoise," represents the slow-moving tortoise winning a race against the hare (who takes a nap because he is convinced that there is no contest), and is usually read as an illustration of how "slow and steady wins the race." Today, however, as our collection suggests, the story may resonate somewhat differently in the context of disability discourse, for example, which might approach the tortoise's "slowness" as an analogy for human beings with physical challenges. Animal characters in ancient animal fables and in the more recent animal narratives examined in this book may therefore find more currency with present-day audiences when we analyze them in relation to disability issues or contemporary views of cultural, gender, and class differences. The contributors in this edited collection have focused on a range of issues, including the relationship between animals and concepts of social justice, the representation of marginalized and dislocated animals, images of the heroic and the monstrous animal, and critiques of animal characters that foster stereotypes, and depictions of the animal or creature in relation to the ethics of care. In their respective chapters, these scholars have both highlighted and erased some of the boundaries between animal/human worlds as presented in narrative film and television.

While this collection does not emphasize literary fiction, the narrative components of literary forms such as a fable—that include character development and various transformations that occur over the course of a narrative, along with aesthetic techniques that reinforce all of these elements—also apply very well to narratives in film and television.

Twentieth-century and twenty-first-century representations of animals in film and television have continued some of the storytelling techniques from earlier literary works and adapted them for screen genres such as anime, comedy, horror, fantasy, and science fiction. The anthropomorphized animal and many of the creatures mentioned in literary works such as *Aesop's Fables*, the Chinese novel *Journey to the West*, *Charlotte's Web*, and *Watership Down* have continued to be prominent in live action film and television. This book covers animals ranging from dogs, rabbits, dolphins, elephants, and mosquitoes to ducks. Some of the animals discussed are beasts of an indeterminate nature, exhibiting characteristics of real animals, often combined with human or otherworldly attributes. These liminal figures are represented in both live action and animated films; they include bear- and pig-like creatures (*The Boy and the Beast*), a mutated leopard (*Kipo and the Age of Wonderbeasts*), a genetically enhanced raccoon (*Guardians of the Galaxy*), and the amphibian-like Asset creature in *The Shape of Water*.

DEFINITION OF THE TERM *ANIMAL*

The somewhat open-ended application of the word *animal* to the host of transitional figures mentioned above leads us to a discussion of the parameters of our understanding of animals as a concept. This book's primary use of the term *animal* refers to non-human animals, although in some cases the creatures presented in the various chapters are hybrid based on a combination of beast-like and human features as discussed in Katsuya Izumi's chapter about the film *The Boy and the Beast*. The inclusion of the hybrid animal concept in this volume allows us to recognize that it is virtually impossible to completely separate the "animal" from human contexts in fiction, even in the case of realistic-looking animals that are represented in live action film/television. The point of view techniques in film/television that enable the fusing of an animal's perspective with a human viewer's and the intervention of genre considerations (such as the science fiction world of *Guardians of the Galaxy*, where a genetically altered raccoon-like creature can exist and behave like a human) make this kind of neat separation difficult. Fictionalized narratives certainly give the creators more latitude to explore the human–animal connections as well as the intersectionality of race, class, gender, and disability in a creative way that facilitates the blurring of boundaries between animal and human.

GENRE/STYLE/AESTHETIC CHOICES AND ANIMALS

As already suggested, representations of animals and their narrative function are shaped or contextualized by genre. Fortunately some genres allow a certain freedom in their representation of real-world subjects that more realistic forms of fiction do not. Rosemary Jackson has pointed out that fantasy (we can include science fiction and horror here too) can offer insight into issues in a way that other more realistic texts do not: "[. . .] the 'value' of fantasy has seemed to reside in precisely this resistance to definition, in its 'free-floating' and escapist qualities. Literary fantasies have appeared to be 'free' from many of the conventions and restraints of more realistic texts [. . .]."[4] Yet fantasy still suggests parallels with actual social issues in the real world: "Like any other text, a literary fantasy is produced within and determined by, its social context. Though it might struggle against the limits of this context, often being articulated upon that very struggle, it cannot be understood in isolation from it."⁵ Part of the ability of fantasy to resonate this way is through defamiliarization, which is a technique that serves as a means of highlighting issues in a different way than the didactic form of a documentary dealing with animal rights, for example. Victor Shklovsky's term *defamiliarization* allows us to consider strange or unusual representations of animals (including hybrid animal-human forms) in fictional narratives and to reflect on the connections between animals and human behavior in our own societies. Shklovsky argued that "The technique of art is to make objects 'unfamiliar,' to make forms difficult, to increase the difficulty and length of perception because the process of perception is an aesthetic end in itself and must be prolonged. Art is a way of experiencing the artfulness of an object."⁶

Bertolt Brecht's Verfremdungseffekt (alienation/distancing effect) operates in a similar way and is discussed in Heather Rolufs and Karin Beeler's chapter; certain cinematography and editing techniques (pov shots, fragmented images, quick cuts) can also produce an alienation effect. In other words, the representation of familiar animals in a strange or disorienting style (which is often determined by genre or medium) can force the viewer to engage critically with what is shown on screen (e.g., social injustice) in a way that transcends the limitation of daily life which often fosters de-sensitization or complacency.

Given the many tools that screen culture has at its disposal to convey the familiar (animal or human behavior) in an altered, strange manner (e.g., as supernatural canines in horror film), perhaps it is not all surprising that every chapter in this edited collection includes examples drawn from fantasy, science fiction, or horror. This speaks not only to the choices of the creative teams who produced these works for a variety of demographically determined audiences but also to the international scholarly interest in the use of these speculative genres to represent animals as a point of intersection with human societal issues.

This volume examines how representations of animal characters in different narrative contexts reflect societal attitudes toward animals as informed by the intersectionality of culture, race, gender, class, and disability. Setting and different historical contexts have also been considered as instrumental elements in shaping the depiction of animals and their narrative function. The discussion in these chapters reveals the ways in which representations of animals in film and television deviate from more conventional character types. With this in mind our contributors have examined a host of characters or paradigmatic representations, including animal heroes, villains, antagonists, victims, and the complex category of the anti-hero. Special attention is paid to how the intersectionality of systems of social privilege and disadvantage operates in these narratives, and to the way animals fulfill or challenge the narrative expectations of various genres in relation to their anthropomorphized and animal traits or behavior. Since modern film and television are noteworthy for their reliance upon genre conventions to attract and maintain audiences, chapter contributions to this volume include a variety of popular genres and formats. In addition to fantasy, science fiction, horror genres, the genres of romance, comedy, and various animated forms have been analyzed in the context of their conventions and in relation to the effect that these structural imperatives have upon the representation of animals. Since this book focuses on visual narratives, there is also consideration of aesthetic features such as cinematography and televisual techniques in the representation of animals and their "stories"; these aesthetic techniques reinforce social issues that need to be brought to the forefront to criticize certain practices and to effect change in our respective societies.

CHAPTER DIVISIONS

Animals in Narrative Film and Television is divided into three sections, although all of the contributions include some consideration of social, gender, race, or ability/disability, and the intersectionality of these issues with animal facets. Genre or style forms an important part of many of these discussions as contributors analyze animals in horror, fantasy, science fiction, comedy, animated film, and animated television.

Part I, "Animal Characters: Racial, Ethnic, and Social Contexts," consists of chapters by Alissa Burger, David Hipple, Jessica Gibson, Heather Rolufs, and Karin Beeler. Burger's "'Beneath the Surface Lies the Future': Narrative, Characterization, and the Natural World with *seaQuest DSV's* Darwin" is a study of *SeaQuest DSV*, a short-lived (1993–1996) live action science fiction television series that follows the adventures of the military personnel and scientists aboard a deep-sea vessel. The main animal character in the series is Darwin, a dolphin who is able to speak with the aid of an electronic translation device. Darwin functions as a "a representation of a dolphin that transcends the limitations of human-animal connection and communication that are currently possible, through Darwin's ability to speak, which opens up new vistas of human-animal interaction." He helps an autistic child during animal-assisted therapy sessions while also functioning as a way of "interrogating the role of training, command and performance." As characters, dolphins affirm "connection and cooperation" therefore offering a way of reflecting on social relations and social justice. David Hipple's "Ducks, Ducks and More Ducks: Comedy and Social Class in Animated TV" examines social convention and the exploits of a vegetarian vampire duck in a UK children's television show. He analyzes animal characters as a way of interrogating "social and cultural matters that might seem awkwardly sensitive in more conventional drama."

Hipple's study of comic technique through language (e.g., dialects), regional, and national stereotypes, and the use of horror tropes in children's television reveals the function of humanoid animal characters in a narrative designed for an audience comprising both children and adults.

The topic of disability and social norms is the focus of Jessica Gibson's "'Don't Just Fly, Soar': Reading Disability in Disney's Animation *Dumbo* (1941) and Live-Action Remake *Dumbo* (2019)." This chapter highlights how Dumbo's journey "aligns with the social model and affirmation model of disability." Gibson demonstrates how Dumbo, the flying elephant with enormous ears, is initially "othered and marginalized because of his physical difference." However, over the course of the narrative of these two films, he becomes a circus star and hero. The circus focus and comparisons between the original animated film and the live action remake allow viewers to see differences in "societal attitudes towards animal welfare."

Heather Rolufs and Karin Beeler's chapter, "Making the Invisible Visible: Displaced and Marginalized Animal Characters in Samuel Fuller's *White Dog* and Kornél Mundruczó's *White God*," reflects on racial and ethnic Others through canine characters that are cast in a variety of roles. These animals are presented as heroes, victims, monsters, and villains at various points in their respective narratives. Rolufs and Beeler engage with the notion that "both films represent the manifestation of different cultural anxieties" and demonstrate that "man's best friend" is used "to unmask systemic issues about displacement and marginalization within societal structures." Beeler and Rolufs address these human–canine relationships in *White Dog* and *White God*, analyzing how canine characters "function in various spaces in order to critique humanity by existing within society and outside of it."

Part II, "Animals and Narrative Functions: Monsters/Victims/Heroes," continues to explore canines as various character types but delves further into the genres of horror and science fiction. In "Worse than Their Bite: Dogs and Horror," Catherine Pugh analyzes the dog's position as "an in-between creature" and how this contributes to the popularity of the canine in horror film and television. She argues that the "horror hound" is a combination of the natural and the supernatural; he serves as a "friend to some" and as an "antagonist to others" and "becomes more than animal, if not quite human." MK Pinder's "The Bad Habits of Rabbits" also considers the animal antagonist while not forgetting their parallel roles as victims. Pinder analyzes animals in the form of monstrous or uncanny rabbits. This chapter investigates the relationship between "ecological anxieties" and the cultural representation of rabbits in films such as *Watership Down*, *Night of the Lepus*, *Donnie Darko*, and David Lynch's *Rabbits*. These animals appear in multiple settings ranging from the countryside of Britain to the Australian landscape. The science fiction, fantasy, and horror films selected present rabbits as the "underestimated tricksters of the animal world," thus establishing some unique representations of the rabbit that are creatively re-imagined but based on their real-world image as an ecological threat.

Re-imagined creatures and beings are also the subject of Jessica Bay and Jonathan Osborn's contribution "Of Animals and Aliens: Identifying with the Nonhuman Other in *Guardians of the Galaxy*." The chapter opens with a consideration of a theory of pets, and this informs Bay's and Osborn's consideration of the animal creatures and aliens in the *Guardians of the Galaxy* franchise. The series of films that are the subject of this chapter tend to aggregate animal and alien creatures under the social function that is a liminal case somewhere between pets and family members.

Part III of this book, "Animal/Human Hybrids and Other Creatures," includes studies of some rather unusual animal characters in animated fantasy and live action science fiction film. The authors consider examples of animal characters and hybrid creatures. Georgia Aitaki, Katsuya Izumi, and Sumor Ziva Sheppard study animals or beast figures in animated film while Monica Sousa focuses on Guillermo del Toro's live action film *The Shape of Water*. Georgia Aitaki's "Hormone Monsters and Animal Antagonists: Animating Teen Horrors and Promoting Eudaimonia in *Big Mouth* (Netflix, 2017–)" examines "anthropomorphized creatures, such as Hormone Monsters and animal antagonists" as "a powerful visual and narrative mechanism" to engage with the "pubertal (emotional and physical) changes" experienced by the human teenagers in this coming of age series. Animal characters such as Depression Kitty (an anthropomorphized cat) and Anxiety Mosquito bring the issues of "teen identity, gender, sexuality, and mental health" to the forefront and serve a didactic function in this narrative. While not animals in the same sense, the Hormone Monsters suggest a kind of "primordial animality" and with their "horns, tails, sharp teeth and hairy bodies" are reminiscent of creatures in *Monsters Inc*. Katsuya Izumi also explores animated screen culture but in the relation to Japanese anime. His chapter, "The Transcendence of the Borders: The Animal Hero in Hosoda Mamoru's *The Boy and the Beast*," undertakes a study of an animated film that incorporates certain genre traits specifically present in the Japanese form known as anime. Izumi examines "various characteristics and hybrid traits that the film uses to depict the Beast Kingdom and the animal characters as preparatory devices for Hosoda (the director) to convey the importance of transcending the borders that exist between different species." He argues that *The Boy and the Beast* can be differentiated from his earlier film *Wolf Children* since Hosoda is not as interested in showing ferociousness of animals "as a cultural construct" as he is in *Wolf Children*. Instead it appears that *The Boy and the Beast* reflects an interest in transcending "the border between the human and animal worlds"; the narratives surrounding the educational contexts and transformative possibilities for characters therefore play an equally important role in the development of animal/beast-like characters and human characters.

Sumor Ziva Sheppard's study of the animated television series "The Esperpento of *Kipo and the Age of Wonderbeasts*" considers the use of the *esperpento* form, "an early, twentieth century, Spanish theatrical genre used to make social critiques that often included racist or antisemitic ideas." Sheppard examines the concept of a human–animal hybrid as a hero in the series, while pointing out how "the very same hybrid visibility" is undercut in the narrative. The chapter reveals that "the function of animals in *Kipo and the Age of Wonderbeasts*—whether anthropomorphized, hybridized, mutated or in their natural state— warns of, rather than promotes, a reality in which human civilization has fully embraced social inclusivity and diversity." Sheppard states, that as a form, anime can encourage anthropomorphism and hybridity, but in the case of this television series, "the animals chosen [including monkeys] align with the perpetuation of racist and misogynistic beliefs."

In the final chapter in this edited volume, "(Un)learning with 'Monsters': Animals, Patriarchal Oppression, and Ethics of Care in Guillermo del Toro's *The Shape of Water*," Monica Sousa explores "animalistic" and animalized qualities in relation to the construction of the monstrous. She analyzes the depiction of an unusual amphibious creature called the Asset in this fantasy film. While he is described as an Amazonian river god, she argues that he "displays animalistic qualities" and is animalized by human beings while in "their care." Sousa's chapter argues that "ethics of care approaches can allow people to learn and unlearn with 'monsters' – animalized/dehumanized beings that are treated as monstrous." The work of animal ethics scholars facilitates a study of del Toro's film, thus encouraging people to "unlearn oppressive anthropocentric attitudes" and to learn how to view other creatures "as subjects worthy of care." Sousa's concluding remarks about the multifaceted way of understanding the term "animal" reinforce the diverse representations of "animals" in this book.

CONCLUSION

Whether functioning as images of heroism, villains, monsters, victims, or something in-between like anti-heroes, animals in live action and animated film and television present complex issues involving race, culture, class, gender, ability/disability, mental health, and animal ethics to their audience. In this collection contributors also show that in screen culture, cinematography can play a key role in reinforcing certain kinds of representation. While some representations rely more heavily on anthropomorphization than others, what remains clear is that the "figure" of the animal offers many of the creators of the films and television shows discussed in this study the opportunity to engage with human–animal relations in ways that recognize hybridity and the transcendence of certain characters or forms. Through the incorporation of animal figures, these screen narratives have gained the ability to critique actions carried out by human beings and teach us how to become more human in our interactions with the non-human creatures that share our world.

NOTES

1. An article in the journal *Animal Conservation* has identified over 500 lost species. T.E. Martin et al., "'Lost Taxa' and Their Conservation Implications," *Animal Conservation* May 16, 2022). Abstract, 1. https://doi.org/10.1111/acv.12788

2. Studies like Margo DeMello's *Animals and Society: An Introduction to Human-Animal Studies* (2nd edition. Margo DeMello. Columbia University Press, 2021), *Animal Places: Lively Cartographies of Human Animal Relations*, eds. Jacob Bull et al. (Routledge, 2018), *Equestrian Cultures: Horses, Human Society, and the Discourse of Modernity*, eds. Kristen Guest and Monica Mattfeld (University of Chicago Press, 2019), *Reading Cats and Dogs: Companion Animals in World Literature*, eds. Francoise Besson et al. (Lexington Books, 2020), *Animal Horror Cinema: Genre, History and Criticism*, eds. Katarina Greggersdotter et al. (Palgrave Macmillan, 2015) and Brett Mills' *Animals on Television* (Palgrave Macmillan, 2017) are just a few of the scholarly works that have contributed to the multidisciplinary interest in animal studies.

3. *Aesop's Fables* are "attributed to the slave Aesop" who was also purported to be mute. Joyce E. Salisbury, *The Beast Within: Animals in the Middle Ages*, 2nd edition (New York: Routledge, 2011), 83.

4. Rosemary Jackson *Fantasy: The Literature of Subversion* (London, New York: Routledge), 1981, 1.

5. Rosemary Jackson, 3.

6. Victor Shklovsky, "Art as Technique," 1917, in *Russian Formalist Criticism: Four Essays,* eds. and trans. Lee T. Lemon and Marion J. Reis (Lincoln: University of Nebraska Press, 1965), 12.

BIBLIOGRAPHY

Jackson, Rosemary. *Fantasy: The Literature of Subversion*. London, New York: Routledge, 1981.

Martin, T. E., Bennett, G. C., Fairbairn, A., and Mooers, A. O., "'Lost Taxa' and Their Conservation Implications." *Animal Conservation*, May 16, 2022. Abstract, 1. https://doi.org/10.1111/acv.12788.

Salisbury, Joyce E. *The Beast Within: Animals in the Middle Ages*. Second Edition. New York: Routledge, 2011.

Shklovsky, Victor. "Art as Technique." In *Russian Formalist Criticism: Four Essays*, edited and translated by Lee T. Lemon and Marion J. Reis, 3–24. Lincoln: University of Nebraska Press, 1965, 3–24.

Part I

ANIMAL CHARACTERS

RACIAL, ETHNIC, AND SOCIAL CONTEXTS

Chapter 1

"Beneath the Surface Lies the Future"

Narrative, Characterization, and the Natural World in seaQuest DSV's Darwin

Alissa Burger

seaQuest DSV was a short-lived (1993–1996) science fiction television series that followed the adventures of military personnel and scientists aboard the eponymous deep-submergence vessel, including the crew's interactions with a range of marine animals, the most notable of which was a dolphin named Darwin. Animals have played a significant role in the science fiction genre, and as Sherryl Vint explains, science fiction creates opportunities for "grappling with alterity and granting subjectivity to the non-human," which often "rais[es] questions about how we interact with living animals, as well as about environmentalism, human/animal symbiosis, and animals as companions or fellow sentient beings."[1]

While primetime television in the 1990s was bursting with science fiction series that explored space, including *Star Trek: The Next Generation* (1987–1994), *Star Trek: Deep Space Nine* (1993–1999), *Babylon 5* (1994–1998), *Star Trek: Voyager* (1995–2001), and *Stargate SG-1* (1997–2007), *seaQuest DSV* set its exploration narrative on Earth, plumbing the depths of the oceans rather than the far reaches of the galaxy.[2] Ryan Britt argues that in a span of television awash with science fiction series, *seaQuest DSV* "was not only an intersection of where sci-fi TV had been at that point, but also a harbinger of where it was going" with a unique "blend of nostalgia and focus on the future."[3] With the first season set in the then-near future of 2018,[4] *seaQuest DSV* presented a world in which nations are brought together under the United Earth Oceans Coalition (UEO), deep-sea exploration and colonization are the norm, and people are able to live, work, and even thrive on the ocean floors. This new frontier naturally comes with a range of challenges and negotiations, including undersea piracy, territorial disputes, and ecological disasters. The *seaQuest* is the UEO's flagship, operated by a crew of military personnel and scientists who work to defuse conflicts, respond to emergencies, and further explore the deep-sea world. While *seaQuest DSV* had several components that should have set the series up for success—including Steven Spielberg as an executive producer, Roy Scheider in a starring role as Captain Nathan Bridger, and Woods Hole Oceanographic Institution's Bob Ballard as a science advisor—the series floundered after the first season, with on-set conflict, sweeping cast changes, and increasingly far-fetched storylines contributing to the series' steep decline and abrupt cancellation in the middle of the third season. While the series has garnered little critical or popular acclaim and has now largely been forgotten, one of its most memorable and inventive elements was the character of Darwin, a bottlenose dolphin who was able to speak through the use of an electronic translator called a vocorder, following a tradition of talking animals in popular culture that allows viewers to imaginatively engage with animals' perspectives and explore the possibility of communication, including how animals would express themselves, what new perceptions they would offer, and how they would respond to and engage with their human counterparts.

Darwin serves a wide range of narrative functions: as an aquatic mammal, he provides insights and perspectives on the ocean and larger natural world that his human crewmates are unable to achieve for themselves, at times even literally speaking for the other marine life he encounters. He is a research subject, a hero, a friend, a crew member, an ambassador for his species with non-*seaQuest* humans, and occasionally a driving force of the narrative itself, such as when he becomes ill after swimming through the emissions of a black smoker,[5] a geological formation that results when hydrothermal vents form chimney-like structures and emit black smoke from iron sulfide deposits.[6] Darwin also has a range of interpersonal relationships and connections with different members of the *seaQuest*'s crew that contribute to and further the series' larger narrative, particularly in the first season. Darwin's most significant relationships and connections are with Captain Nathan Bridger and teen genius Lucas Wolenczak (Jonathan Brandis). These two characters view and engage with Darwin in different ways, which highlights multiple facets of Darwin's unique personality while also revealing the significance others ascribe to him in their interactions through the anthropocentric perspective of these human–animal connections. Finally, there are two episodes in which Darwin is threatened by non-*seaQuest* humans who look to him for knowledge and enlightenment, first by a black market trader known as The Regulator (played by John Bedford Lloyd)[7] and later by war criminal Milos Tezlof (played by William Shatner).[8] Darwin's development both as an independent character and through the human–animal interactions and relationships featured in the series provide the opportunity to critically consider Darwin's representation and significance within these larger interpersonal and social contexts.

DOLPHINS IN POPULAR CULTURE

The representation of Darwin—both as a character and in his interaction with the human characters within the series—builds on a long tradition of historical accounts and cultural representations of dolphins. Humankind has long been fascinated with dolphins, with representations of these animals appearing in the art and culture of a wide range of ancient civilizations, from Greeks and Romans to Aboriginal Australians and Pacific Islanders.[9] An exploration of the artifacts from these cultures reveals that "Dolphins were painted on palace walls, sculpted into statues, stamped on gold coins, tattooed on bodies."[10] Our present day is no different. In *Voices of the Ocean: A Journey into the Wild and Haunting World of Dolphins*, Susan Casey embarks on a quest to understand not just dolphins themselves but also the significance ascribed to them and the affinities people form with these animals. As Casey reflects at the start of this endeavor, "Once I started paying attention to dolphins, I began to notice them everywhere. They were no strangers to the headlines, and extremely popular on the internet,"[11] as well as in art, culture, and current events, running the gamut from heroes to victims. These connections and representations take a wide range of forms, from advocating for animal rights to captive performance, near-deification to anthropomorphized projection. Regardless of the specific impulse or ascribed significance, humans' perennial fascination with dolphins is undeniable.

Popular culture representations of animals have a significant impact on how humans understand those animals. As Marie-France Boissonneault argues, "The ability of human beings to relate to nonhuman animals is often correlated with the level of attention that specific species are awarded through various media interpretations."[12] As a result, the roles and representations of animals of all kinds in popular culture is deserving of critical consideration. This influence is the central focus of the article "Dolphins in Popular Literature and Media" by John Fraser, Diana Reiss, Paul Boyle, Katherine Lemcke, Jessica Sickler, Elizabeth Elliot, Barbara Newman, and Sarah Gruber. Fraser et al. conducted "a review of popular media to ascertain the common themes used to characterize dolphins in literature, television, movies, and music to ascertain whether such themes provide reinforcement for common misconceptions"[13] and how these representations might shape people's beliefs about dolphins. These representations and misinformed perceptions can be cause for concern, as these impressions can directly influence individuals' understanding of, empathy with, and response to dolphins. This exposure to representations of dolphins may elicit different responses from individuals, ranging from a desire to view them in captivity, attempts to interact with them in ways that may disregard the health and safety of the animals themselves, or the investment individuals may feel in conservation and protection efforts. Fraser et al. express concern that "the pervasiveness of exaggerated portrayals of dolphins in popular culture, whether positive or negative, could make it difficult for the public to distinguish fact from fiction and might pose a barrier for science learning,"[14] while Boissonneault's reservation is a more general worry that "in attributing select human behaviours to 'animal' performers, consumers may not always have an accurate assessment of animal behaviour [,] which in turn may not be in the best interest of the portrayed nonhuman species."[15] Just as representation matters in portraying and understanding the diverse range of human experiences, the representation of animals matters as well, and is a central force in shaping how people perceive, respond to, and engage with these animals, in both representation and in real life.

Fraser et al. identified four main themes in the representation of dolphins in literature and popular culture that influence individuals' perceptions and understanding of these animals, including:

1. Dolphin as peer to humans, of equal intelligence or at least capable of communicating with humans or helping humans;
2. Dolphin as representative of peace, unconditional love, or an idealized freedom in harmony with the natural order;
3. Dolphin as naïve or innocent, in which they are subordinate and vulnerable; and
4. Dolphin as superior to humans, associated with a higher power or intelligence.[16]

These themes are large in scope and often contradictory: dolphins are smarter than humans but also more innocent and less sophisticated, "superior" but also "subordinate and vulnerable."[17] This is a combination that reveals more about humans than it does about the dolphins themselves, and through these representations, readers and viewers "have the opportunity to examine deep-seated cultural and personal beliefs about our relationships with animals and theirs with us."[18] In the case of dolphins specifically, the trends identified by Fraser et al. suggest that as humans, we yearn for something bigger and wiser than ourselves, while at the same time wanting that something to be manageable, accessible, and cute, and when taken to amoral extremes, controllable and exploitable.

Popular culture has a plentiful and varied range of dolphin representations. Flipper first swam into the hearts and minds of adoring audiences in the film *Flipper* (1963), with accounts of his heroism further explored in *Flipper's*

New Adventure (1964), the television series *Flipper* (1964–1968), the film *Flipper* (1996), and the television series *Flipper: The New Adventures* (1995-2000). Dolphins abound in young adult literature, including Scott O'Dell's *Island of the Blue Dolphins* (1960), Karen Hesse's *The Music of Dolphins* (1996), and Ben M. Baglio's *Dolphin Diaries* series (2002–2003), where the focus is often on the affinity and relationships between dolphins and the novels' young protagonists, who invariably have a "special connection" with the dolphins they encounter, following an established pattern of representation of "nonhuman animals displaying human-like qualities and behaviours . . . geared toward younger audiences."[19] For young readers interested in true dolphin tales, there's Margaret Davidson's classic *Nine True Dolphin Stories* (1950). The fourth book of Douglas Adams's *Hitchhiker's Guide to the Galaxy* series is titled *So Long, and Thanks for All the Fish* (1985), a parting salvo attributed to the Earth's dolphins as they disappear from the planet prior to its annihilation (and memorably included as a jaunty tune in the 2005 film adaptation *The Hitchhiker's Guide to the Galaxy*). There are also numerous books touting the metaphysical power of dolphins, including Timothy Wyllie's *Dolphins, ETs and Angels: Adventures Among Spiritual Intelligences* (1988) and *Dolphins, Telepathy, and Underwater Birthing* (1993), Amanda Cochrane and Karena Callen's *Dolphins and Their Power to Heal* (1994), and Frank Joseph's *Our Dolphin Ancestors: Keepers of Lost Knowledge and Healing Wisdom* (2016). Across this wide range of representations—whether on the page or onscreen, fiction or reality, and regardless of their specific intended audience—these dolphin narratives tell readers and viewers more about how humans think about dolphins and the meaning humans ascribe to these animals than they do about the dolphins themselves.

SEAQUEST DSV AND DARWIN

With Darwin, *seaQuest DSV* builds on these established traditions, including emphasis of dolphin intelligence and the dolphin–human bond, combined with the science fiction genre's promise of technology that can expand the boundaries of knowledge and engagement between beings. As with these previous representations of dolphins, the meaning ascribed to Darwin by different characters is also revealing, reflecting the human characters' needs, desires, and motivations.

Darwin is a bottlenose dolphin. After Bridger rescued Darwin from a fishing net, the two became companions, with Bridger able to communicate with Darwin through hand signals. Bridger is a decorated naval captain and designed the *seaQuest*, though he became a recluse following the loss of his wife and son, and on his isolated island hideaway, Darwin is the only other living being with whom he regularly interacts, a connection with the sea and the research he loves.

When Bridger is brought onboard the *seaQuest*, his colleague UEO Admiral Noyce (Richard Herd) brings Darwin along as well, though deep-sea ecologist Andrew Thaler notes that this is "in clear violation of CITES and the Marine Mammal Protection Act."[20] Noyce has also used subterfuge to get Bridger onboard, offering a tour of the vessel when his real intent is to manipulate Bridger into a high-stakes military showdown situation that he hopes will force Bridger to assume captaincy of the *seaQuest*, bringing Darwin along as an added incentive for Bridger to stay and as a way to make him feel "at home" onboard. This is not an auspicious beginning in the UEO's interactions with Bridger or Darwin. Both man and dolphin are overtly controlled, managed, and made to serve military aims, including Darwin tagging an enemy ship with a tracking device so the *seaQuest* can fire torpedoes after the vessel's high-tech systems are sabotaged.[21] Within this paradigm, the UEO sees both Bridger and Darwin as tools, a means to an end.[22]

These problematic interactions create conflict but also set the tone for subversion in *seaQuest DSV*: Bridger takes control of the *seaQuest* on his own terms and Darwin becomes a well-developed character who forms relationships with a wide range of crew members in a pattern of animal representation that reinforces that "Each species, as well as every individual member of that species, has a unique point of view."[23] The subversion and the active negotiation of UEO expectations and demands also reflect the dual purpose of the *seaQuest* as a vessel that is committed to both military intervention and scientific exploration, which often results in tension and contradictory priorities among different factions of the crew. The development of these relationships and Darwin's ability to express his own thoughts, feelings, and perspective are amplified through the use of a device called a vo-corder, which allows interspecies communication by translating Darwin's clicks and whistles into human-accessible language and speech. This engagement builds on previous research into dolphin communication among other members of their own species and mimicry in dolphin interactions with humans,[24] though the "translation" of the vo-corder is pure science fiction. Darwin is a central figure in this negotiation, becoming an equal and peer as both a subject of and collaborator in these military maneuvers and scientific explorations.

One productive way of considering this range of representations is through Darwin's interactions and relationships with his fellow crew members and other humans. Notably, while many science fiction narratives featuring animals depict female characters having more nurturing or maternal relationships with these animal characters than their male human counterparts do, this is not the case in *seaQuest*: while Kristin Westphalen (Stephanie Beacham) does nurture Darwin and look out for his best interest, Bridger and Lucas are both protective of Darwin as well, and Westphalen is just as likely as the male characters to engage in scientific research and philosophical conversations with Darwin, with each of these characters incorporating affection and an ethics of care in their personal and professional interactions with Darwin.

Nathan Bridger

Darwin's initial and longest-standing human relationship is with Captain Nathan Bridger. Their relationship initially began in a rescuer/rescued dichotomy, when Bridger released Darwin from a fishing net in which the dolphin had become entrapped. This event embodies Fraser et al.'s representational theme of dolphin vulnerability[25] and reinforces "the human/animal divide."[26] Within this paradigm of human–animal interaction, such representations "imply a superiority of humans to these animals, giving humans responsibility over the care, protection, and well being of dolphins."[27] This difference is prominent in their first onscreen interaction, with Bridger the trainer and Darwin the trainee, as Darwin follows Bridger's hand-signal instructions.[28] Before Bridger and Darwin join the crew of the *seaQuest*, their communication is exclusively one-way. There is a clear camaraderie and affinity between Bridger and Darwin, but the human–animal divide remains a significant barrier in their interactions and understanding of one another. When Bridger discovers that Noyce has had Darwin brought aboard the *seaQuest*, his initial response is outraged and possessive, as he refers to Darwin as "my dolphin."[29]

However, once aboard the *seaQuest*, there are two changes that dramatically resituate Bridger and Darwin's relationship: the ability to verbally communicate through use of the vo-corder and Darwin's new position aboard the *seaQuest* as a skilled crew member. When the *seaQuest*'s targeting technology is sabotaged and the only way to fire torpedoes at an enemy sub with any accuracy is through Darwin's tagging the other ship with a homing device, instead of simply giving Darwin the hand motion commands that he developed on the island, Bridger is able to speak with Darwin, explain what he is asking the dolphin to do, and ask Darwin whether he is willing to do so.[30] In this shift from command to conversation, Darwin has increased agency, able to consent or decline the mission Bridger is setting for him. Debra L. Merskin argues that "the connection between Us and Them, of whatever species, is powerful as a motivator of attitudes and ultimately behaviors and has a powerful connection to social justice."[31] This newly developed and collaborative relationship between Bridger and Darwin reframes their previous interactions and relationship—as well as real-world interactions and relationships between humans and dolphins in a variety of contexts, from captive performance to encounters in the wild—by interrogating the role of training, command, and performance. While Darwin is able to communicate and agree to the task before him, this communication remains problematic, as "this new form of communication helps the crew use Darwin even more effectively for their own purposes. . . . Darwin's poetic nature is somewhat humanly determined by the technology that allows him to speak, a technology that co-opts his agency toward creating human, logocentric worlds."[32] Bridger is resistant to this reading and notes that both his hand signals and this technologically enabled conversation pose requests rather than commands, with Darwin free to acquiesce or refuse with no fear of repercussion, but as Westphalen points out, Darwin wants to please Bridger, which complicates notions of free will and agency being ascribed to Darwin, even when he is able to speak for himself.

In addition to their own connection and shared history, Bridger and Darwin engage in some larger philosophical discussions as well, though the language of these is limited. In the episode "The Devil's Window," Darwin becomes sick after swimming through the emissions from a black smoker and when he tries to explain how he is feeling and what is going on to Bridger and others, his communication is cryptic, with Darwin repeating the phrase "Light is dark and one."[33] In this case, even though Darwin is able to speak, he is not able to effectively communicate with Bridger because their frames of reference and understanding of the world around them are so fundamentally different. The limitations of human–animal communication are cast into stark relief in this episode and in the end, Bridger determines that the only way to save Darwin's life is to use the *seaQuest*'s technology to find and reunite Darwin with his pod, from whom he was separated when he became entangled in the fishing net. This proves successful, as the pod cares for Darwin and provides him with a type of seaweed that serves as a natural cure for the bacteria Darwin has encountered. Darwin is able to bring back and share this seaweed with the crew of the *seaQuest*, thus contributing to and furthering human knowledge as well. The fact that Darwin has been reunited with his pod and actively chooses to return to the *seaQuest* and Bridger further develops Darwin's agency and choice: he is not with Bridger because he needs the human to care for him or protect him in the absence of his pod, but rather because he chooses to be.[34] In a later episode titled "The Good Death," Darwin works with Bridger and the crew of the *seaQuest* to help human rights activists who are fighting to protect children from governmental death squads. Bridger uses Darwin as a sounding board for trying to make sense of human cruelty, with Darwin responding that human evil is inconsequential because "bad sinks, the future floats," before committing himself to the mission with his reassurance that "Darwin help."[35] Despite the limitations of this translated speech, there is a clear interaction and exchange of ideas, an interspecies understanding and sharing of perspectives, and a relationship defined by collaboration rather than command.

Darwin's contributions to the larger aims of the *seaQuest* also alter Bridger and Darwin's relationship. While Bridger never describes Darwin as a pet, his claim of "my dolphin"[36] emphasizes the singularity of their relationship with one another in their lives on the island. When Bridger and Darwin come aboard the *seaQuest*, this relationship changes in notable ways. Darwin begins to form relationships and close bonds with other crew members, particularly Lucas Wolenczak, a brilliant teenage boy in need of connection and camaraderie with someone other than the adults onboard, whose interactions with Lucas are often hierarchically structured and paternalistic. Bridger's relationship with Darwin becomes just one of many human–animal relationships, with Darwin no longer solely dependent upon Bridger for that human connection and free to explore and express other elements of his personality in these diverse relationships. In addition, in joining *seaQuest*, Darwin becomes a crew member, capable of assisting in emergency situations and contributing to the mission of the *seaQuest* and its crew. In the first season alone, Darwin demonstrates collaborative rescue maneuvers for a UEO inspector,[37] finds missing crew members,[38] locates a missing and disabled submarine full of stranded children,[39] runs interference with hostile divers,[40] helps coordinate subversive response when *seaQuest* is boarded by ecoterrorists and all traditional communications are taken off-line,[41] and translates alien communications.[42] These are all contributions that no other crew member would be able to make and actions which have a profound impact on the success of the *seaQuest*'s mission, essential in saving the lives of both Darwin's fellow *seaQuest* crewmates and other humans in need. In one respect, this frames Darwin within a representational trend in which "animals are thought of more by what they mean to us"[43] as humans rather than on their own terms because Darwin's behavior clearly serves human needs. However, this behavior also positions him as an equal, a valuable and appreciated member of the *seaQuest*'s crew.

Lucas Wolenczak

Darwin's other sustained and central relationship in *seaQuest DSV* is with Lucas Wolenczak, a teen genius whose workaholic father sent him to the *seaQuest* to keep the boy out of trouble. Lucas designed the vo-corder that allows Darwin to communicate with humans but beyond that, Darwin and Lucas also share a unique relationship as two outsiders aboard the *seaQuest*. While Darwin is the only nonhuman crew member, Lucas often finds himself excluded from the larger action on board, dismissed as just a "kid" despite his central role in managing the vessel's technology and his ability to track down all kinds of information, including encrypted and confidential files that no one else can access. In some ways, Lucas and Darwin are in a similar position, finding out who they are in relationship to the adult humans onboard and how they can most productively express themselves and contribute to the *seaQuest*'s mission. Darwin and Lucas quickly become fast friends, with Darwin frequently following Lucas around the *seaQuest* by swimming through the seawater tubes that cut through the vessel (evidence that Bridger was invested in human–dolphin collaboration—at least for military purposes—even before he befriended Darwin specifically). A stretch of these tubes runs along the wall of Lucas's quarters, directly above his bunk, meaning that in addition to their face-to-face interactions and conversations in Darwin's pool area, Lucas and Darwin can enjoy one another's company in this more informal setting as well. Lucas describes Darwin as "a friend," telling an onboard visitor that he and Darwin "sorta stick together."[44] This is a different, less hierarchical relationship than the one Darwin shares with Bridger, characterized by fun and play, rather than training, and Lucas's conversations with Darwin are informal, punctuated with curiosity, teasing, and jokes.

While many of Darwin's conversations with Bridger are philosophical in nature and his interactions with other crew members are predominantly objective-focused, Darwin's relationship with Lucas is largely social. They talk, play, and have fun together. When Lucas takes a new high-speed submersible for a spin, Darwin swims along with him,[45] and they frequently swim and play together in Darwin's pool area onboard. Lucas and Darwin also share a yearning for and preoccupation with the world outside of the *seaQuest*, while still valuing their relationships and connections onboard. For example, in one episode, Lucas has the opportunity to spend time with kids his own age when the *seaQuest* stops to drop off supplies at an undersea school full of teen geniuses.[46] Bridger's reluctance is protective and paternalistic, but Darwin's response to Lucas's impending absence is more complicated. There is initial worry and trepidation, as Darwin inquires "Lucas leave pod?" before he affirms Lucas's need to see the world outside of the *seaQuest* and the inevitability of leaving the community, as Darwin reflects that there is a "big ocean, big fun."[47] Just as Darwin needed to leave the *seaQuest* and temporarily rejoin his pod for his own safety and well-being, as well as to be able to determine for himself where he wants to be, he understands and validates Lucas's need to do the same. While Lucas is a genius, he is still a teenager and has social needs that are not being met on the *seaQuest*, thus echoing Darwin's own isolation from his familial pod and other members of his species more generally. Darwin and Lucas support one another and provide camaraderie since both are isolated from the larger crew, but they simultaneously support one another's social needs beyond their individual relationship as well, respecting one another's need for separation, distance, and species-based connections: Lucas with other teens and Darwin with other dolphins.

Lucas's relationship with Darwin is also professional, since he is the inventor of the vo-corder that allows Darwin to communicate with humans. Lucas and Dr. Kristin Westphalen, the *seaQuest*'s lead scientist, model empathetic scientific practice in their engagement with Darwin, actively collaborating with the dolphin as they work to build his language base and communicate with him. These interactions of scientific research and discovery blur the lines between several of the categories established by Fraser et al., as Lucas and Westphalen are concerned with Darwin's vulnerability and seek to protect him, while simultaneously treating him like an equal and being keen to learn all that he has to offer through his unique perspective and intelligence.[48]

While Lucas and Darwin's relationship is largely defined by friendship and scientific collaboration, this relationship is still at times problematically possessive. When Darwin is kidnapped by a black market trader called The Regulator, Lucas demands that the other man give back "my dolphin,"[49] echoing Bridger's earlier claim of ownership and suggesting that while the human–animal divide is blurred to some degree in these interactions, the foundational anthropocentric hierarchy remains firmly in place.

The Regulator and Milos Tezlof

While the majority of the *seaQuest*'s crew members understand and engage with Darwin as an individual, outsiders view Darwin differently and often project or ascribe their own meanings onto him with potentially disastrous results. In each case, the ways in which these humans interact with and attempt to take ownership of Darwin in different ways also reflect larger discourses about dolphins in both real life and popular culture.

The Regulator is a black market trader who has cultivated an aura of mystery and travels the oceans with an orangutan companion named Verne. In spite of this legendary status and the awe with which many crew members—particularly Lucas—view The Regulator, he and Bridger have crossed paths before, which enables Bridger to share The Regulator's real name (Leslie Ferina) and his dark past, including that he faked his own death when his unethical tests on animals got him driven out of the scientific community. In the case of The Regulator, he has dual motivations for his interest in Darwin, which work at cross purposes and reveal more about The Regulator himself than they do about Darwin. His first comment to Lucas after overhearing Darwin speaking is that "you shouldn't hold creatures against their will,"[50] despite the fact that he himself keeps the orangutan Verne in captivity. However, in The Regulator's further interactions with Darwin, it becomes clear that he sees dolphins in general and Darwin specifically as "superior to humans in intelligence, communication abilities, and/or spiritual purpose."[51]

While Bridger, Lucas, and other members of the *seaQuest* crew appreciate Darwin's intelligence and value his unique perspective, they do not elevate Darwin's intelligence to superhuman levels, instead engaging in these connections and knowledge building as collaborative and dynamically engaged. In contrast, The Regulator reveres Darwin and believes him to be the key to unlocking the secrets of and validating his own belief in "spherical evolution."[52] The Regulator pleads with Darwin for insight, saying "No mind is as advanced as yours. Complex communication, cycling faster than I can blink .... But what really matters here and now is that you can talk. Speak to me, Darwin, open my eyes."[53] Thwarted by the limitations of his own intelligence and ingenuity, he is now desperately turning to Darwin for the answers, willing to both kidnap and coerce the dolphin to reveal the secrets of the universe to him. While Bridger and Lucas are able to tell The Regulator about Darwin and explain his ability to communicate with humans in non-metaphysical terms, the episode ends with a self-reflective and redemptive moment for The Regulator and the possibility that he might not have been far off in his estimation of Darwin's cosmic wisdom, when Darwin tells The Regulator that he can find the center of the universe "inside you."[54] This interaction also allows The Regulator to reclaim his humanity, as he forsakes his enigmatic professional name to introduce himself to Darwin by his real name (Leslie).

In a later episode, Darwin also catches the attention of war criminal Milos Tezlof. While *seaQuest DSV* largely avoids metaphysical representations of dolphins, this episode begins with several of the *seaQuest*'s crew members having the same dream about Darwin, as Bridger, Lucas, Westphalen, Lieutenant Junior Grade Tim O'Neill (Ted Raimi), and Sensor Chief Miguel Ortiz (Marco Sanchez) are all drawn to the dolphin through this dream. In addition to building on Sigmund Freud's observation of "how frequently animals appeared in the dreams of children (and adults),"[55] this representation follows the popular culture trend identified by Fraser et al. in which the superiority of dolphins to humans is explored through dolphins being ascribed "specific abilities and competencies beyond the capabilities of humans ... includ[ing] inter-species communication, telepathy, extraterrestrial communication, healing powers, and spiritual powers."[56] In the episode "Hide and Seek," Westphalen and Malcolm Lansdowne (Robert Engels) are at Lansdowne's estate when they are accosted by Tezlof,[57] who wants to take Lansdowne's dolphins for military use, echoing the real-life use of dolphins in combat, including the U.S. Navy's "military dolphin program"[58] and their historic use in the Vietnam War. While Tezlof's initial impulse is acquisitive and destructive, his perspective begins to change when he sees his non-verbal son Caesar (played by Christopher James Miller) responding to interaction and contact with one of the dolphins.

Caesar's non-verbal state can be read as a combination of unarticulated trauma and autism. Following this initial contact with one of Lansdowne's dolphins, Tezlof and his son board the *seaQuest*, where Caesar is able to connect and swim with Darwin, which has a calming and therapeutic effect on the child. There is a well-established history of animal-assisted therapy being productively used with children, particularly those on the autism spectrum and those who have experienced trauma. Researchers have found that children with autism "seek interaction with animals more often than with humans and inanimate objects,"[59] and as a result, animals can "serve as an initial catalyst for social interactions," increasing the child's comfort within their environment, and resulting in lowered stress and anxiety.[60] Animal-assisted therapy has proven similarly effective in treating individuals who have experienced trauma, with therapeutic approaches based on "a common understanding regarding the significance of animals in providing emotional security, psychophysiological and affect regulation, neurological recalibration, and other behavioral response of humans to our social environment."[61] Through his interactions with Darwin, Caesar expresses curiosity and enjoyment, as he begins to laugh and even vocalize following his engagement and play with Darwin.[62]

While this furthers the representation of dolphins in general and Darwin specifically as possessing metaphysical intelligence and ability, Tezlof's default remains one of conquest, as he attempts to kidnap Darwin, using the possessive term "your dolphin" as he makes his demand.[63] This discourse of superiority/inferiority informs his understanding of and interaction with humans as well, as he refers to Caesar as a "curse," a broken child in need of being "heal[ed]" and made "whole."[64] Members of seaQuest ask Darwin for his assistance and he actively chooses to help Caesar, engaging with a machine that enables the projection of Caesar's trauma. Tezlov is a violent dictator and war criminal, and when there was a coup to overthrow him, Caesar lost his mother, who Tezlof sacrificed when he fled with his son. While this new knowledge doesn't resolve Caesar's trauma, it does enable him to speak, as he calls out for his mother. With Milos and Caesar Tezlof, Darwin is symbolic of their fractured relationship, as the sins of the father have resulted in the trauma of the son, but he is also a metaphysical means of healing, as the dolphin's therapeutic swimming with Caesar and the projection of the boy's non-verbal communication allow them to reconnect and reconcile.[65]

Both The Regulator and Tezlof ascribe significance to Darwin that expands his presence beyond his identity as a dolphin, and they project these meanings onto Darwin before they have established any personal connection or relationship with him. As a result, their interactions with Darwin are filtered through their own flawed expectations, rather than Darwin's actual individual identity. In each of these cases, that engagement follows Fraser et al.'s pattern of dolphins "as superior to humans, associated with a higher power or intelligence,"⁶⁶ thus speaking directly to a lack that these men have identified within themselves. They turn to Darwin for answers that they cannot find elsewhere, whether through their own intellectual and philosophical reflection (The Regulator) or in their relationships with others (Tezlof).

CONCLUSION

seaQuest DSV presents a range of perceptions through the ways human characters interact with Darwin and the relationships they form with him. As a series that imagined the near future, *seaQuest DSV*'s representations of a dolphin lead to a consideration of the thoughts humans have about animals, both in that specific historical moment and in looking forward to what human/ nonhuman–animal relationships might become. As a result of the series' science fiction context, Darwin occupies a distinctly liminal space, in which he has many of the characteristics of a real dolphin but is also capable of unrealistic feats, such as the translation of Darwin's communication into human speech. The interactions of characters with Darwin on *seaQuest DSV* reflect several predominant perceptions of and beliefs about dolphins in general, including their complex connections with humans outlined by Fraser et al., as peers, emissaries of the natural world, animals in need of protection, and creatures capable of metaphysical perception.⁶⁷ Both Bridger and Lucas see Darwin as a valued friend, while also at times speaking of him in possessive or acquisitive terms ("my dolphin"). He is reunited with his pod, but chooses to return to his human friends aboard the *seaQuest*, claiming two family units and contexts of belonging. When Bridger loses faith in humanity, Darwin helps him regain it, demonstrating a belief in the human race that the captain himself struggles to maintain. Darwin has military use and capability but also effectively facilitates connection and communication between hostile parties, as in his engagement with The Regulator and Milos Tezlof. He is a scientific marvel and at least in the eyes of some of the crew members, The Regulator, and Tezlof, a metaphysical ambassador of greater wisdom than their own.

Darwin offers a representation of a dolphin than transcends the limitations of human–animal connection and communication that are currently possible, through Darwin's ability to speak, which opens up new vistas of human–animal interaction. While this is remarkable in and of itself, what the series presents as even more important is *what* Darwin says and the perspective he shares, which is one that validates and affirms humanity. Both the characters of *seaQuest DSV* and the series' viewers adore Darwin not just for who he is as an individual but for what he tells us about ourselves: that we are worth talking to, that other species on the planet desire a connection with us as well, and that we haven't messed the world up quite so badly that it cannot be salvaged through interspecies connection and cooperation. Darwin is a beacon of hope, an ambassador for his species, a believer in humanity, and a reminder of all that could still be possible.

NOTES

1. Sherryl Vint, "'The Animals in That Country': Science Fiction and Animals Studies," *Science Fiction Studies* 35, no. 2 (2008), 178.

2. The series does include an alien-based episode in Season One (Episode 22, "Such Great Patience") and the end of Season Two sees the *seaQuest* transported to the far reaches of the galaxy by an alien spacecraft.

3. Ryan Britt, "Why *seaQuest DSV* is the Ultimate '90s Sci-Fi Show," *SyFy.com*, 4 June 2019, https://www.syfy.com/syfywire/why-seaquest-dsv-is-the-ultimate-90s-sci-fi-show.

4. The third season jumps forward in time, which prompted the re-titling of the series to *seaQuest 2032*.

5. *seaQuest*, Episode 1.3, "The Devil's Window."

6. "What is a Hydrothermal Vent?," *National Ocean Service*, n.d., https://oceanservice.noaa.gov/facts/vents.html.

7. *seaQuest*, Episode 1.11, "The Regulator."

8. *seaQuest*, Episode 1.19, "Hide and Seek."

9. Susan Casey, *Voices of the Ocean: A Journey into the Wild and Haunting World of Dolphins* (New York: Doubleday, 2015), 12.

10. Casey, *Voices of the Ocean*, 12.

11. Casey, *Voices of the Ocean*, 8.

12. Marie-France Boissonneault, *Every Living Being: Representations of Nonhuman Animals in the Exploration of Human Well-Being* (Portland, OR: Inkwater Press, 2010), 237.

13. John Fraser et al., "Dolphins in Popular Literature and Media," *Society and Animals* 14, no. 4 (2006), 323.

14. Fraser et al., "Dolphins in Popular Literature and Media," 323.

15. Boissonnealt, *Every Living Being*, 25.

16. Fraser et al., "Dolphins in Popular Literature and Media," 327.

17. Fraser et al., "Dolphins in Popular Literature and Media," 327.

18. Debra L. Merskin, *Seeing Species: Re-presentations of Animals in Media & Popular Culture* (New York: Peter Lang, 2018), xiv.

19. Boissonnealt, *Every Living Being*, 99.

20. Andrew Thaler, "Deep-Sea Ecologist Rewatches seaQuest DSV: Episodes 1 & 2: 'To Be or Not to Be,'" *The Mary Sue*, 2 April 2016, https://www.themarysue.com/deep-see-ecologist-seaquest/.

21. *seaQuest*, Episode 1.2, "To Be or Not to Be, Part Two."

22. This is a pattern of exploitation that extends to other crew members in this situation as well, as Noyce asks Commander Jonathan Ford (Don Franklin), to feign arrogance and incompetence in order to push Bridger into taking control. This subterfuge is particularly problematic because as a Black man, Ford is one of the only high-ranking officers of color on *seaQuest*. Ford heroically stood up to his former captain when she attempted to launch an unauthorized nuclear strike, and he has now been put in this well-deserved position of power only to be asked to compromise his morals and integrity so that this power can be passed on to Bridger, who clearly and repeatedly says that he does not want it.

23. Merskin, *Seeing Species*, 23.

24. Research in this area has been going on for decades, and studies focused on dolphin language-learning, mimicry, and the signature-whistle hypothesis include D.G. Richards, J.P. Wolz and L.M. Herman's "Vocal Mimicry of Computer-Generated Sounds and Vocal Labeling of Objects by the Bottlenosed Dolphin, Tursiops Truncatus," *Journal of Comparative Psychology* 98, no. 1 (1984), 10–28, D. Reiss and B. McCowan's "Spontaneous Vocal Mimicry and Production by Bottlenose Dolphins (Tursiops Truncatus): Evidence for Vocal Learning," *Journal of Comparative Psychology* 104, no. 3 (1993), 301–312 and Brian K. Branstetter et al.'s "Recognition of Frequency Modulated Whistle-Like Sounds by a Bottlenose Dolphin (Tursiops Truncatus) and Humans with Transformations in Amplitude, Duration and Frequency," *PLoS ONE* 11, no. 2 (2016), 1–23.

25. Fraser et al., "Dolphins in Popular Literature and Media," 327.

26. Merskin, *Seeing Species*, 5.

27. Fraser et al., "Dolphins in Popular Literature and Media," 331.

28. *seaQuest*, Episode 1.1., "To Be or Not to Be, Part One."

29. "To Be or Not to Be, Part One."

30. "To Be or Not to Be, Part Two."

31. Merskin, *Seeing Species*, 21.

32. Sean Morey, "Speculative Zoopoetics," in *Rhetorical Speculations: The Future of Rhetoric, Writing, and Technology*, ed. Scott Sundvall (Logan: Utah University Press, 2019), 57.

33. "The Devil's Window."

34. "The Devil's Window."

35. *seaQuest*, Episode 1.23, "The Good Death."

36. "To Be or Not to Be, Part One."

37. *seaQuest*, Episode 1.6, "Treasures of the Tonga Trench."

38. *seaQuest*, Episode 1.7, "Bad Water."

39. "Bad Water."

40. *seaQuest*, Episode 1.14, "Better Than a Martian."

41. *seaQuest*, Episode 1.15, "Nothing But the Truth."

42. "Such Great Patience."

43. Merskin, *Seeing Species*, xvi.

44. *seaQuest*, Episode 1.7, "Brothers and Sisters."

45. *seaQuest*, Episode 1.17, "The Stinger."

46. *seaQuest*, Episode 1.13, "Photon Bullet."

47. "Photon Bullet."
48. Fraser et al., "Dolphins in Popular Literature and Media," 327.
49. "The Regulator."
50. "The Regulator."
51. Fraser et al., "Dolphins in Popular Literature and Media," 333.
52. "The Regulator."
53. "The Regulator."
54. "The Reguator."
55. Gail F. Melson and Aubrey H. Fine, "Animals in the Lives of Children," *Handbook on Animal-Assisted Therapy: Foundations and Guidelines for Animal-Assisted Interventions*, 4th edition, ed. Aubrey H. Fine (Boston: Academic Press, 2015), 181.
56. Fraser et al., "Dolphins in Popular Literature and Media," 334.
57. There is also an erotic undercurrent in this particular interaction, as the connection between Westphalen and Lansdowne is at least partially romantic in nature, with Lansdowne preparing to kiss Westphalen as she engages with a virtual reality experience he has created to allow humans to swim with dolphins ("Hide and Seek").
58. Thaler, "Deep-Sea Ecololgist Rewatches *seaQuest DSV*."
59. Mirena Dimolareva and Thomas J. Dunn, "Animal-Assisted Interventions for School-Aged Children with Autism Spectrum Disorder: A Meta-Analysis," *Journal of Autism and Developmental Disorders* 51 (2021), 2436.
60. Temple Grandin et al., "The Roles of Animals for Individuals with Autism Spectrum Disorder," *Handbook on Animal-Assisted Therapy: Foundations and Guidelines for Animal-Assisted Interventions*, 4th edition, ed. Aubrey H. Fine (Boston: Academic Press, 2015), 226.
61. Philip Tedeschi et al., "Treating Human Trauma with the Help of Animals: Trauma Informed Intervention for Child Maltreatment and Adult Post-Traumatic Stress," *Handbook on Animal-Assisted Therapy: Foundations and Guidelines for Animal-Assisted Interventions*, 4th edition, ed. Aubrey H. Fine (Boston: Academic Press, 2015), 305.
62. "Hide and Seek."
63. "Hide and Seek."
64. "Hide and Seek."
65. While Darwin in instrumental is reconnecting Tezlof and his son, this reconciliation is temporary, with Tezlof about to be executed for his war crimes. As a result, this is a truncated and incomplete trauma narrative, with Caesar about to lose his only surviving parent. While the crew of the *seaQuest* promise that they will ensure Caesar is turned over to someone who will take good care of him, who this is, what this will look like, and what Caesar's life moving forward will be—particularly if he no longer has the therapeutic connection with dolphins in general or Darwin specifically—remain unaddressed ("Hide and Seek").
66. Fraser et al., "Dolphins in Popular Literature and Media," 327.
67. Fraser et al., "Dolphins in Popular Literature and Media," 327.

BIBLIOGRAPHY

Boissonneault, Marie-France. *Every Living Being: Representations of Nonhuman Animals in the Exploration of Human Well-Being.* Portland, OR: Inkwater Press, 2010.

Branstetter, Brian K., Caroline M. DeLong, Brandon Dziedzic, Amy Black, and Kimberly Bakhtiari. "Recognition of Frequency Modulated Whistle-Like Sounds by a Bottlenose Dolphin (Tursiops Truncatus) and Humans With Transformations in Amplitude, Duration and Frequency." *PLoS ONE* 11, no. 2 (2016): 1–23.

Britt, Ryan. "Why *seaQuest DSV* is the Ultimate '90s Sci-Fi Show'." *SyFy.com*, June 4, 2019. https://www.syfy.com/syfywire/why-seaquest-dsv-is-the-ultimate-90s-sci-fi-show.

Casey, Susan. *Voices of the Ocean: A Journey into the Wild and Haunting World of Dolphins.* New York: Doubleday, 2015.

Dimolareva, Mirena, and Thomas J. Dunn. "Animal-Assisted Interventions for School-Aged Children With Autism Spectrum Disorder: A Meta-Analysis." *Journal of Autism and Developmental Disorders* 51 (2021): 2436–2449.

Fraser, John, Diana Reiss, Paul Boyle, Katherine Lemcke, Jessica Sickler, Elizabeth Elliott, Barbara Newman, and Sarah Gruber. "Dolphins in Popular Literature and Media." *Society and Animals* 14, no. 4 (2006): 321–349.

Grandin, Temple, Aubrey H. Fine, Marguerite E. O'Haire, Gretchen Carlisle, and Christine M. Bowers. "The Roles of Animals for Individuals With Autism Spectrum Disorder." In *Handbook on Animal-Assisted Therapy: Foundations and Guidelines for Animal-Assisted Interventions*, 4th ed., edited by Aubrey H. Fine. Boston: Academic Press, 2015, 225–236.

Melson, Gail F., and Aubrey H. Fine. "Animals in the Lives of Children." In *Handbook on Animal-Assisted Therapy: Foundations and Guidelines for Animal-Assisted Interventions*, 4th ed., edited by Aubrey H. Fine. Boston: Academic Press, 2015, 181–194.

Merskin, Debra L. *Seeing Species: Re-Presentations of Animals in Media & Popular Culture.* New York: Peter Lang, 2018.

Morey, Sean. "Speculative Zoopoetics." In *Rhetorical Speculations: The Future of Rhetoric, Writing, and Technology*, edited by Scott Sundvall. Logan: Utah University Press, 2019, 45–66.

Reiss, D., and B. McCowan. "Spontaneous Vocal Mimicry and Production by Bottlenose Dolphins (Tursiops Truncatus): Evidence for Vocal Learning." *Journal of Comparative Psychology* 104, no. 3 (1993): 301–312.

Richards, D. G., J. P. Wolz, and L. M. Herman. "Vocal Mimicry of Computer-Generated Sounds and Vocal Labeling of Objects by the Bottlenosed Dolphin, Tursiops Truncatus." *Journal of Comparative Psychology* 98, no. 1 (1984): 10–28.

seaQuest DSV. Created by Rockne S. O'Bannon. Perf. Roy Scheider, Jonathan Brandis, Stephanie Beacham, Frank Welker. Universal, 1993–1996.

Tedeschi, Philip, Meredith L. Sisa, Meg Daley Olmert, Nancy Parish-Plass, and Rick Yount. "Treating Human Trauma With the Help of Animals: Trauma Informed

Intervention for Child Maltreatment and Adult Post-Traumatic Stress." In *Handbook on Animal-Assisted Therapy: Foundations and Guidelines for Animal-Assisted Interventions*, 4th ed., edited by Aubrey H. Fine. Boston: Academic Press, 2015, 305–319.

Thaler, Andrew. "Deep-Sea Ecologist Rewatches seaQuest DSV: Episodes 1 & 2: 'To Be or Not to Be.'" *The Mary Sue*, April 2, 2016. https://www.themarysue.com/deep-see-ecologist-seaquest/.

Vint, Sherryl. "'The Animals in That Country': Science Fiction and Animals Studies." *Science Fiction Studies* 35, no. 2 (2008): 177–188.

"What is a Hydrothermal Vent?" *National Ocean Service*. n.d. https://oceanservice.noaa.gov/ facts/vents.html.

Chapter 2

Ducks, Ducks and More Ducks
Comedy and Social Class in Animated TV
David Hipple

CONTEXT AND FORMAT

The 1988–1993 British animated series *Count Duckula* concerns the exploits of the eponymous vegetarian vampire duck. It exemplifies the disingenuous ability of material involving animal characters to interrogate social and cultural matters that might seem awkwardly sensitive in more conventional drama. Most characters inhabit class and occupational positions reflecting British stereotypes, variously signaled by factors such as dress and dialect. This discussion addresses only the twenty-six-episode 1988–1989 first series (of four), the only one to be issued on DVD outside Region 2 (Region 1 in 2005, and 4 in 2007). This initial series clearly introduces the vampiric duck character's reinforcement of some comical conventions, while also creating unique elements through Count Duckula's anti-hero status.

Count Duckula was commissioned from Cosgrove Hall Films by Nickelodeon, an American cable company.[1] Though Cosgrove Hall was based in a Manchester suburb, it was owned by Thames Television, a London-serving regional company in the UK's commercial Independent Television (ITV) network of the time. ITV broadcasters were funded by advertising, in contrast to the publicly financed BBC. Every episode involves the interaction of Duckula himself, his butler Igor (of course!), and his housekeeper Nanny. Their respective characters are expressed in part by their physical appearances as outlined below. It quickly becomes evident that Igor has served the Duckula line for a *very* long time, presiding over many of the Count's reincarnation ceremonies, and later it seems that Nanny *might* be equally long-lived. Igor is dedicated to the Duckulas' time-honored practice of evil, constantly trying to tempt the present incumbent back toward merciless hunting and bloodletting. Nanny, by contrast, is single-mindedly devoted to protecting and coddling

Duckula. The home of these characters is described in the titles sequence's narration, over a shot of an apparently ramshackle citadel atop a lonely mountain: "Castle Duckula: home for many centuries to a dreadful dynasty of vicious vampire ducks: *the Counts of Duckula!*" The Castle quickly becomes something of a character in its own right: conveniently for writers, it can teleport to anywhere in the world (and can even return itself from outer space), though sometimes disorientating characters by misinterpreting instructions and materializing somewhere unintended.

Recurring guest characters include a band of four thieving crows who constantly try to rob the Castle, a boatload of pirate penguins (witty use of an aquatic bird species), and Duckula's nemesis Dr. Von Goosewing. This character is obviously derived from the heroic Dutch vampire hunter Abraham Van Helsing in Bram Stoker's novel *Dracula*, here mutated into a German goose. He is a rather deranged scientist-cum-engineer with delusions of competence, who has appointed himself the nemesis of a vampire who is in fact entirely harmless.

The central hybrid duck/vampire is presented with character traits and an animation style largely distinct from earlier visual portrayals of duck characters in television or film. *Count Duckula*'s central character is an aristocratic duck, proprietor of a crumbling Transylvanian castle, and was originally an occasional guest presence in a series where animal characters adopted roles familiar from traditional spy adventures. There he was a conventional (other than being a duck) vampiric villain. Tweaked for his own series, Duckula was transformed into this *vegetarian* vampire, instantly creating contradictions (see below) within a light-hearted form of comedy aimed at both children and adults. This is not to say that those two groups should be seen as separate.

THEORIES OF COMEDY, FOR OLDER AND YOUNGER AUDIENCES

Rebecca Farley energetically opposes a conventional idea that "cartoons" in particular are consciously aimed at *separate* (if often co-present) audiences with distinct sensibilities in a process generally termed *double-coding*: for example, slapstick violence to entertain children and satire for adults.[2] "In refusing to privilege content, approaching cartoons in terms of play also avoids the double-coding tendency to intellectualize the pleasures of the text. In play mode, the popular entertainment value of a program is located primarily in trivialities," encompassing *all* of "spoof products, songs, satire, and extravagant stretch-and-squash" *plus* "an engagingly self-aware celebration of their own production apparatus."[3] Farley argues that narratives are not necessarily contrived with concurrent but unrelated levels of significance, but function simultaneously and richly on *complementary* levels. This seemingly simple suggestion is nonetheless contested. Jason Mittell, for example, argues that, "Regardless of this interpretation, the producers and critics of this era [the 1950s and 60s, in his analysis] did clearly view dual appeals in cartoons as the key to their success."[4] Even given Mittell's evidence, however, this orthodoxy could still produce workable results for mistaken reasons.[5]

Addressing sitcoms in general (not just animation), Brett Mills accepts Farley's analytical position as supporting a "Relief Theory" of the social value of comedy:

> Adults are just as capable of enjoying violence, and the distinction that is made is therefore an attempt to distinguish between forms of humour which, as [*The Simpsons*, 1989–present] shows, can happily exist side by side. Indeed, the Relief Theory would argue that society's desire to categorise such jokes as childish shows precisely how repressed we are about these topics, which in turn demonstrates the need for our acceptance of them.[6]

Relief Theory mainly unpacks a narrative's address to its audience(s), with widely accessible narrative layers. Mills presents analytical perspectives that illuminate *Count Duckula*'s humor in other ways. The ancient Superiority Theory emphasizes challenges arising from the artificiality of class systems (while also inscribing the audience's superiority to the characters). Incongruity Theory underlines the frustration that *all* plans seem to backfire on those with the hubristic nerve to attempt them. And Cue Theory reminds us that technical tropes (a laugh track, a pregnant pause, a glance to camera) *prompt* us to *be amused*.

Nonetheless, Relief Theory suggests a progression from mid-twentieth-century oppositions of immature and sophisticated audiences toward a more integrated 1980s view represented in *Count Duckula* that multiple types of absurdity can coexist, including approaches to violence. In a 2012 interview, for example, Matt Groening discusses related thinking baked-into *The Simpsons*: "My attitude is that things can be improbable but not physically impossible; it's OK for Homer to fall off a cliff and survive, but he's got to be pretty banged up. There's got to be blood [. . . although . . .] we violate that rule a lot."[7]

Another decade later, such dilemmas are so widely understood that even in courtroom dialogue Johnny Depp can use them to explain a viewing experience shared with his three-year-old daughter: "For example Wile E Coyote gets a boulder dropped on his head, and he's completely crushed, but they cut to the next scene and he's just got a little bandage on his head. [Depp mimes these events and chuckles affectionately.] [. . .] Whether you were five or 95, you didn't ask a question: 'Oh, Wile E Coyote. . .? *Of course* he's still alive!'"[8]

POPULAR DUCK FOREBEARS

During the opening titles, a Narrator explains that whenever a Duckula is killed (each is nominally immortal, although vulnerable to a stake through the heart or exposure to sunlight), he can be reincarnated "by means of a secret rite that can be performed once per century."[9] The Narrator states simply that "The latest reincarnation did not run according to plan," while the screen shows that Nanny absent-mindedly handed Igor tomato ketchup instead of the ritual blood. This sequence also sets up the role of accents in characterizing social relationships, by briskly establishing Igor's sonorous Received Pronunciation (RP),[10] while Nanny's west country accent implies a humble yokel background.

The narration then gives way to an energetic theme song, including these lines:

He won't bite beast or man
'Cos he's a vegetari-*an*,
And things never go to plan
For . . . *DUCKULA*.[11]

All of this smoothly allows Duckula to function as a comical anti-hero—inevitably feared and hunted by some (simply for being the latest of his vampiric line), but in fact entirely well-meaning. Two threads of adaptation provide insight into this animal-based narrative's ability to imbue conventional dramatic forms with counterintuitive perspectives. We can explore Duckula's immediate ancestry within entertainment products, after specifically locating him among duck characters.

Surprising though this might seem to normal humans, published tales of sapient[12] ducks with extraordinary skills were far from new, even in 1988, quite apart from Disney's renowned character Donald (and his family) and Warner Bros.'s Daffy. Of course, one might argue that no duck character can now be introduced without comparison with Donald—just as any detective character might be compared with Sherlock Holmes, or any space captain with James Kirk—but in all these cases, it is worth considering each instance in its own context.

Comics-savvy readers will be aware of the extremely popular character Howard the Duck, created by Steve Gerber and Val Meyerik. Howard's first story was published by Marvel in 1973, and he attained his own full comic in 1976. Howard is a disaffected alien warrior marooned on Earth, stuck with heroically (although, like Batman or Judge Dredd, with no actual superpowers) making the best way he can through a world full of vulnerably inept humans and miscellaneous extravagant threats. After almost fifty years at the time of this writing, through a number of publishing incarnations and several hiatuses, there is no indication that Howard's heroic stories are exhausted.

Alas, the most high-profile public exposure for Howard the Duck was as the title character of Willard Huyck's film *Howard the Duck*, or in Europe as *Howard: a New Breed of Hero* (1986). That film attracted considerable opprobrium, although financially it did scrape through on box office receipts, and it can still be sincerely admired for having ambitiously taken on a startling number of narrative and technical challenges in trying to satisfy the mass audience long before purveyors of entirely fantastic narratives could have dreamed of such films' current ascendancy in the marketplace. (Happily for Howard, recent fleeting appearances in the Marvel Cinematic Universe suggest that he might yet have a successful big-screen resurgence.)[13]

Within that period, a lesser-known departure for Howard the Duck was his adoption in disguise by one of the most celebrated fantasy roleplaying games, as neatly summarized by Michael O'Brien.[14] Sapient ducks inspired by Howard were present as a race of characters from the first edition of *RuneQuest* (1978), developed by Greg Stafford as a roleplaying extension of his huge existing wargame *White Bear and Red Moon* (1975) dealing with the long history and mythology of his fantasy world Glorantha (very much as JRR Tolkien originally developed Middle-earth as a setting for his invented philological projects).[15] When *White Bear and Red Moon* was redeveloped as *Dragon Pass* in 1980, three new military units were "Ducks," "Ducks," and "More Ducks." Chaosium, the publisher, took prudent tactical steps to distance these games from the original *Howard the Duck* comics, whose creators had already come to an understanding with Disney to avoid conflict over the image of Donald Duck. The marketplace for duck-based heroes, albeit rather small, was keenly contested.

It is unknown whether the creators of *Count Duckula* would have known about Howard and his *RuneQuest* legacy when originally developing this character in 1982 for a few appearances in a different TV series. It is certain, however, that they and their American sponsors would have been aware of the flopped 1986 film by the time of reinventing Duckula for his own series in 1988. It must have been decided that the new product and its intended audience were sufficiently distinct to be uncontaminated by any superficial association. Coincidentally, the following text from the third edition of *RuneQuest*, describing the mysterious status of ducks in Glorantha, happens also to work to frame some of the most obvious issues surrounding the simple existence of Count Duckula's illustrious line: "Legend claims that these odd creatures were cursed during premortal times. It is unclear whether they were humans cursed with feathers and webbed feet or ordinary ducks cursed with intelligence and flightlessness."[16]

BACKGROUND, ADAPTATION, AND EVOLUTION

Count Duckula first appears in the earlier Cosgrove Hall series *Danger Mouse* (1981–1992). Here David Jason plays the lead character with a Received Pronunciation accent as a suave, calm, ever-competent international spy, a pastiche of lead character John Drake in the spy thriller series *Danger Man* (1960–1968). Danger Mouse's speech is always profoundly measured, much like Patrick McGoohan's characteristically intense performance as Drake.

The first stylistic transition toward *Count Duckula*, then, was *Danger Man*'s small-screen interpretation of James Bond-style adventure (predating the later cinematic juggernaut). Ian Fleming was involved in early discussions toward what became *Danger Man*, and McGoohan heavily influenced the shift from a Bond-type hard-drinking, womanizing killer to Drake as a more principled superspy.[17] This led to *Danger Mouse*'s anthropomorphic human-sized mouse. The success of that "performance" (the combination of visuals and voice work) relies on recognizably appropriating the presence of a well-known live-action lead, but with imaginative latitude provided by animation and therefore allegorical scope to attribute traits and abilities to anthropomorphic *animals*. Dramatic possibilities of cultural essentialism are suddenly fully available in well-established ways: Disney's big cats are lithe and calculating, for example; foxes are nimble and clever; snakes are stealthy and untrustworthy—and all of these exaggerated traits can be reflected in combined visual and vocal design. The broadly science fictional setting thus created meant that Danger Mouse's screen adventures could be as fantastic as anyone might wish, with the audience's necessary acceptance that this is a superbly talented quasi-human *mouse*, constantly battling in a world full of animal-style characters to foil the schemes of a criminal mastermind toad. With those elements in place, just about any reasonably rational stories are permitted.[18]

In *Danger Mouse* Jason also voices the intermittent guest character Count Duckula: a vain, capricious vampire with indeterminately American intonation, and also with a stammer that Jason might have borrowed from many sources, including Porky Pig or his own co-star Ronnie Barker's character in the live-action sitcom *Open All Hours* (1976–1985). The overall character design survived almost intact into *Count Duckula*. *Danger Mouse* was popular, and was bought by the American children's cable TV company Nickelodeon, immediately interested in possible further material from the same source. Brian Cosgrove describes Geri (Geraldine) Laybourne, Nickelodeon's manager at the time, with a special personal interest in children's programming, exploring possibilities for co-production. Laybourne was uninterested in Cosgrove Hall's new projects but was very taken with an illustration of Count Duckula: "'That's the one I want,' she said," Cosgrove reports, "and she wouldn't be moved—that was what she wanted!"[19] Clearly, the character's *look* suggested viable narratives to Laybourne, with solid financial considerations in mind; Nickelodeon, fully operational since 1979, had changed its marketplace stance and started accepting commercial advertising in 1984. From *Danger Mouse* Laybourne evidently derived faith in Cosgrove Hall's ability to create appealing narratives with the broadened fantasy possibilities of animal characters.

The most pointed use of this scope in *Count Duckula* is a particularly surreal comical tic. In *Danger Mouse* much of the humor slithers past in evasively dry, understated puns. In *Count Duckula*, by contrast, with no logical warning the sapient but apparently partially mechanical bats Dmitri and Sviatislav (honorary birds, it seems, thanks to their wings) routinely slide on rails out of a cuckoo clock and, in a close two-shot, deliver painfully contrived stand-up jokes about the current plot to an invisible (and in fact inexplicable, but still audibly delighted) audience. This audience is never observed in the show's main action, and conceivably exists *only* in the imagination of the bats.[20] They remark on the main action while never contributing to it (although the clock is part of the castle's teleporting mechanism, as explained in "Down Under Duckula").[21] The series's narrative strategy thus elevates its unreality to a point where communities of talking birds seem relatively straightforward to accommodate.

Now we should examine Cosgrove Hall's transplantation of Count Duckula from *Danger Mouse* to his own series, beginning with his first appearance. In "The Four Tasks of Danger Mouse,"[22] the eponymous secret agent is coerced into several more or less magical quests to save the life of his kidnapped sidekick Penfold. The fourth task imposed (and the third accomplished) is to procure "two feathers from a vampire duck."[23] Arriving in Transylvania, Danger Mouse mutters to himself: "How can I get two feathers from something that doesn't even *exist*? Huh! Vampire duck!" A bright green duck immediately materializes, yelling, "All right! All right! Who called so loud?"[24]

It is worth considering how Duckula was later reimagined, in more or less emphatic ways, and how such changes together accomplish a distinctive visual design. Even though most visual strokes of the *character* were carried-over to the spinoff series, it is significant that the *series* adopted a new presentation overall. In visual style and narrative rhythm, *Danger Mouse* had looked back as a parodic if affectionate celebration of the likes of *Danger Man* and *The Avengers* (1961–1969). Its stories were steadily purposeful, although with its own slightly soft-focus, elegantly curved classic dignity. By contrast, and regardless of its much more magical narrative world, *Count Duckula* took on a more modern, no-nonsense, angular look, also with more adventurous range in vocal performances (addressed separately below).

Senior Producer/Director John Doyle acknowledges this wholesale shift in visual style for *Count Duckula*, attributing it to adoption of "the loose drawing style" of backgrounds in animated productions like *101 Dalmatians*, with artists' drawings being transferred by other illustrators to transparent cels,[25] and color then being introduced behind (whether airbrushed, or colored paper, or textured cardboard), "to give that really graphic style."[26] Doyle is explaining *Count Duckula*'s vivid luminosity, as compared to *Danger Mouse*'s muted, pastel visual surface, constituting something like conventional cinematography's hyperreality: consider the unignorable glow of the quasi-magical live-action moments in Jean-Pierre Jeunet's *Amélie* (2001) or Ron Howard's *A Beautiful Mind* (2001), for example. In a setting so *constantly* sumptuously colorful, a world of talking birds seems easy enough to take on board. In its own way, the contemporaneous animated series *Æon Flux* (1991–1995) achieved something similar: regularly dwelling on the most minute of physical details (even while humans are depicted with grotesque angularity) eases the credibility of a baroque city of mutants.

DUCKULA AS LEAD CHARACTER

In his brief appearances in *Danger Mouse* Duckula had fangs, a flexible extending neck, and an ability to become gaseous on a whim, all features that were removed for *Count Duckula* (although he can still teleport).[27] The seminal character change is Duckula's vegetarianism, explaining his lack of visible fangs in this incarnation (except when he is drugged by Von Goosewing in "Dr Goosewing and Mr Duck").[28] This development remains uncredited, though Cosgrove attributes it elsewhere: "When [*Count Duckula*] went into production, of course one of the guys had the bright idea of making him a vegetarian as well, which turns the whole business of vampirism on its head. [. . .] It made it more acceptable for a child audience, too, and we could be sillier with it."[29]

This joke works in two main ways. The minor target is the fact that ducks are primarily understood as herbivorous and entirely unthreatening. Whether or not they actively take part, British (and presumably American) children are familiar at least with the *idea* of feeding bread to ducks, and are unlikely to know that some ducks might eat insects, and even frogs. In any case, ducks are generally not hunters, hence the originating *Danger Mouse* joke about the basic absurdity of a vampire duck. The second and larger point, equally accessible to children, is specifically about vampires. The *Dracula*-based stereotypes that *Count Duckula* deploys very freely were already so embedded in visual culture that they had been smoothly lampooned in, for example, the hit Hollywood romcom *Love at First Bite* (1979) almost a decade before *Count Duckula*. Of course *everybody knows* that *proper* vampires are remorseless nocturnal predators who regard humans merely as prey. We can immediately embrace as delightfully absurd the whole idea of a nominal vampire fixated on helping people, living on broccoli sandwiches, and achieving a showbiz career (and this one is a *duck*).

Almost a decade after *Count Duckula*, the series *Buffy the Vampire Slayer* (1997–2003) would introduce the character Angel, a vampire cursed with the restoration of his human soul, bringing with it compassion and guilt, and thus creating enormous emotional conflict. That fueled much serious drama and later poised comedy—and the character's own spinoff series (1999–2004)—but *Count Duckula*'s out-and-out genre absurdism generated humorous potential from the start.

Here, one important trait transferred from *Danger Mouse* was Duckula's craving for fame. When originally asked to donate two of his own feathers, he will consider the request if Danger Mouse can get him on television: "You will be astounded! I will produce *not* rabbits out of hats . . . but *hats*, ha-ha, out of *rabbits*! Lo! Abra . . . ca . . . thingy!"[30] and he pulls a huge top hat out of the mouth of a live, baffled, and conspicuously upset rabbit (whose facial expression, in its small way, shows that creatures in this world can always exhibit a degree of sentience, if not the sapience of the social, talking birds).

The Count is so keen to prove his performance potential that he seals himself in a coffin-shaped box and demands to be sawn in half. Danger Mouse complies. When he then asks whether being cut in half *lengthwise* was what Duckula really wanted, he is told, "Not entirely . . . but no matter!"[31] Duckula simply reconstitutes himself and goes on to give an audition piece as Hamlet. The prop skull (of Yorick, of course) enthusiastically takes a bow (in midair) alongside Duckula, irritating him: "Cease! Go! Avaunt! *I* am the star, so kindly leave the stage!"[32] Danger Mouse hesitantly suggests, "I don't think that television is quite ready for you yet,"[33] and tricks the Count into playing a booby-trapped harmonica that he happens to have brought along: "OK, Mr Showbiz: *this* will put you *among the stars*."[34] The harmonica blows up in Duckula's mouth, but of course the vampire survives the explosion, and Danger Mouse gets the two feathers that he came for. Timely sunrise thwarts the vengeful Duckula, who must fly back to his castle (atop a craggy peak, much as in the spinoff series), still frustrated in his quest for celebrity.

The paradoxical credibility of animal characters allows most of these features to be adapted into a new series focused on a vegetarian vampire. *Count Duckula*'s first episode "No Sax Please We're Egyptian"[35] is driven by the jaded, dispirited Count finding fresh impetus in a project to locate the Mystic Saxophone, an ancient Egyptian relic with the power to enchant any listener. With such an artifact in his hands, Duckula could escape lonely exile as a mysterious Count in remote Transylvania and gain the adulation of huge metropolitan audiences. This is not as repellent a motivation as it might first seem, especially in a children's series. In *Mork & Mindy* (1978–1982) the alien visitor Mork primarily wants to help and love people, while overcoming the inadvertent egoism and preconceptions energizing his hopes. The equally lovable Duckula desperately wants to contribute to society, but keeps running up against the boundaries of his isolation and his own awkward mix of idealism and vanity. Duckula inevitably makes one hubristic mistake after another, frequently connected with his desire for popularity, but even that can lead to him being sincerely *too kind* for his own good. Where, for example, *Wacky Races* (1968–1969) amusingly but simplistically depicts the cheating Dick Dastardly *never* learning his lesson and always suffering for it, *Count Duckula* presents an anti-hero typically striving to be in some sense better than he really is—and often failing horribly, but still deciding to *strive better* anyway. This is set out explicitly in "Town Hall Terrors" after Igor encourages Duckula to feed on an unconscious villager: "Igor, I've told you a thousand times: *this* Duckula is not the teeth-sinking kind. I want to *help* people, not *eat* them!"[36]

We find a character of noble background, tragically unable to take advantage of his inherited pedigree as all of his ancestors trivially did, and the audience will have been quick to absorb the disadvantaged irony of heroic duck-kind doing their best in a difficult world and despite their inherent harmlessness, a paradoxical situation that (as mentioned above) has been used in other contexts.

Igor, reinforcing the hereditary role of the faithful family retainer, regularly reminds everyone of the good old days when the incumbent Duckula would casually impose his will on commoners. Igor adopts a consistently (if usually fairly discreet) paternalistic role, for example, in "Dr. Von Goosewing's Invisible Ray": "He is not your 'Little Duckyboos,' Nanny. He is the *Master*—and *no*, he is not 'all right,' as I fear that he is further betraying his evil destiny by wasting his time on yoga when he should be practising the *black arts* of the *vampire*."[37]

This attitude creates a very convincing setting for accessibly conscientious philosophy, testament to Geri Laybourne's commitment to children's television. Where Dick Dastardly is a resentful adult (we never find out what made him so bitter) repeatedly trying (and failing) to wangle superficial "victory" by any means possible, Duckula is a childlike soul trying to progress in a grownup world that is usually only visible to him from far away. Thanks to his bungled resurrection he can't do anything about (and in fact embraces) being vegetarian, so most of the (un)natural vampiric *potency* of his ancient heritage is neutralized, and he can fall back only on uncoordinated but still unshakeable self-belief. The resulting complex of challenges would be hard to sell in mainstream drama, but we can accept it for a duck in a world of talking birds.

BIRD CHARACTERS

Among its many functions, *Count Duckula*'s titles sequence smoothly establishes the convention that all characters seem to be caricatures of birds of various kinds—at least in that they all have beaks, while otherwise being anthropomorphic in physical abilities (like Donald, Daffy, Howard). Anthropomorphism replaces wings with arms and hands, and "Jungle Duck" confirms (through the near-naked Tarzan) that all birds' torsos seem to be humanoid[38] (also hinted-at throughout by visual suggestions of Nanny's heavy bosom). In the same episode Igor fears certain potentially "anthropophagous" wild plants, which he explains as meaning "*man*-eating." This is not an imaginary world populated by sapient birds, then, so much as a surreal version of our own world in elaborate costume. This disorientating conflation is reinforced in "A Fright at the Opera" when Duckula narrowly avoids falling through a trapdoor: "I *said* that was a *stupid* place to leave a manhole. Or a duckhole, even."[39] At the same time, however, this world claims affiliation with other animated worlds where impossible feats are accidentally but routinely accomplished, and characters can sustain poison, electrocution or crushing without significant harm.

One witty exception to the "sapient birds" rule occurs in "Down Under Duckula,"[40] with the introduction of Bill Platypus—incidentally, a joke that adults can explain to children, in the mixed-audience model considered above. In "The Vampire Strikes Back" our heroes narrowly escape being eaten by the crew of an Oids spaceship.[41] They then visit Planet Cute and encounter Adorable Amy, who resembles a puppy, and her sickeningly cute retinue of talking rabbits—but these are all clearly aliens, excused from the terrestrial flightless-avian model. Similarly the sapience of the stand-up bats might be excused by their seeming at least partially mechanical. The only seemingly *human* character in the series appears in "Hardluck Hotel."[42] The hotel manager is clearly an even-more-exaggerated homage to the character Basil Fawlty as played by John Cleese in the celebrated BBC sitcom *Fawlty Towers* (1975, 1979), then a reasonably recent broadcast and already highly acclaimed. This exception seems justified by the fact that Fawlty was a larger-than-life caricature in the first place,[43] so here *Count Duckula* neatly claims kinship with the broader parade of classic British comedy.

Even if his name were not such a clue, Duckula's flat beak marks him as some kind of duck, and Igor is equally obviously a vulture: hunched, with a pink bald patch, and generally sinister. (The opening of "Dr Goosewing and Mr Duck," shows that Igor routinely sleeps in the fridge.[44]) Nanny is a less visually identifiable huge blob of a character, with her right wing/arm permanently in a sling—but in "One Stormy Night" she clucks gently while dozing off to sleep,[45] and in "Transylvanian Homesick Blues" she complains about a lumpy seat, to which a very muffled Igor responds, "You'd be lumpy, too, if you'd been sat on by a great fat hen."[46] Nanny's species is entirely appropriate, since she is blunderingly obsessed with smotheringly mothering Duckula.

Duckula resembles a real duck no more than Danger Mouse does a mouse. He is an anthropomorphic caricature of a duck with no sincere naturalistic accuracy: his species-relevant visual signifiers are a flat beak and palmate feet (accompanied by a slapping sound effect whenever he moves around a scene). His duckish identity is most consistently reasserted by the opening titles' narration, and by Nanny addressing her adored "Duckyboos."

Much the same vagueness goes for the visual representations of vultures, crows, penguins, among others throughout the series. Indeed, few characters seem to represent particular species at all. For example, Quasimodo, the "Hunchbudgie of Notre Dame,"[47] is identified by the episode title rather than by any significant details of appearance, and the Commodore in "Jungle Duck"[48] *might* (judging by his wattles) be a turkey, but it is impossible to be sure. While most characters are generically bird-like, distinguishing attributes often function mainly to indicate social distinction, not always with species-specific insinuations.

ACCENTS

Duckula's American accent, though surprising for Transylvanian nobility, probably served mainly to provide David Jason with a totally contrasting vocal gamut to Danger Mouse's RP for what was just a bit-part, avoiding confusion for the audience, and serving as a cheaper option than hiring another actor. All concerned, however, must have been aware of Jason's delivery closely approximating Mel Blanc's for Daffy Duck. This resemblance would have provided reassuring orientation toward Daffy's famous series (sharing a popular screen world with Bugs Bunny and Porky Pig), given Duckula's similarly impulsive nature, while heightening the absurdity of Duckula's vegetarian vampirism. (This parallel also locates *Count Duckula* on the extreme end of cartoon violence, as discussed above.)

In 1988 British families were thoroughly accustomed to American characters being represented in popular TV material, from westerns to science fiction to domestic comedy, so were literally at home with Duckula's accent. The British TV experience then spanned only the four terrestrial channels: BBC1, BBC2, the independent network (with regional variations), and the recently introduced Channel 4 (from 1982). Even with VCRs widespread and the video hire market thriving, the national TV palette was much more homogeneous than now, including much American material, so in itself Duckula's accent was unremarkable (and not a production design challenge for adaptation from *Danger Mouse*). After all, in *Count Duckula* it was also painless to accept that what little we ever see of "Transylvania" is a tiny microcosm of English social stereotypes, from the toffee-nosed butler to the nearby village's bumpkin peasants.

Also, into the 1980s and beyond, on British TV American accents could serve as indicators of *authority*,[49] even in domestically produced material. Voluminous evidence exists in Gerry Anderson's prolific science fictional output (both live action and marionette), most famously in *Thunderbirds* (1965–1966). With this cultural resonance, especially in fantastic settings, a character's American accent would assuredly connote diegetic *agency*, and often heroism.[50] *Count Duckula* ironically presents a lead character whose accent suggests effective leadership and who proceeds through the world with brash energy—but who is ineffectual nonetheless. This further tortures the contrast of his being an irresistible vampire by inherited ability, but also fundamentally just a harmless duck.

The titles sequence immediately shows how accents can emphasize character, including the unvarying factors of Nanny's all-encompassing bewilderment in a west-country accent (in British stereotypes connoting a yokel of rustic stock), Igor's snooty, disapproving condescension, and Duckula's pathological enthusiasms suggesting an American TV teenager.[51] The titles' brasher-than-brash musical approach prepares the audience for this.

This world's well-bred duck dynasty displays quite a variety of accents. Merganser in "No Sax Please We're Egyptian"[52] is a crusty English toff. Don Diego in "Vampire Vacation"[53] is of course loftily Spanish. In "One Stormy Night,"[54] an accidentally resurrected ancestral Duckula (also voiced by Jason) sounds fairly similar to *our* Duckula, but with perhaps a slightly Germanic twang (perhaps the hereditary tendency of the Transylvanian family branch). Rory McDuckula, "the scourge of the glens"[55] is posh-Scottish to the point of initially being willfully unintelligible to Duckula (another British joke about passive-aggressive social friction). When a wayward rollercoaster takes our cast to prehistoric times in "Transylvanian Homesick Blues,"[56] the very first vampire (there is no explanation as to his origin, or that of the stone coffin in which he resides) already resembles Duckula and speaks English well, in what seems a heavy Lancashire accent. Although duck-form appears to indicate aristocratic lineage most consistently, as individuals the Duckulas always seem free to express as they wish with no need ever to think about their speech.

SOCIAL CLASS

Like all sitcoms, *Count Duckula* is in some measure a comedy of manners.[57] Whether or not characters understand or even recognize their relative social stations, they are all trapped in a structure based on arbitrary status. *Count*

Duckula gleefully uses British class conventions to set up problems to which characters can be oblivious, since they proceed so uncritically. Duckula himself demonstrates this obliviousness, even though he vividly represents a preeminent stratum of position that Igor slavishly upholds, and of which Von Goosewing seems to be a member *manqué*.

Duckula almost always wears a white dress shirt with waistcoat and red bow tie, and a black, high-collared cloak with purple lining, although this can occasionally vary for plot purposes. At all times, Duckula's costume (or even the occasional lack of it) reflects his privileged (if also impoverished) standing. His attire and his sprawling gothic abode (however run-down) are the main visual ways in which the *Count's* aristocratic position is constantly visually reinscribed. Duckula's flexibly goofy duck-face (onscreen his wide beak is useful for this) never goes anywhere without such simultaneous social confirmation. He begins "Restoration Comedy,"[58] for example, in pyjamas and floppy nightcap—minor emblems of luxury (cf. Ebenezer Scrooge's night attire in *A Christmas Carol*). In "Castle Duckula Open to the Public"[59] he initially wears only a shower cap—conceivably undignified, except that he is being bathed by his housekeeper. He then spends some time with, unashamedly, just a towel around his pudgy waist (like Tarzan, demonstrating that he is bird-like only in his legs and beak). Such expressions of identity extend to other aspects of Duckula's bodily presence: he has black center-parted hair (in his own series bulked-up from the sparser *Danger Mouse* version), and a voluminously expressive, big-eyed face to accompany his emotionally impulsive and unthinkingly *entitled* vocal delivery. In fact, all of the vampire ducks, both present and historical (even the stone-age ones, by their own contemporary standards), are well-dressed—and so are Igor and Von Goosewing, who in their different ways are defined by the nobility while not being *of* it: despite mutual frictions they *all* occupy and define a class space distinct from (most obviously) Nanny, the thieving crows, and the villagers in Ye Tooth and Jugular pub below the castle.

Besuited Igor despises the hoi polloi in a way that Duckula would never approve, and the common people are too far outside Von Goosewing's sphere for him to know how to deal with them maturely: when in "One Stormy Night" he has mistaken an ancient Duckula for an ordinary "young lady" he addresses "her" with patronizing obliviousness as "Cheeky."[60] And in "A Fright at the Opera" Igor remonstrates with his old friend Krool over his plans for destruction: "Please don't go on: you're making me jealous. Oh, how I miss a little evil! It's so long since I did anything really wicked. If only my master were half as malevolent as his father, and his father's father."[61] It should be noted that Igor's style of pining for pure evil has been carefully designed for a children's series. When it comes down to it, even Igor recognizes his own propensity for ill-doing as a matter of personal taste, secondary to his social and professional obligations, however irksome those might be at times. Later in the same episode Igor learns of the Phantom's plan to have the Opera House blown up when the prima donna Elvira hits a high C. He laments to himself: "It is my duty to protect the Duckulas, *even that one*. [...] Curses! I have no alternative but to stop Elvira from singing. And just when I was enjoying myself!"[62]

It has already seemed easy to appreciate Igor's fundamental malevolence, given that he is clearly a vulture with all the stereotypical unpleasantness that implies. At the same time, however, it is also easy to accept the message that rational responsibility trumps preference. That is to say, the metaphor of innately embodied predilections defined by animal form also creates the space for a lesson of civilized self-discipline. This point is driven home quite powerfully in the following episode, "Dr Goosewing and Mr Duck," when Von Goosewing's potion causes everyone to take on traits antithetical to their norms.[63] It is genuinely disconcerting to find Igor being helplessly emotional, and to see both Duckula and Von Goosewing really demonstrating vampiric appetite and ferocity.

The patrons of Ye Tooth and Jugular don't similarly discriminate. Shabbily dressed, they gather in the undirected fashion familiar in pubs everywhere to discuss trivialities in accents much like Nanny's (though not quite as broad, so implicitly not so entirely stupid), or lumpenly bemoan their plight in the shadow of the Castle. To them the present Count is automatically equivalent to all of his predecessors, as they launch into yet another chorus of "One Man Went to Kill, Went to Kill a Vampire."[64] In the context of a children's series, incidentally, it is charming that the pub regulars adapt as a drinking song something that all British children (and accompanying parents!) recognize from early schooling. While oafish, the peasants are also innocently likable. The same goes for the crow burglars, who in their shambolic cockney fashion never actually do any harm. And that is also true of the pirate penguins, whose primary occupation is to sail the seas while threateningly *talkin' loike poirates*. Both of these groups serve mainly to provide contrast to the privileged but helpless aristocracy, and within that fundamental tension absolutely nobody ever manages to advance their own interests significantly, although there is endless scope for them all to struggle.

All of this reflects the narrative latitude afforded by an enthusiastically nonsensical ecology of broadly sketched animal characters (almost all of them birds). The only well-established diet is Duckula's, with his predilection for broccoli sandwiches—and that only upends the conventional vampire stereotype. Although Nanny constantly provides him with snacks such as biscuits, cocoa and cereal, it remains unclear what sustains her and Igor (although the latter at least enjoys the occasional tot of blood—but even then apparently as something of a minor delicacy). The villagers near the castle seem to live on beer, as do the Australians in "Down Under Duckula,"[65] and nobody anywhere seems to farm anything, at least for any useful purpose. In "Down Under Duckula" it is far from obvious why Bill Platypus maintains a wallaby patch at all.

Minor though this point might seem, it helps to illustrate the narrative freedom that can be possible in a landscape of fantasy animals. For comparison, the super-strong Desperate Dan (long-running character in the British children's comic *The Dandy*) can have a borderline-credible penchant for "cow pie" (including the horns), and Popeye can similarly favor spinach for strength. Even the simplified diet of Popeye's friend Wimpy, however, must lean toward a conceivably realistic preference for hamburgers. These generally human characters must in some sense reflect needs and behaviors recognizable from our own society. The characters in *Count Duckula* are not thus constrained, so the writers have the best of both worlds: they can perform caricatures of realistic all-too-human foibles in an exaggerated ecology that seems to work by magic.

In this setting, the essentialism enabled by animal-style analogues can be tactically inverted to disrupt the assumptions that they originally suggested. In "Dr Goosewing and Mr Duck" (1·22), the alarming destabilization of both Duckula and Von Goosewing becoming vampiric is leavened by Igor becoming sentimental and the magnificently dim-witted mother-hen Nanny loquaciously droning on about Goethe and Hegel. This suddenly subverts the menial positioning of the laboring classes: we *like* Nanny's vacuous mother-hen cooing, when applied appropriately to protecting "Duckyboos." With Duckula and Igor back to normal before she is, we can sympathize with their opposed but equal torment in enduring interminable philosophy. As so often in sitcoms, we understand the reassuring safety in what was initially presented as precarious dysfunctionality.

Children might recognize in Duckula a creative but inexpert kindred spirit indefatigably trying hard to be *liked*, generally wishing to enjoy *something*, and hoping to be good at *anything at all*, while his elders (within the dynamic of this incarnation) strive to mold him. In that perspective Igor is something of a father figure, vicariously ambitious for his ward's vocational and social development, alongside Nanny as the unfalteringly devoted (if fabulously stupid) "mother."

The absurdist appeal of these narratives to all ages is illustrated in "Dr Von Goosewing's Invisible Ray" where Duckula stamps on the enormous dining table and throws a tantrum after Igor admits that he swats insects into the "vegetarian" soups: "I am sick to death of you interfering in my life! I am sick and tired of you trying to get me back to being the vampire I was when I was my father. I'm fed up to the back teeth with not being able to get any peace or live a normal life with a proper job to go to, and a little wife and family around me!"⁶⁶ In the same episode Von Goosewing launches another inept attack with an invisibility ray whose usefulness is not at all obvious. Igor explains: "He's just doing his job, sir, as a vampire hunter. Now, if *you* were to accept *your* role in life, there'd be no problem, Milord."⁶⁷ Duckula retorts: "I am *not* gonna become a *vampire* just to keep you and that lunatic Goosewing happy. I am gonna become a famous magician, if only to make you and Goosewing and that brainless Nanny disappear."⁶⁸

CONCLUSION

Even given its superficially sinister background of vampirism and general-purpose evil, this relentlessly positive (if constantly normative) address to children by ITV contrasts strikingly with the slightly earlier and far darker BBC series *Willo the Wisp* (1981), also based in a supernatural setting: a wood populated by anthropomorphic animals, this time with the addition of an overweight fairy (and at some point just about *every* character, including the fairy herself, engages in what is now termed "fat-shaming"). That can certainly be seen as more *edgy*: arbitrarily sinister and less inclined to suggest comforting standards of any kind. Opportunities to give lessons for constructive behavior tend to give way to reminders that life is mercurial and that wariness is a wise general policy. *Willo the Wisp* refuses even to *imply* any possibility of moral clarity, while simultaneously offering a vivid and paradoxical message (personified by Evil Edna, a witch manifesting as a walking television) that, in its basic nature, TV narrative is both untrustworthy and corrupting.

By contrast *Count Duckula* presents a world that is infuriatingly challenging and almost always frustrating, but where characters learn and grow through *doing the right thing*. This is possible only because the population of indestructible animals can experiment in ways completely unavailable to a naturalistic cast, achieved through a combination of many strategies, including those discussed here: exaggerated visual style, ridicule of narrow judgment, and merciless use of stereotypical dialects to rehearse a high-contrast version of social class structure for both interrogation and amusement.

It is noteworthy that, at the 2012 BAFTA Children's Awards, Brian Cosgrove accepted (really on behalf of Cosgrove Hall) a Special Award for outstanding creative contribution.⁶⁹ Where other series can be genuinely and creatively disturbing in their own ways, *Count Duckula*'s bizarre world of cranky, talking birds is from the outset a powerfully suggestive landscape in which to position a set of variously venal and incompetent characters vividly enacting, in fancy dress, the real world that older viewers already sigh about, and into which the younger portion of its audience will eventually arrive.

NOTES

1. "Cosgrove Hall" indicates not a place, as the words imply, but company proprietors and producers Mark Hall and Brian Cosgrove.
2. Rebecca Farley, "From Fred and Wilma to Ren and Stimpy: What Makes a Cartoon 'Prime Time,'?" Carole A Stabile and Mark Harrison (eds), *Prime Time Animation: Television Animation and American Culture* (Abingdon: Routledge, 2003), 147–164.
3. Farley (2003, 160).
4. Jason Mittell, *Genre and Television: From Cop Shows to Cartoons in American Culture* (New York: Routledge, 2004), 212 note 50.
5. Compare a similarly specious assessment of science fiction, held by blinkered producers of TV series *V* and *War of the Worlds*: "As long as we have aliens, ray guns and spaceships, we're *guaranteed the sci-fi audience automatically*."— quoted by J Michael Straczynski: "The Profession of Science Fiction 48: Approaching Babylon," *Foundation* 64 (Summer 1995), 5–19, 6.
6. Brett Mills, *The Sitcom* (Edinburgh: Edinburgh University Press, 2009), 92.
7. Robert Lloyd, "'The Simpsons': Q&A with Matt Groening on reaching 500 episodes," 20 February 2012, https://latimesblogs.latimes.com/showtracker/2012/02/qa-matt-groening-on-the-simpsons-at-500.html, accessed 15 May 2022.
8. Law&Crime Network, "Johnny Depp Explains How He Got Into Acting & Talks Pirate of the Caribbean," 19 April 2022, https://www.youtube.com/watch?v=b6yt8aWPiIE, accessed 15 May 2022.
9. One gentle running joke is that Duckula has *been* all of his own ancestors. This point is extravagantly yet inadequately elaborated in "Transylvanian Homesick Blues" (1.4).
10. Received Pronunciation ("RP") is an arguably superannuated twentieth-century standard for English pronunciation in the UK. It is closely equivalent to what used to be called "BBC English," from the days when BBC presenters were trained to speak crisply and interchangeably with no regional dialect, supporting the BBC's nationwide mission (since establishment in 1922) to "inform, educate and entertain" (in that order). RP is sometimes described as having "no accent," meaningful only regarding its relative neutrality. In truth RP's accent indeterminately suggests south-eastern England, consistent with the BBC's London-based benevolent authority. In practice RP's supposed neutrality therefore connotes a kind of *correctness* in speech and thinking, backhandedly marking regional dialects as inferior. All of this only reinforces existing stereotypes such as the west country's farming dimwits, the north's cultural deficiency, and cockneys being lovable scamps.
11. "Titles Sequence," *Count Duckula*, "No Sax Please We're Egyptian," 1.1, Cosgrove Hall, 1988–93.
12. This discussion uses the notion of *sapience* to distinguish "animals" capable of speech and reasoning (even if poorly in some cases) from those that display merely a cartoon level of rudimentary *sentience*, even including goal-orientated planning.

13. Howard makes cameo appearances in *Guardians of the Galaxy* (2014), *Guardians of the Galaxy Vol.2* (2017) and *Avengers: Endgame* (2019).

14. Michael O'Brien, "Out of the Suitcase #2: Ducks, Ducks, and more Ducks," 22 December 2020, https://www.chaosium.com/blogout-of-the-suitcase-2-ducks-ducks-and-more-ducks/, accessed 19 April 2022.

15. *RuneQuest* was one of the very early roleplaying systems that presented coherent mechanics and an intelligible setting, challenging the derivative and over-complicated mishmash of the nevertheless groundbreaking *Dungeons & Dragons*.

16. Steve Perrin et al., *RuneQuest Fantasy Roleplaying Adventure, Third Edition* (Nottingham: Games Workshop, 1987), 58.

17. It is a rather charming coincidence that the iconic character John *Drake* had such significance in the development of an extremely popular vampire *duck*.

18. Contrary to some assumptions, science fiction is a fundamentally logical and *realistic* genre, where rules apply and consequences can be severe. Writers and producers taking a superficial "anything goes" approach to science fiction produce narratives that seem deflatingly arbitrary.

19. *Brian Cosgrove Interview*, included (with no production credits) on Disc Three of the Region 2 DVD set *Count Duckula: The Complete Collection*, 2008.

20. This reflects *Count Duckula*'s playful twisting of its relationship with its own audience. The bats' audience exists, if at all, somewhere never explained. Towser the werewolf *does* exist, and contributes to the action, but never appears onscreen. Dr Von Goosewing always has to fulfil the duties of his never-seen servant Heinrich—who *might* (but we can't tell) exist only in Von Goosewing's imagination. The very first proto-Duckula vampire's origin (along with his palaeolithic coffin) goes completely unexplained. The narrative blatantly dangles such mysteries in front of the audience.

21. *Count Duckula,* 1.8. Episodes are identified as x.y, where y is the episode number in series x. All *Count Duckula* episodes referenced in this specific discussion are drawn from the first series (of four).

22. Pinning down individual *Danger Mouse* "episode" details is hard, with stories originally spread over multiple very short broadcast segments. DVD credits: *Close Encounters of the Absurd Kind!* (Pearson Television International, Ltd, 2001), "The Four Tasks of Danger Mouse," scr. Brian Trueman; dir. Brian Cosgrove, 1980. This *Danger Mouse* DVD compilation also features the first *Count Duckula* episode, "No Sax Please We're Egyptian."

23. The first three achievements demanded are to collect (1) four hairs from a yeti, (2) a twig from a witch's broom, and (3) a piece of the dreaded fog monster of Old London Town. "The Four Tasks of Danger Mouse."

24. "The Four Tasks of Danger Mouse."

25. "Cels" (short for 'celluloid') are transparent plastic sheets on which artists draw or paint individual moments of narrative action, which are then photographed onto film one frame at a time to create animated sequences. A cel's transparency permits several to be overlaid in a single shot, and/or a background image to be placed behind.

26. *John Doyle Interview*, included (with no production credits) on Disc Three of the Region 2 DVD set *Count Duckula: The Complete Collection*, 2008.

27. In a single unexplained scene-setting action in "Restoration Comedy" (1.5) Duckula impulsively transports himself out of his pyjamas, into his normal clothes, *and* into a phone box distant from the Castle (which is visible in the background). Narratively this is a wonderful use of a character who tends never to think twice (or sometimes at all) about anything, and certainly not his innate supernatural abilities.

28. Episode 1.22.
29. *Brian Cosgrove Interview*, 2008.
30. "The Four Tasks of Danger Mouse."
31. "The Four Tasks of Danger Mouse."
32. "The Four Tasks of Danger Mouse."
33. "The Four Tasks of Danger Mouse."
34. "The Four Tasks of Danger Mouse."
35. Episode 1.1.
36. Episode 1.23.
37. Episode 1.7.
38. Episode 1.19.
39. Episode 1.21.
40. Episode 1.8.
41. Episode 1.14.
42. Episode 1.15.
43. John Cleese explains that his character Basil Fawlty derives from "the rudest man I've ever come across," manager of a hotel where the Monty Python team once stayed, who seemed to think that, "This hotel would run *really well* if we weren't constantly bothered by these *guests*." "John Cleese Interview Pt. One | Parkinson | BBC Studios," https://www.youtube.com/watch?v=c1yKb_77Sf0, accessed 26 October 2021.
44. Episode 1.22.
45. Episode 1.3.
46. Episode 1.4.
47. Episode 1.16.
48. Episode 1.19.
49. This cultural assumption can be seen coming unstuck in the stunt-casting of Fred Ward in *Invasion: Earth* (1998), for example—although still effective with Robert Vaughan being cast in *Hustle* (2004–12).
50. This convention came full-circle with the film *Team America: World Police* (Trey Parker, 2004), stylistically spoofing *Thunderbirds* to satirize American interventionist foreign policy.
51. *Count Duckula* does not convey an anti-American tone. Although it does take easy pot-shots at stereotypes such as wealthy and imperious tourists, one-dimensional intellectual nerds and scheming fraudsters, these are more than balanced by Duckula's unrealistically lovable determination to make the world better for everyone.
52. Episode 1.1.
53. Episode 1.2.
54. Episode 1.3.
55. "The Ghost of McCastle McDuckula," 1.11.

56. Episode 1.4.
57. The episode title "Restoration Comedy" (1.5) is undoubtedly a sly nod to this fact, even though it is primarily a pun about literally restoring the Castle.
58. Episode 1.5.
59. Episode 1.10.
60. Episode 1.3.
61. Episode 1.21.
62. Episode 1.21.
63. Episode 1.22.
64. "Igor's Busy Day" 1.12. The producers clearly assume that this will be recognized by all British children (and their parents) as modifying the educational counting song "One Man Went to Mow," which works rather like "Ten Green Bottles" but in reverse, creating a potentially infinite performance:

    One man went to mow, went to mow a meadow
    One man and his dog went to mow a meadow
    Two men went to mow, went to mow a meadow
    Two men, one man and his dog went to mow a meadow
    Three men went to mow, went to mow a meadow
    Three men, two men, one man and his dog . . . (etc.)

65. Episode 1.8.
66. Episode 1.7.
67. Episode 1.7.
68. Episode 1.7.
69. "Brian Cosgrove - Special Award Recipient in 2012," 18 November 2012, https://www.bafta.org/children/awards/brian-cosgrove-special-award-recipient-in-2012, accessed 17 April 2022. Video of David Jason presenting the award can be found at https://www.youtube.com/watch?v=7gaa4rWKv5U, accessed 17 April 2022.

BIBLIOGRAPHY

Æon Flux. Colossal Pictures/MTV Animation, 1991–1995.
Angel. Mutant Enemy Productions/Greenwolf Corp/David Greenwalt Productions/Kuzui Enterprises/Sandollar Television, 1999–2004.
Buffy the Vampire Slayer. Mutant Enemy Productions/Sandollar Television/Kuzui Enterprises/20th Century Fox Television, 1997–2003.
Cosgrove, Brian. *Brian Cosgrove Interview*, Included (With No Production Credits) on Disc Three of the Region 2 DVD Set *Count Duckula: the Complete Collection*. Fremantle Media, 2008.
Count Duckula. Cosgrove Hall, 1988–1993.
"No Sax Please We're Egyptian" (1.1).
"Vampire Vacation" (1.2).
"One Stormy Night" (1.3).
"Transylvanian Homesick Blues" (1.4).
"Restoration Comedy" (1.5).

"Dr. Von Goosewing's Invisible Ray" (1.7).
"Down Under Duckula" (1.8).
"Castle Duckula Open to the Public" (1.10).
"The Ghost of McCastle McDuckula" (1.11).
"Igor's Busy Day" (1.12).
"The Vampire Strikes Back" (1.14).
"Hardluck Hotel" (1.15).
"Hunchbudgie of Notre Dame" (1.16)
"Jungle Duck" (1.19).
"A Fright at the Opera" (1.21).
"Dr Goosewing and Mr Duck" (1.22).
"Town Hall Terrors" (1.23).
Daffy Duck. Warner Bros., 1937–Present.
Danger Man. Incorporated Television Company, 1960–1968.
Danger Mouse. Cosgrove Hall, 1981–1992.
"The Four Tasks of Danger Mouse" DVD Credits: *Close Encounters of the Absurd Kind!* Pearson Television International, Ltd, 2001. "The Four Tasks of Danger Mouse," scr. Brian Trueman; dir. Brian Cosgrove, 1980. This *Danger Mouse* DVD Compilation Also Features the First *Count Duckula* Episode, "No Sax Please We're Egyptian."
Doyle, John. *John Doyle Interview*, Included (With No Production Credits) on Disc Three of the Region 2 DVD Set *Count Duckula: the Complete Collection*. Fremantle Media, 2008.
Dragoti, Stan, director. *Love at First Bite*. Melvin Simon Productions, 1979.
Farley, Rebecca. "From Fred and Wilma to Ren and Stimpy: What Makes a Cartoon 'Prime Time'?" In *Prime Time Animation: Television Animation and American Culture*, edited by Carole A Stabile and Mark Harrison, 147–164. Abingdon: Routledge, 2003.
Fawlty Towers. BBC, 1975, 1979.
Gerber, Steve, and Val Mayerik. 1976–present. *Howard the Duck*. New York: Marvel.
Gunn, James, director. *Guardians of the Galaxy*. Marvel Studios, 2014.
Gunn, James, director. *Guardians of the Galaxy, Vol. 2*. Marvel Studios, 2017.
Howard, Ron, director. *A Beautiful Mind*. Universal Pictures/DreamWorks Pictures/Imagine Entertainment, 2001.
Huyck, William, director. *Howard the Duck*. Lucasfilm, 1986.
Jeunet, Jean-Pierre, director. *Amélie*. Claudie Ossard Productions/UGC, 2001.
Law & Crime Network. "Johnny Depp Explains How He Got Into Acting & Talks Pirate [*sic*] of the Caribbean." 2022. https://www.youtube.com/watch?v=b6yt8aWPiIE.
Lloyd, Robert. "'The Simpsons': Q&A With Matt Groening on Reaching 500 Episodes." 2012. https://latimesblogs.latimes.com/showtracker/2012/02/qa-matt-groening-on-the-simpsons-at-500.html.

Mills, Brett. *The Sitcom*. Edinburgh: Edinburgh University Press, 2009.
Mittell, Jason. *Genre and Television: From Cop Shows to Cartoons in American Culture*. New York: Routledge, 2004.
Mork & Mindy. Henderson Production Company, Inc./Miller-Milkis Productions/Miller-Milkis-Boyett Productions/Paramount Television, 1978–1982.
O'Brien, Michael. 2020. "Out of the Suitcase #2: Ducks, Ducks, and More Ducks." https://www.chaosium.com/blogout-of-the-suitcase-2-ducks-ducks-and-more-ducks/.
Open All Hours. BBC, 1976–1985.
Parker, Trey, director. *Team America: World Police*. Scott Rudin Productions/Braniff Productions, 2004.
Perrin, Steve, Greg Stafford, Lynn Willis, Sandy Petersen, Steve Henderson, and Warren James. 1987. *RuneQuest Fantasy Roleplaying Adventure, Third Edition*. Nottingham: Games Workshop.
Russo, Anthony, and Joe Russo, directors. *Avengers: Endgame*. Marvel Studios, 2019.
Stafford, Greg. 1975. *White Bear and Red Moon*. Ann Arbor, MI: Chaosium.
Stafford, Greg. 1981. *Dragon Pass*. Ann Arbor, MI: Chaosium, 1981.
Straczynski, J. Michael. 1995. "The Profession of Science Fiction 48: Approaching Babylon." *Foundation* 64 (1995): 5–19.
The Dandy. 1937–2007. Dundee: DC Thompson.
The Simpsons. Gracie Films/20th Television/20th Television Animation, 1989–Present.
Thunderbirds. AP Films, 1965–1966.
Wacky Races. Hanna-Barbera Productions/Heatter-Quigley Productions, 1968–1969.
Willo the Wisp. BBC, 1981.

Chapter 3

"Don't Just Fly, Soar"

Reading Disability in Disney's Animation Dumbo *(1941) and Live-Action Remake* Dumbo *(2019)*

Jessica Gibson

"Exploring examples where the text does not explicitly name a particular impairment or condition, but where disability structures the logic of the narrative or ways of seeing and knowing in the text"[1] is stated by Alice Hall as a way of engaging with and exploring disability. Indeed, critical disability theory enables an examination into the ambiguous experience and definition of *disability* by challenging the expected social norms and understanding the role of the body in such representations. As Sally Chivers and Nicole Markotic assert, *disability* is an important category of analysis even when disability may not be explicitly or overtly present.[2] This is the case for Dumbo, the flying elephant with large ears in the Disney animated film *Dumbo*[3] (1941) and live-action remake *Dumbo*[4] (2019). A close reading of both films can reveal how Dumbo's physical difference is treated negatively by others and thus draws parallels to the experience of disability. This chapter explores several key aspects of Dumbo's journey to highlight how it aligns with the social model and affirmation model of disability. Dumbo's narrative depicts him as the protagonist who at first is othered and marginalized because of his physical difference. However, through his individual talent, he learns to use his ability to become the star of the circus and ultimate hero. By focusing on circus performing animals, this chapter also highlights the changes made between the original and live-action remake that reflect societal attitudes toward animal welfare.

CRITICAL DISABILITY THEORY— MEDICAL VERSUS SOCIAL

In disability studies, there are two central models of disability that have enabled scholars and disabled people to contextualize the experience of disability. First, the medical model views disability as an individual problem in need of diagnosis and cure.[5] When an individual does not fit within the norms of society, through medical model thinking, they must fix themselves to reintegrate back into society. A person with an impairment, then, is disabled by their impairment which creates a fear in society, oppressing those with impairments in the process. The social model, on the other hand, identifies disability as a social construct. Through the social model of disability, it is barriers in society and discriminatory attitudes that cause people with impairments to become disabled,[6] rather than an individual's actual impairment or difference. The social model has played a vital role in the disability rights movement and has been utilized as an important tool highlighting oppression, exclusion, and discrimination faced by disabled people. And thus, disability has moved from a medical problem to a social justice issue.

Critical disability theory is based upon the assumption that disability is caused by the disadvantage experienced by people with impairments and the social environment that does not accommodate for all individuals, as demonstrated in the social model. If someone does not conform to the expectation of normalcy, they become disabled by the world around them. The *concept of normalcy*, developed by Lennard J. Davis,[7] emphasizes the dominance of the able-bodied which is embedded throughout our lives in society and culture. He focuses particularly on culture, including literature, film, and media, highlighting how they have become so ingrained in our society that we forget to interrogate them. In *Enforcing Normalcy*,[8] Davis challenges the hegemony of normalcy. The concept of normalcy, then, is used to show how the disabled body is deviant, othered, and stereotyped in culture as it does not conform to the expected norms of the superior, the able-bodied. This is useful as a framework for analyzing texts where a character does not conform to the expected levels of normalcy because of a physical difference. As Davis emphasizes, texts that do not claim to be about disability can still be read through the concept of normalcy because where bodily difference is highlighted, the expected normalcy is disrupted. Certainly, as Colin Cameron claims, "normalcy requires impairments to be identified as abnormality."[9]

The Affirmation Model of Disability

The affirmation model of disability, first created by John Swain and Sally French[10] and further developed by Colin Cameron, views disability and impairment as a non-tragic, positive social identity.[11] This builds upon the social model in which disability is caused by society but rejects the assumption of negativity associated with an individual's impairment or disability. The affirmation model describes impairment as a common and ordinary part of human life that differs from the cultural normalcy of embodiment but should be expected,[12] rather than as an individual problem that needs to be cured as emphasized in the medical model. And thus, an individual's disability or difference can be embraced and celebrated. The affirmation model of disability is beneficial for film analysis as it allows narratives and characters to be identified that represent disability pride.[13] This chapter argues that *Dumbo* provides a representation of physical difference that aligns with the social model and the affirmation model of disability.

Dumbo (1941)

Dumbo is Walt Disney Animation Studio's fourth feature-length animated film. Released in 1941, the animation follows the story of Dumbo, a young elephant with big ears, who is initially bullied and excluded for his physical difference until he realizes he can use them to fly. He uses his ability to become the star of the circus and is subsequently loved by everyone. The animated film is an adaptation of an illustrated Roll-a-Book titled *Dumbo, the Flying Elephant* by Helen Aberson and Harold Pearl.[14] The film was rushed into production by the Walt Disney Animation Studio due to the high costs and low box office returns of *Pinocchio* and *Fantasia*—as a result of the loss of foreign markets due to World War II.[15] The studio was in need of quick profit so much so that if *Dumbo* had followed the failures of its predecessors, Disney would have been out of business. Walt Disney knew that the studio needed a low-cost blockbuster hit and put *Dumbo* into production at the same time as *Bambi*, using less experienced animators, lower-quality animation, and no special effects.[16] At the time, the Disney studio was on the verge of a labor strike. The film was near completion when the strike began on May 29, 1941.[17] *Dumbo* was released in cinemas on October 23, 1941, to favorable, positive reviews helping to win back audiences and make a profit. And it turned out that *Dumbo* was Walt Disney Animation's most profitable film of the 1940s;[18] however, this popularity quickly ended after the unexpected attack on Pearl Harbor that occurred less than seven weeks after its release.[19]

The 1941 animated film begins with storks delivering newborn babies to the circus animals, but Mrs Jumbo receives her baby late. When the baby elephant arrives, the other elephants call him cute and adorable until he sneezes, which reveals his extra-large ears. The elephants gasp and say, "Is it possible? Isn't there some mistake?" and "just look at those ears, aren't they funny!"[20] One elephant then calls the baby elephant Dumbo, teasing him for the size of his ears. Later, as they arrive at the circus, the public continues to laugh at Dumbo—however he is young and naïve, unaware they are being mean toward him. It is at this moment that Mrs Jumbo gets angry, resulting in her getting locked away in a carriage labeled "mad elephant" and separated from Dumbo for simply trying to protect him. At this point in the film, it is evident that Dumbo's society has become disabling. He is bullied, discriminated against, and marginalized for his physical difference. Through the social model of disability, we can see how Dumbo is treated and excluded within his society. He is labeled a "freak" (figure 3.1), laughed at, and ultimately given the name Dumbo because of the size of his ears. Dumbo's physical difference is read as a disability because of this negative treatment. This reinforces stereotypes of viewing unusual bodies and "freaks" as something that should be pitied, feared, or viewed as monstrous.[21] These stereotypes among others are still recycled in mainstream media to this day. [22]

From Clown to Star of the Circus

Disney's animated feature *Dumbo* follows several Hollywood films set in a circus, namely Charlie Chaplin's *The Circus* (1928) and Todd Browning's *Freaks* (1932), with the latter drawing much attention from scholars in disability studies due to its representation of disability as monstrous.[23] The circus, sideshow, and freak show have historically presented unusual

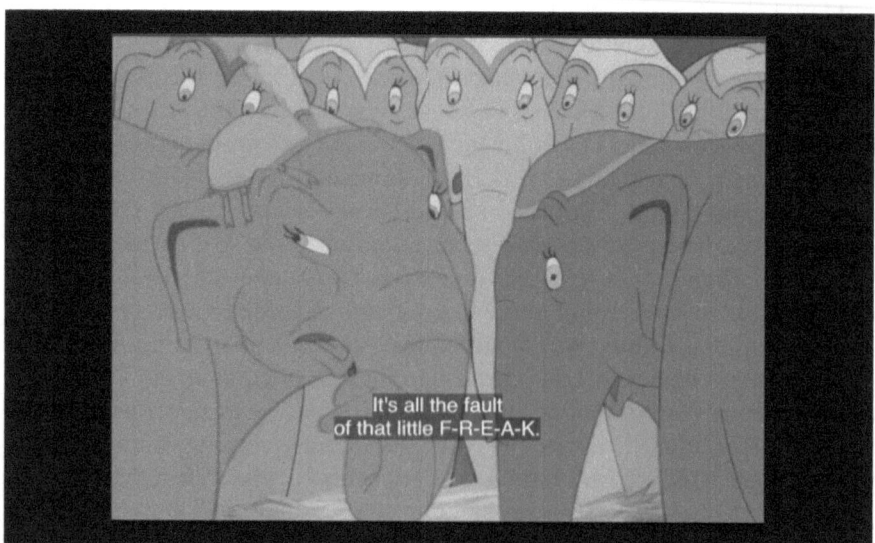

Figure 3.1 Elephants Calling Dumbo a Freak after His Ears Are Revealed. *Source: Dumbo, RKO Radio Pictures, 1941. Screenshot captured by author.*

bodies as entertainment. Elizabeth Stephens argues that twenty-first-century sideshows have moved away from "born" freaks to "self-made" freaks representing the wider shift in society.[24] This is further argued by Rosemarie Garland-Thompson who notes that the discourse of the extraordinary body in freak shows changed from a spectacle to medical.[25] Indeed, the cultural image shifted from "freaks" and "monsters" to sick people that were in need of medical intervention and cure—this is now known as the *medical model of disability*.

The ridicule of Dumbo's ears continues, depicting them as a source of shame and pity. Dumbo is then comforted by Timothy Q. Mouse who asks, "What's the matter with his ears? I don't see nothing wrong with them." He continues to say to Dumbo, "it ain't nobody's fault you've got big ears."[26] Timothy befriends Dumbo and protects him when other elephants continue to bully him for his physical difference. Dumbo continues to be oppressed when he is given the role of a clown in the circus, wearing a costume that hides his ears. However, when he trips and falls, revealing his large ears, the audiences laugh at him. This emphasizes the treatment toward Dumbo's physical difference because even though he is part of a circus where social behaviors are challenged and deviance is accepted, Dumbo is still ridiculed for his difference. Mikhail Bakhtin's carnival and carnivalesque concept explains how the carnival is a dystopian landscape celebrating all that exists and a place where social behaviors and values are turned upside down.[27] In *Dumbo*, the circus is a fun space where the concept of normal is contested as it participates in the carnivalesque. And so, although Dumbo is part of a circus where there are clowns of all shapes and sizes, his over-sized ears still do not conform to the level of normalcy within this society.

The next scene shows Dumbo and Timothy returning from the circus and taking a drink from a nearby bucket without realizing the clowns have dropped champagne into the water. This leads to both Dumbo and Timothy becoming drunk—an interesting plot point for a children's film. They then hallucinate and through their point of view, viewers of the film see the "Pink Elephants on Parade" musical number. The following morning, Dumbo and Timothy are awakened by five black crows and realize they are up in a tree. Questioning how they got there, Timothy guesses Dumbo flew them to the top when they were hallucinating. In modern versions of *Dumbo*, including picture books and the live-action remake, it is clear that Disney wanted to erase this problematic scene which depicts Dumbo, a young anthropomorphized elephant, getting drunk. The picture book of Walt Disney's *Dumbo* by Treasure Cove Stories[28] replaced the drinking and hallucinating Pink Elephant scene with Dumbo practicing to run, jump and hop, and trying to fly until he falls asleep and dreams of flying. In the live-action film, there is much more focus on the humans, and there are no anthropomorphized animals; therefore, Timothy the Mouse doesn't play a major role, and there is no Pink Elephant scene.

In the animation of *Dumbo*, once Dumbo and Timothy realize that they are up a tree, Timothy believes it could have been Dumbo's ears that got them up there—unaware at this point that he can actually fly. The crows joke and mock Timothy and Dumbo with the musical sequence "When I See an Elephant Fly." The crows have since been labeled as a negative racial stereotype[29] for several reasons; the lead crow is named Jim Crow after the Jim Crow laws that enforced racial segregation in the South of the United States in the 1870s to 1950s, and they were voiced by Cliff Edwards, a White man who was putting on his best "black voice" and thus assigning African American stereotypes to anthropomorphized birds. Indeed, Kheli R. Willetts states how Disney provides viewers with a caricatured portrayal of Blackness that mocked the legal process toward any racial equality.[30] On the other hand, however, Douglas Brode argues that characters such as Timothy the mouse and the five crows are presented as equals or sometimes as superior to other characters which shows how Disney animation contained radical ideas representing race, gender, sexuality, and difference.[31] Nevertheless, since October 2020, the original animation has featured a content advisory on Disney+ indicating that the film contains scenes that negatively depict people and cultures. It states that "these stereotypes were wrong then and are wrong now."[32] One could argue that this is a step in the right direction for the fact that Disney is recognizing that older representations are problematic and that they can be used as tools to help audiences learn and create conversations about inclusivity.[33] In the original *Dumbo*, the crows are the ones that help Dumbo whereas the other characters in the circus, particularly the elephants, only laugh at him. Ultimately, the crows help Dumbo to fly by giving him a "magic" feather. Dumbo then holds onto the magic feather which gives him the courage to fly, much to the joy of the crows and Timothy.

When Dumbo returns to the circus, he is still made to dress like a clown but this time he clutches on to the magic feather with Timothy by his side, ready to fly. As he falls from the building, as part of the circus act, he loses the feather. Timothy then shouts "Dumbo! Come on, fly! Open them ears!" and "The magic feather was just a gag. You can fly!"[34] And just as Dumbo was about to fall to the ground, he uses his ears to fly, making the audience gasp with surprise. He flies around the circus scaring the clowns and making the audience cheer. The clowns are now the comedic part of the show, not Dumbo. Dumbo even gets his revenge on the elephants that first named him Dumbo by shooting peanuts at them. Dumbo becomes a star, making headline news and Timothy Q. Mouse, now his manager, signs a Hollywood contract. In the closing scene of the film, the traveling circus, including the elephants that were unkind to Dumbo, appears happy after the reveal of

Dumbo's ability and overnight success. The final shot shows Mrs Jumbo in a private and luxury carriage at the back of the train—removed from the carriage labeled mad elephant—with Dumbo flying above followed by the crows who join in singing "When I See an Elephant Fly." The crows wave goodbye to the train and Dumbo joins Mrs Jumbo in the carriage as it travels to another destination for another circus show. The ending implies that although Mrs Jumbo and Dumbo were mistreated by the circus—locked up, bullied, and forced to perform as a clown—they are happy to continue as part of the traveling circus. However, when the live-action remake of *Dumbo* was announced in 2015, an open letter was sent to director Tim Burton from PETA, People for the Ethical Treatment of Animals, asking for changes to be made to the ending so that Mrs Jumbo and Dumbo were not depicted in captivity but free in the wild, as elephants should be.[35]

Dumbo's ability to fly is celebrated by the circus that welcomes him back as the star of the show—rather than the clown. He uses his ability to triumph and becomes confident in his own identity and uniqueness; however, as Nicholas Sammond argues,[36] Dumbo goes back to the same circus that once ridiculed him and treated both him and his mother badly. The individual success that Dumbo has now conforms to the expectations in his society of the circus because it is also benefiting the success of the circus. From this, we see how Dumbo's ears caused him to become discriminated against as they did not fit the norms of his society within the system of the film. However, Dumbo stays true to himself and uses his difference to become a valuable member of the circus rather than giving in to the expectations that were first alluded to in the film—that his difference degraded him to a clown, in need of pity, and labeled as a freak. By remaining true to himself, Dumbo embraces his difference which is then accepted by others. And thus, through the affirmation model of disability, we can see how Dumbo's physical difference becomes a positive part of his identity that is celebrated. Ultimately, Dumbo's journey is one of self-identify and embracing difference.

Dumbo's journey shows how he overcomes his physical difference, using his ears to fly and become the star of the circus. This can be identified as a supercrip stereotype of disability which Jack A. Nelson states "deals with a heart-warming struggle of someone likeable facing the trauma of a disability, who through great courage, stamina, and determination either succeeds in triumphing or succumbs heroically."[37] Indeed, Dumbo's journey displays him struggling with acceptance, striving toward the ability to fly, and ultimately learning to fly, enabling him to overcome the trauma and negativity he initially faced. However, this depiction could be beneficial for individuals, particularly younger children, which is the primary audience of this film. Victoria Lucas discusses the first time she watched *Dumbo* when she was nine years old and how representations like this have the potential to help individuals accept who they are, overcome stigma, and become a role model for disabled people:

> Like me, Dumbo had an extremely enlarged facial feature. His large ears made him clumsy and awkward, and the other elephants considered him a "freak." But then he discovered that those big funny ears could make him fly (which in my opinion makes this the best disability film ever). For the first time, I'd found someone I could relate to. I didn't realize it then, but I had reclaimed him as a disabled role model.[38]

Live-Action Dumbo (2019)

In 2019, Disney released five live-action remakes of their animated films: *Dumbo*, *Aladdin*, *The Lion King*, *Maleficent: Mistress of Evil*, and *Lady and the Tramp*. This follows a common trend in which Disney are reimagining their classic animated films. The live-action films are predominately longer and expand upon original narratives. This provides Disney with a chance to develop or disregard parts of the original animation that are now viewed as outdated or problematic such as the Siamese cat scene in *Lady and the Tramp* and the crow scene in *Dumbo*. Disney released their streaming service, Disney+, in November 2019 to compete with the likes of Netflix and Amazon Prime. The timing of their service could not have been more perfect for the company's finances as the COVID-19 outbreak was declared a pandemic on March 11, 2020.[39] Disney was hit with billion-dollar losses due to theme park and cinema closures in addition to filming delays. As people around the world were told to stay at home to protect themselves and others, Disney+ became an outlet for fans. Indeed, by August 2020, Disney+ had surpassed 60 million subscribers and by March 2022, this had increased to 129.8 million subscribers worldwide.[40] The on-demand video service provides users access to the "Disney vault" featuring films and television programs from Walt Disney Studios, Walt Disney Television, Pixar, Star Wars, Marvel, National Geographic, and 21st Century Fox. With Disney+, Disney has a platform to create and release exclusive content which was particularly beneficial during the COVID-19 pandemic. Releases including *Mulan*, *Raya and the Last Dragon*, *Cruella*, *Black Widow*, and *Jungle Cruise* all became available for exclusive premium access on Disney+ because they could not be shown in cinemas due to the pandemic. Since the release of Disney+, the Disney catalogue has become ever more accessible, and, thus, is in more need of critical analysis due to the exponential rise in viewers. Additionally, in October 2020, Disney added a content warning to some of their classic animated films, including *Dumbo*, *Peter Pan*, *Lady and the Tramp*, *The Jungle Book*, *Aladdin*, *Swiss Family Robinson*, and *The Aristocats* because of their outdated cultural depictions.[41]

Although the narrative follows the same journey for Dumbo in Tim Burton's CGI and live-action hybrid *Dumbo*, there is more depth and development of other characters and the surrounding narrative of the circus. That is, Dumbo, the flying elephant, still becomes the star of the circus when he learns to fly, overcoming the bullies that first ridiculed his large ears, but the focus turns much more to the humans of the circus, humanity, and animal welfare. Now set in Medici Brothers' Traveling Circus, this version of *Dumbo* introduces viewers to Holt Farrier, an amputee returning from World War I. Played by Colin Farrell, Holt is a war veteran who lost his left arm during battle. His children, Joe and Milly, are hesitant when they first see him after returning from war; they have already lost their mother to the Spanish flu, but Holt points at his face reminding them that "it's still me."[42] As Holt returns to the circus as an amputee, he is quickly given a prosthetic arm by Max Medici, the circus owner, who implies that it is best not to scare the kids who come to see the show. Max, who is played by Danny DeVito, bought the elephant Mrs Jumbo, who at the time was pregnant. Now given birth, the circus performers gather around to see the baby elephant. When his big ears become visible, Max asks, "What is that?" to which the children reply, "Baby Jumbo."[43] Max responds, "I already got fake freaks in the freak show. I don't need a real one in the centre ring"[44] (see Figure 3.2) demonstrating the association being made between Dumbo's physical difference and otherness.

In the next scene, Joe and Millie are playing with Baby Jumbo when he inhales a feather, causing him to sneeze and flap his ears for a few seconds allowing him to fly. Later, in the circus show, Baby Jumbo is dressed up as a baby with an outfit that covers his ears. When he spots a feather in the

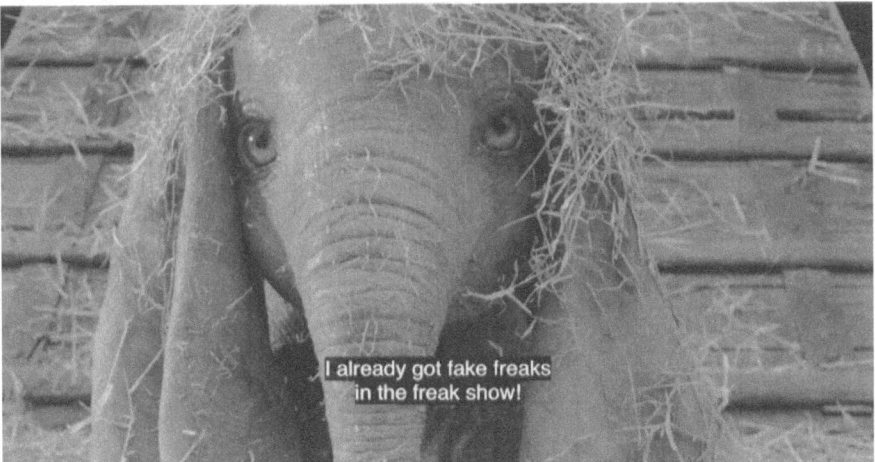

Figure 3.2 CGI Dumbo, Circus Owner, Max Shouts, "I already got fake freaks in the freak show!" *Source: Dumbo, Walt Disney Studios Motion Pictures, 2019. Screenshot captured by author.*

audience, he takes it, inhales it, and ends up sneezing. He falls out of the wooden pram into the center of the circus ring with his ears on show. As this happens, the sign on the pram saying "Dear Baby Jumbo" breaks causing the D to fall into the place of the J, displaying Dumbo. This is pointed out by the audience, causing hysteria at the expense of the baby elephant now named Dumbo.

As the live-action remake is far longer than the original, the narrative expands upon the original storyline of a circus featuring a flying elephant. This includes the addition of Dreamland, an amusement park that collaborates with the Medici Brothers' Traveling Circus after interest was sparked when people found out that Dumbo could fly. The first performance at the amusement park does not go to plan when Dumbo nearly falls and flies out of the circus because he hears Mrs Jumbo calling. Instead of getting locked in a carriage labeled "mad elephant" as is depicted in the original, Mrs Jumbo is sent to an exhibit in Nightmare Island within the amusement park. V. A. Vandevere, the owner of Dreamland, played by Michael Keaton, threatens to kill Mrs Jumbo. And so, the circus performers of the Medici Brothers' Travelling Circus make a plan to get Mrs Jumbo out and reunite her with Dumbo. As anger ensues, a fire breaks out destroying the park. Dumbo, now able to fly without the help of a feather, saves Holt and his family. Dumbo and Mrs Jumbo are then taken to the harbor where they board a ship, taking them to their native home in India. This is a welcome addition that depicts the elephants as free animals in the wild rather than being held captive in a traveling circus as shown in the animation. The emphasis on this change was encouraged by PETA who had urged Tim Burton to change the original ending in the live-action film. As demonstrated, the original depicts Mrs Jumbo and Dumbo continuing to be part of the traveling circus despite their mistreatment. The change in ending illustrates that Disney, and Tim Burton in particular, may have listened to PETA's requests.[45] Both the revised ending and the use of CGI rather than real elephants in the live-action film help support the cause toward ending animal captivity.

In the ending scenes of the live-action *Dumbo*, the circus is up and running again, now called the Medici Family circus. Max Medici welcomes the audience back to the circus, stating how the circus believes no wild animals should be held in captivity. This is highlighted with the release of mice from their cages and birds flying free. The circus has subtle references to Dumbo, the flying elephant, including a live film showing him flying. Holt performs in the circus with a prosthetic arm; however, this is a new, automated prosthetic that is rather unrealistic. Throughout the film, Holt's journey as an amputee is progressive. At one point, he rejects the use of his prosthetic arm and is shown as capable of doing everything he wants to achieve, including climbing the circus tent to help Dumbo escape, and finding love with his new partner, Collette, the circus performer. However, the final scene indicates that he has forgotten everything he has learned about himself and his disability. The use of Holt's disability is a well-meant addition to the narrative, but the use of a futuristic prosthetic has the unfortunate effect of erasing his impairment and his journey throughout the film. Why did he need the prosthetic arm if he was able to perform in the circus and find love without it?

The final scene shows Mrs Jumbo and Dumbo with other elephants in the wild. Dumbo flies among the elephants who trumpet as he passes them, depicting a sign of acceptance. As he flies back to Mrs Jumbo, this signifies the journey they have made together. They are now free from any harm or ridicule they encountered in the circus, and Dumbo can live, and fly authentically. Disney's revised end highlights the development and improvements that can be made to their existing narratives taken from classic animated films. And this particular revision highlights the changes in attitudes toward performing animals from the 1940s to the twenty-first century.

Disney's animated *Dumbo* is a story of difference and inclusion that journeys through self-discovery and social acceptance. This theme has continued to be a key element for Disney's animated films that followed, including *Beauty and the Beast* (1991), *The Hunchback of Notre Dame* (1996), and *Frozen* (2013). The live-action *Dumbo* enabled a richer narrative that addressed social issues, including animal welfare. This chapter has argued that *Dumbo* can be read as a disability narrative because of the treatment of the elephant's physical difference. By learning to fly, Dumbo overcomes his bullies and ultimately, celebrates his difference. The *Dumbo* film can therefore teach the audience to feel better about themselves regardless of negative societal attitudes. Viewers of these films may not have the magical ability to fly like Dumbo, but they may be inspired to overcome social stigma and affirm divergence from "normalcy," whatever form that divergence may take.

NOTES

1. Alice Hall, *The Routledge Companion to Literature and Disability*, 1st edition (London: Routledge, 2020), 2.

2. Sally Chivers and Nicole Markotić, "Introduction," in *The Problem Body: Projecting Disability on Film*, ed. Sally Chivers and Nicole Markotić (Columbus: Ohio State University Press, 2010), 12.

3. *Dumbo*, directed by Ben Sharpsteen, 1942. 64 min. https://www.disneyplus.com/movies/dumbo/31AXKmGUOnjh

4. *Dumbo*, directed by Tim Burton, 2019. 1hr., 57 min. https://www.disneyplus.com/movies/dumbo/1JtOLaonibHo

5. Colin Barnes and Geof Mercer, *Exploring Disability: A Sociological Introduction*, 2nd edition, ed. Colin Barnes and Geof Mercer (Cambridge: Polity Press, 2010).

6. Mike Oliver, "The Social Model of Disability: Thirty Years On," *Disability and Society* 28, no. 7 (October 2013): 1024–26. doi: 10.1080/09687599.2013.818773.

7. Lennard. J. Davis, "Constructing Normalcy: The Bell Curve, the Novel, and the Invention 3 of the Disabled Body in the Nineteenth Century," in *The Disability Studies Reader*, 2nd edition, ed. Lennard. J. Davis (Oxon: Routledge, 2006), 3–16.

8. Lennard. J. Davis, *Enforcing Normalcy: Disability, Deafness, and the Body* (London: Verso, 1995).

9. Colin Cameron, "Normalcy," in *Disability Studies: A Student's Guide*, ed. Colin Cameron (London: SAGE Publications Inc., 2014), 107–9.

10. John Swain and Sally French, "Towards an Affirmation Model of Disability," *Disability & Society* 15, no. 4 (2010): 569–82. doi: 10.1080/09687590050058189.

11. Colin Cameron, "The Affirmation Model," in *Disability Studies: A Student's Guide*, ed. Cameron Colin (London: SAGE Publications Ltd, 2014), 4–7.

12. Cameron, *"The Affirmation Model,"* 4–7.

13. Jordan Alice and Kate Ellis, "Subverting the Monster: Reading Shrek as a Disability Fairy Tale," *M/C Journal* 24, no. 5 (2021), https://doi.org/10.5204/mcj.2828.

14. Helen Pearl and Harold Pearl, *Dumbo, the Flying Elephant* (New York: Roll-a-book Publishers Inc, 1939).

15. Janet Wasko, *Understanding Disney: The Manufacture of Fantasy*, 2nd edition (Cambridge: Polity Press, 2020).

16. Michael Barrier, *The Animated Man: A Life of Walt Disney* (Berkeley and Los Angeles, CA: University of California Press, 2007).

17. Barrier, "The Animated Man."

18. Wasko, *Understanding Disney: The Manufacture of Fantasy*.

19. Alan Bryman, *Disney & His Worlds* (London: Routledge, 1995).

20. *Dumbo*, 00:10:44 - 00:10:46.

21. Rosemarie Garland-Thomson, *Freakery: Cultural Spectacles of the Extraordinary Body* (London: NYU Press, 1996).

22. Beth A. Haller, *Representing Disability in an Ableist World: Essays on Mass Media* (Louisville: The Advocado Press, 2010).

23. Christopher R. Smit and Anthony Enns, *Screening Disability : Essays on Cinema and Disability* (Oxford: University Press of America, 2001).

24. Elizabeth Stephens, "Twenty-First Century Freak Show: Recent Transformations in the Exhibition of Non-Normative Bodies," *Disability Studies Quarterly* 25, no. 3 (2005), https://dsq-sds.org/article/view/580/757.

25. Garland-Thomson, *Freakery: Cultural Spectacles of the Extraordinary Body*.

26. *Dumbo*, 00:21:41.

27. Mikhail Bakhtin, *Rabelais and His World* (Bloomington: Indiana University Press, 1984).

28. A Treasure Cove Story, *Walt Disney's Dumbo* (London: Centum Books, 2018).

29. Mia Adessa Towbin et al., "Images of Gender, Race, Age, and Sexual Orientation in Disney Feature-Length Animated Films," *Journal of Feminist Family Therapy* 15, no. 4 (2004): 32. doi: 10.1300/J086v15n04_02.

30. Kheli R. Willets, "Cannibals and Coons: Blackness in the Early Days of Walt Disney," in *Diversity in Disney Films: Critical Essays on Race, Ethnicity, Gender,*

Sexuality and Disability, ed. Johnson Cheu (Jefferson: McFarland & Company, Inc., Publishers, 2013), 9–22.

31. Douglas Brode, *Multiculturalism and the Mouse: Race and Sex in Disney Entertainment*, 1st edition (Austin: University of Texas Press, 2005).

32. *Dumbo*, https://www.disneyplus.com/movies/dumbo/3lAXKmGUOnjh

33. "Stories Matter," The Walt Disney Company, accessed November 2, 2021, https://storiesmatter.thewaltdisneycompany.com/

34. *Dumbo*, 00:01:18 – 00:01:26.

35. "A new ending for Tim Burton's live-action 'Dumbo'?," PETA, accessed September 18, 2021, https://www.peta.org/blog/peta-asks-tim-burton-to-change-ending-of-dumbo-and-implores-him-to-use-cgi-instead-of-live-elephants/

36. Nicholas Sammond, "Dumbo, Disney, and Difference," in *The Oxford Handbook of Children's Literature*, ed. Lynne Vallone and Julia Mickenberg (Oxford: Oxford University Press, 2011), 147–66.

37. J. A. Nelson, "Broken Images: Portrayals of Those with Disabilities in American Media," in *The Disabled, the Media, and the Information Age*, ed. A. Jack Nelson (Westport: Greenwood Press, 1994), 1–24.

38. Victoria Lucas, "Reclaiming Nemo," Ouch! It's a Disability Thing, August 14, 2004, https://www.bbc.co.uk/ouch/features/reclaiming_nemo.shtml

39. "Coronavirus confirmed as pandemic by World Health Organization," BBC News, accessed September 26, 2021, https://www.bbc.co.uk/news/world-51839944

40. Julia Stoll, "Disney+ subscriber numbers worldwide 2021-2022," Statista, March 28, 2022, https://www.statista.com/statistics/1095372/disney-plus-number-of-subscribers-us/

41. "Disney updates content warning for racism in classic films," BBC News, October 16, 2020, https://www.bbc.co.uk/news/world-us-canada-54566087

42. *Dumbo*, 00:04:18.

43. *Dumbo*, 00:14:36 – 00:14:38.

44. *Dumbo*, 00:14:40 – 00:14:44.

45. "Three Quotes That Prove Tim Burton's 'Dumbo' is worth the tears," PETA, accessed September 19, 2021, https://www.peta.org/blog/disney-tim-burton-dumbo-remake-win-for-elephants/

BIBLIOGRAPHY

Alice, Jordan, and Kate Ellis. "Subverting the Monster: Reading Shrek as a Disability Fairy Tale." *M/C Journal* 24, no. 5 (2021), https://doi.org/10.5204/mcj.2828.

Bakhtin, Mikhail. *Rabelais and His World*. Bloomington: Indiana University Press, 1984.

Barnes, Colin, and Geof Mercer. *Exploring Disability: A Sociological Introduction*. Edited by Colin Barnes and Geof Mercer. 2nd ed. Cambridge: Polity Press, 2010.

Barrier, Michael. *The Animated Man a Life of Walt Disney*. Berkeley and Los Angeles, California: University of California Press, 2007.

Brode, Douglas. *Multiculturalism and the Mouse: Race and Sex in Disney Entertainment.* 1st ed. Austin: University of Texas Press, 2005.

Bryman, Alan. *Disney & His Worlds.* London: Routledge, 1995.

Cameron, Colin. "Normalcy." In *Disability Studies: A Student's Guide*, edited by Colin Cameron, 107–109. London: SAGE Publications Inc., 2014.

———. "The Affirmation Model." In *Disability Studies: A Student's Guide*, edited by Cameron Colin, 4–7. London: SAGE Publications Ltd, 2014.

Chivers, Sally, and Nicole Markotić. "Introduction." In *The Problem Body: Projecting Disability on Film*, edited by Sally Chivers and Nicole Markotić, 12. Columbus: Ohio State University Press, 2010.

Davis, Lennard J. "Constructing Normalcy: The Bell Curve, the Novel, and the Invention 3 of the Disabled Body in the Nineteenth Century." In *The Disability Studies Reader*, edited by Lennard J. Davis, 2nd ed., 3–16. Oxon: Routledge, 2006.

———. *Enforcing Normalcy: Disability, Deafness, and the Body.* London: Verso, 1995.

Garland-Thomson, Rosemarie. *Freakery: Cultural Spectacles of the Extraordinary Body.* London: New York University Press, 1996.

Hall, Alice. *The Routledge Companion to Literature and Disability.* 1st ed. London: Routledge, 2020.

Haller, Beth A. *Representing Disability in an Ableist World: Essays on Mass Media.* Louisville: The Advocado Press, 2010.

Nelson, J. A. "Broken Images: Portrayals of Those With Disabilities in American Media." In *The Disabled, the Media, and the Information Age*, edited by A. Jack Nelson, 1–24. Westport: Greenwood Press, 1994.

Oliver, Mike. "The Social Model of Disability: Thirty Years On." *Disability and Society* 28, no. 7 (October 2013): 1024–1026. https://doi.org/10.1080/09687599.2013.818773.

Sammond, Nicholas. "Dumbo, Disney, and Difference." In *The Oxford Handbook of Children's Literature*, edited by Lynne Vallone and Julia Mickenberg, 147–166. Oxford: Oxford University Press, 2011. https://doi.org/10.1093/OXFORDHB/9780195379785.013.0008.

Smit, Christopher R., and Anthony Enns. *Screening Disability : Essays on Cinema and Disability.* Oxford: University Press of America, 2001.

Stephens, Elizabeth. "Twenty-First Century Freak Show: Recent Transformations in the Exhibition of Non-Normative Bodies." *Disability Studies Quarterly* 25, no. 3 (June 15, 2005). https://dsq-sds.org/article/view/580/757.

Swain, John, and Sally French. "Towards an Affirmation Model of Disability." *Disability & Society* 15, no. 4 (2010): 569–582. https://doi.org/10.1080/09687590050058189.

Towbin, Mia Adessa, Shelley A. Haddock, Toni Schindler Zimmerman, Lori K. Lund, and Litsa Renee Tanner. "Images of Gender, Race, Age, and Sexual Orientation in Disney Feature-Length Animated Films." *Journal of Feminist Family Therapy* 15, no. 4 (2004): 19–44. https://doi.org/10.1300/J086v15n04_02.

Wasko, Janet. *Understanding Disney: The Manufacture of Fantasy*. 2nd ed. Cambridge: Polity Press, 2020.
Willets, Kheli R. "Cannibals and Coons: Blackness in the Early Days of Walt Disney." In *Diversity in Disney Films: Critical Essays on Race, Ethnicity, Gender, Sexuality and Disability*, edited by Johnson Cheu, 9–22. Jefferson: McFarland & Company, Inc., Publishers, 2013.

Chapter 4

Making the Invisible Visible
Displaced and Marginalized Animal Characters in Samuel Fuller's White Dog and Kornél Mundruczó's White God

Heather Rolufs and Karin Beeler

Animal characters, specifically canine characters, have a long history in film. While many films and television series feature dogs as prominent characters (e.g., *Lassie Come Home*, *The Adventures of Rin Tin Tin*, *Cujo*) and imbue these animals with heroic or villainous qualities, they are also used to reflect the best and worst of humanity by forcing viewers to see fissures within societal infrastructures. Samuel Fuller's *White Dog* (1982) and Kornél Mundruczó's *White God* (2014) both use canine characters to explore the complexities of racism, marginalization, and displacement within societal structures. Fuller's film, *White Dog* (1982), adapted from Romain Gary's novella, tells the story of a stray White German Shepherd that is hit by a car and taken in by the driver, Julie. His past is unknown, but it is revealed that he is a "White Dog"[1] trained to attack Black people. Metaphorically, the dog is being used to reflect racial and cultural anxieties that stem from a complicated history between Black people and dogs in America. The dog also depicts othering and displacement as it is never given a name or identity beyond "White Dog." In this sense, the dog becomes a compromised figure that has been displaced and marginalized, having no place anywhere within society. His inability to navigate the different rules causes him to become unstable and unable to acquire any agency. As a result, the character becomes less of a dog and more of a monstrous other. Kornél Mundruczó's Hungarian film, *White God* (2014), takes a slightly different approach to racism, displacement, and marginalization in society by telling the story of Hagen, a mixed-breed dog in Budapest who is the companion of a young girl named Lili. Unlike the White Dog, Hagen has a name (a sense of identity) and good home life until he and Lili have to stay with Lili's father. Then it is revealed that mixed-breed dogs are subject to taxes (unlike purebred dogs), and while Lili does her best to keep Hagen, she is forced to abandon him. He sees the cruelty his "kind" faces through his displacement, which includes marginalization, beatings, dog fighting, and imprisonment. As a result, he and other mixed breeds trigger an uprising against the humans or "[W]hite gods,"[2] thus functioning as anthropomorphized canine characters who resist injustice. The issues pertaining to racism and marginalization are depicted through mixed-breed dogs as they are afforded fewer freedoms and are expected to adhere to more rules; in a sense these restrictions serve as a parallel to the kinds of restrictions/biases experienced by immigrants around the world, including marginalized groups such as the Roma and ethnic Romanians in Hungary. *White God*'s focus on the treatment of displaced mixed-breed dogs is crucial as Hagen's navigation of a society constructed to exclude him due to his breed and species highlights the injustices that other marginalized populations face. Exploring how the canine characters in both films represent the manifestation of different cultural anxieties will suggest that "man's best friend" is being used to unmask systemic issues about displacement and marginalization within societal structures. These human–canine relationships will reveal how the categories of hero, anti-hero, and villain might apply to the White Dog and to Hagen as they experience displacement. In doing so, this chapter will highlight how the canine characters utilize the established and often romanticized human-dog bond to force the viewer to see and face what they do not want to see about themselves and society by making visible the need to see it.

The exploration of dog characters in film is not new. *Lassie Come Home* (1943), *the Rin Tin Tin* films (e.g., *Where the North Begins* ([1923])), *Benji* (1974), *Beethoven* (1992), *Old Yeller* (1957), *My Dog Skip* (2000), *Cujo* (1982), *A Dog's Purpose* (2019), *Hachiko* (2009), *Marley and Me* (2008), and other such films have been studied and analyzed for the plethora of cinematic tropes they employ. Adrienne L. McLean's edited collection *Cinematic Canines*, in particular, provides a closer look at the movie industry (the good, the bad, and the ugly) and the influence that dog films have on society and culture. Caleb Chodosh in "Good Boy: Canine Representations in Cinema" points out that "depictions of dogs vary wildly in pop culture . . . Dogs have been commercialized, anthropomorphized, weaponized, and racialized. Dogs on film have transcended genre to serve as a proxy for what we fear and value about humanity itself."[3] Canine characters in film can be multifaceted as they "can be equally compelling as heroes, villains, or romantic leads."[4] Dogs on screen are "both driven by culture and impact culture in a circular feedback loop."[5] Katarina Gregersdotter, Johan Höglund, and Nicklas Hållén's *Animal Horror Cinema* explores how animal narratives are used to "provoke fear and suspense . . . [by] often engag[ing] with social (human) issues and address[ing] problems such as racism and sexism."⁶ Sam Fuller, the director of *White Dog*, made a point of addressing racism in many of his films and pushing back against an industry that at the time would have preferred that he be less provocative. Despite these efforts, as Lisa Dombrowski states he "was not a maker of typical social-problem films and rejected treating subjects with sanitized white gloves."⁷ Instead he preferred "stylistic punctuation, and emphasizing spectacle and emotion" that offer the viewer "a slap in the face rather than a reassuring message."⁸ *White Dog*, specifically, drew critical attention due to unfounded rumors of racist content and "Black civil-rights leaders feared [the film] might provoke racist activity."⁹ Paramount became reluctant to release the film due to pressure from the NAACP. Fuller maintained that his revision of *White Dog* was a "strongly anti-racist film."¹⁰ While members of the NAACP did acknowledge that they did not find the film inherently racist, they argued that the "unintended readings of the film . . . 'could cause a distribution problem if the Black population were to collectively voice an objection to the subject matter,'"¹¹ which sealed its fate. Ultimately, *White Dog* was shelved for over a decade before finally receiving limited release and even then, it was not available on DVD until 2008.

Fuller's *White Dog* (1982) has become the subject of discussion and analysis more recently due to the critical lens focused on Hollywood and America regarding systemic racism. Education and academia have been focused on examining equity, societal infrastructures, and power dynamics and, in doing so, have provided a new lens and vocabulary with which to examine race within society and culture. While it should be noted that we are viewing this film, and the film *White God*, through a White lens ourselves, the study of canine characters gives us the ability to examine both the films and, to an extent, our privilege, in order to focus the discussion on racism and speciesism. In addition, the interest in animal narratives within film provides another avenue to explore the complexities of animal characters and their ability to communicate truths about humanity. In the case of canine narratives, the adaptation of Stephen King's *Cujo* (1982), coincidentally released the same year as Fuller's *White Dog*, tells the story of the domesticated dog who is bitten by a rabies-infected bat. As a result, Cujo turns on a family in a horrifying escalation of Old Yeller-esque magnitude. Breed does carry some significance here due to the dog's size and its historic role/partnership with humans. The Saint Bernard is a very large and powerful molosser breed that worked beside people assisting with search and rescue in the Swiss Alps.¹² These "good dog" characteristics are important because it makes the idea of the dog turning on people that much more unthinkable and horrifying. Cujo, like *Old Yeller*, becomes a monster who can only be stopped by being shot. In both Disney's *Old Yeller* (1957) and Fuller's *White Dog* (1982), the canine characters share the same outcome, which reinforces what Doble characterizes as "the control of dogs through rabies discourse—[by] demonstrate[ing] how dogs have been used as vehicles and agents of white societal concerns." [13] When the "infected" dog loses control and cannot abide by human societal rules, it becomes displaced from its domesticated role as trusted protector of the White nuclear family. The dog is no longer "man's best friend" but the monstrous other that threatens the domestic home. Though still tragic, when the dog becomes the monstrous other, this transformed state gives the human characters "permission" to kill the animal, but only because there was no other choice. For some reason, even in horror, there needs to be a rationale for killing the monstrous canine character, as that is the only way the audience will accept the outcome since dogs have such a long history as trusted companions.

In the case of Fuller's *White Dog,* rabies is replaced by racism, re-envisioning Doble's "rabies discourse"[14] by adding racial components to elements of the horror genre in order to add complexity to its canine character. Again, breed is important here because historically, the German Shepherd shares a special bond with people as protectors, enforcers, and reflections/projections of cultural anxieties. As Aaron Skabelund points out, "people often do not recognize or forget that animal breeds, like human races, are contingent, constantly changing, culturally constructed categories that are inextricably interconnected to state formation, class structures, and national identities."[15] In some ways, the German Shepherd's "identity [was] both extremely malleable but also very stable; the dog became associated with a number of different political regimes but for many of the same reasons—whether revered for supposed purity of blood, loyalty, and courage, or despised as a symbol of oppressive authority."[16] Additionally, the breed could be viewed "as an agent and symbol of political racism and repression."[17] The breed was "metaphorically manipulated" by humans as a way to "to define, discipline, and enforce political and social boundaries."[18] As a result, the German Shepherd Dog "provided people [with] a powerful way to regulate human society . . . when notions of social, [and] racial hierarch[ies] were often important to the ideological mechanisms of control."[19] It is due to the breed's employment as an "agent of social control" that it began to symbolize certain actions, like policing, and therefore, became synonymous with the term "'Police Dog.'"[20] Generally, when people think of a police dog, they think of the German Shepherd which upholds the idea of the dog as a manifestation of societal control; in that sense, the German Shepherd embodies both literal and figurative interpretations of control/enforcement, which are then mirrored on screen.

Fuller's metaphorical interpretation of the breed creates a character that navigates the space of displacement and marginalization through the concept of the stray. The dog is introduced to the audience as a stray, which does not have a home until Julie's character attempts to give him one. Like most strays, his history is unknown, but he does display characteristics known to his breed when he protects Julie from an intruder, and thus acquires the status of a heroic animal. Julie's bond with the dog is solidified here, and the audience connects with the dog through Julie's character. The White Dog protects Julie and seems to view her as a resource, as she provides a safe place for him to rest, which is evident by how deeply he sleeps with the TV blaring even though Julie is being attacked in the other room by the intruder. However, what is interesting is that his connection to her is a little more ambiguous due to his roaming behavior. He chases after a rabbit at one point in the film, leaving Julie running after him only to lose him in the ravine. She searches for him everywhere to no avail. Meanwhile, having lost the rabbit, the dog has wandered into a deserted street when he comes across a Black man in a service truck and proceeds to attack him without cause. He then returns to Julie's home covered in blood, and she thinks he has been in a fight with an animal and cleans him up. His return reveals that he was never lost; he knew his way back to Julie's, which suggests a certain independence and a lack of connection with her character. While he did return, it was on his terms.

In addition to his portrayal as a stray, the White Dog's color is significant. The "acceptable" colors for German Shepherds registered with various kennel clubs around the world typically include dark colors. The American Kennel club (AKC) standard indicates that "strong rich colors are preferred" and that "white dogs must be disqualified"[21] (American Kennel Club "Official Standard of the German Shepherd Dog"). However, the White German Shepherd does have a following. There are clubs dedicated to White German Shepherds, but there is also a history of discrimination against the breed. This outlier status therefore reinforces the White Dog's role as a stray in the film and might even emphasize the conflicting images of the dog as both hero and victim (in one instance) and villain/monster in another. It also creates a duality between the idea of purity and taint, prejudice and acceptance, and could be a way to align the White Dog mythos with racial disparity allowing the character to occupy multiple positions as hero/victim, villain/monster/other. However, most viewers not familiar with the AKC breed standard of the German Shepherd would probably see the main purpose of the dog's "Whiteness" as a symbol of racist White supremacy since the dog attacks Black people. Julie concludes that the dog is triggered to attack Black people when she witnesses the dog attack her colleague while they are shooting a scene. Even though she is encouraged by her boyfriend to surrender him to the pound, she feels obligated to help him, so she seeks out Keys, a professional animal trainer, who is Black. What is bizarre is that she feels so bonded to the dog that she is willing to seek out a professional trainer, but she never gives the dog a name. Throughout the entire film, the dog is referred to as "the dog" or "White Dog," limiting the dog's identity to his appearance and behavior, while maintaining a certain amount of distance between the audience and the canine character. In a sense, naming a dog personalizes it, humanizes it, and makes it an individual, suggesting that Fuller's choice to maintain that generalized distance between the canine character, the human characters, and the audience was deliberate. At the very least, it created uncomfortable tension and allowed the canine character the ability to slip between the image of man's best friend and monstrous other. The dog is able to occupy multiple spaces but is ultimately displaced from them all. Susan Schwertfeger notes that "the dog's representation oscillates between animal/non-human and human. . .its state is deliberately kept ambiguous and cannot be determined exactly as subject (attacker) or object (instrument), because its condition and actions are initiated through the manipulation by man."[22] In this sense, the dog becomes "othered," a compromised figure that has been displaced and marginalized, having no place anywhere within society. Whether it is Julie, Keys, or his former racist owner, humans constantly manipulate the dog, making him both villain and victim. His inability to navigate the different human rules causes him to become unstable and limits his agency. As a result, the character becomes less of a dog and more of a monstrous other.

When the White Dog is viewed as a symbol of White displacement, this is one of the few if only times that "White" and, to a degree, "White hate" can be considered through a displaced lens. The American societal infrastructure created by Euro-centric White men renders the idea of White people being marginalized, displaced, or excluded unlikely due to a system that has placed Whiteness at the center. The idea of a White German Shepherd becoming the White, and in a sense, "pure" manifestation of institutionalized racism and hatred is interesting as much as it is complicated, given the more common color variations, such as black, black and tan, and sable, and the employment of the breed today "by police departments and their varied specialized units to . . . be at the forefront of 'policing the color-line.'"[23] The German Shepherd is, ultimately, interwoven into the fabric of society where systemic racism permeates. Fuller forces the audience to "see" the systemic racism that surrounds them by using a canine character to expose "the perversion of weaponizing an ideology . . . by playing with audience expectations of what a dog can and can't be."[24] Can a dog be racist? No, but as Chodosh argues, "it can be conditioned to be,"[25] which is why the audience can "accept" this possibility even if it makes them uncomfortable because it is ultimately, humans, White humans, that have created this "racist" dog. The German Shepherd's breed history as an agent of oppression/social control is visually illustrated through its relationship to the Black character, Joe. Joe shows Julie a scar on his leg and tells her that when he was fourteen that a "'White Dog did it'"[26] and Keys then proceeds to explain the history/creation of White Dogs to Julie: "Well, over a hundred years ago, they raised dogs to catch runaway slaves. Then they progressed—to track down runaway black convicts."[27] The scene is meant to convince Julie, and by proxy, the audience, that humans were responsible for the dog's behavior or, as Keys puts it, that the dog was turned into a monster by "'a two-legged racist.'"[28] Julie, of course, asks if they were trained to attack any other "colors," but Keys replies, "No, dogs live in a black-and-white world. Unlike ours, they live it visually and not racially."[29] At the time *White Dog* was produced, this could be taken literally and figuratively as it was believed that dogs could only see in black and white, but now, it is common knowledge that dogs only have two photoreceptors "one is sensitive blue and the other to greenish-yellow."[30] Therefore, they see things "most strongly when it is in the range of blue and green."[31] However, figuratively speaking, Keys's comment reinforces what was mentioned above; dogs cannot be racist, but they can be taught to reinforce a human's racist belief system and, in a way, can become an extension of that racism. While this seemingly takes away the dog's agency or choice, at the same time, the White Dog character had limited agency, and this begs the question as to whether it was ever supposed to and if not, why not? Keys's subsequent explanation of how the White Dog was conditioned to hate Black people by a "two legged racist"[32] who paid Black people to beat the dog as a puppy serves to highlight to the audience that hate is not born; it is created. The canine character has a dual function here by suggesting that no one is inherently racist, but that people (and dogs) are products of their environments and experiences. That said, this in no way excuses the dog's behavior in the film but it seems to be an attempt by Fuller to make the audience "see" how systemic racism functions within society and how it bleeds into everything. Julie, a rather ingenuous White woman, is confused as she does not understand how someone "can turn a dog into a racist."[33] Her disgust that someone could train a dog to hate a race of people is demonstrated when she is confronted by the dog's original owner, and his young granddaughters, who have finally come to reclaim the dog: "You sick son of a bitch . . . You got two puppies there. You gonna teach 'em to be as sick as you are?! . . . [You] turned that dog into a monster! A killer!"[34] Fuller further uses this scene in an attempt to highlight that racism is learned by drawing a parallel between the previous owner's granddaughters and the puppies who were taught to hate: "Do you know what your grandfather did to that dog? He turned that dog into a monster! . . . Don't you let him turn you into monsters either! Don't listen to a damn word he says about anything!"[35] While Julie's White privilege allows her the ability to pick and choose what she sees, it is interesting that she does not call the previous owner a "monster" but instead refers to him as being "sick."[36] Julie suggests that monsters are shaped or created; in other words, the owner had turned the dog into a monster—thus her warning to the girls to not let him turn them in monsters. Fuller's film presents racism as a form of hate and fear and argues that racist behaviors are taught and learned. Therefore, Fuller's use of the White Dog character emphasizes and explores how hate, more specifically, racism, is socially constructed and embedded into social structures that make the film more than a typical dog film or even more than just a horror film.

This schism is vividly depicted in the final scenes when the dog snarls and visually fights its "programming" to attack. The tension is created through music, rapid cuts between the dog's bared teeth and Keys's hold on the gun that he raises and points at the dog numerous times. While this sequence was supposed to increase the intensity of the scene, it also illustrates that Keys never fully trusted that the dog was completely cured. The dog's death at the end of the film is layered as Keys both fails and succeeds. He did "cure" the dog of his "racial" programming, as the dog was able to be in the presence of Black men without attacking them, but he could not cure him of the hate instilled by humans, as the dog ends up attacking Mr. Carruthers for no reason, forcing Keys to shoot him. Fuller stages the dog dramatically by framing the prone figure of the White Dog in the arena with his head upside down and displaying a fixed snarl that never relaxes, even in death. The snarl remains etched in his face as the camera pulls back. We also see a brown collar dividing the dog's head from his body and acting as a vertical division line that occupies the center of the frame. Blood is shown on either side of the collar, on the dog's muzzle, and on his body. Thus, the image of the White Dog with the grotesquely twisted face and bloody body becomes representative of systemic issues that continue to persist within American societal structures. The ending upsets the audience's expectation that the dog can be healed or cured of its "disease" and therefore questions the idea that racism can be eradicated. However, the final image of the dog could also be suggesting that eliminating racism is not that simple, especially when society is built on systems that privilege White culture. Fuller himself is White, and while he is using his position to critically comment on racism, especially within the industry, he is limited to his White lens and as a result, any power that Keys's character has is muted as there is no way to negate Fuller's control over Keys's character and his actions. Additionally, one could also critique Keys's obsessive need to cure the monster within the dog as he is focusing on the consequence of racist programming rather than concentrating on the human monster or villain responsible for the programming. In that sense, the film could end only one way because the dog character was never the root cause of racism; therefore, "curing" him would have less of an impact than his death. In death, the canine character's last function is making the invisible damage of systemic hate and fear visible and uncomfortable by daring the audience to see what they are afraid to acknowledge within themselves. Unlike *Old Yeller*, which alleviates the sadness associated with the death of the dog through the family's acquisition of another dog, *White Dog* does not provide this kind of relief. Instead, the audience is forced to search for some kind of meaning, and none of the interpretations appear to provide comfort; the ending is confusing and makes the audience question the film's message. Perhaps that is exactly what Fuller wanted: to use the dog character to make the audience start asking questions about the cause and effects of racism, regardless of whether the answers are readily available. As a result, the canine character becomes a force that the audience cannot ignore or turn away from. Dog characters highlight Donna Haraway's point that "[d]ogs, in their historic complexity, matter here . . . they are here to live with. Partners in the crime of human evolution,"[37] if only to provide the mirror with which to show humanity how much it still needs grow and evolve.

Over thirty years after the release of *White Dog,* Hungarian director Kornél Mundruczó's film *White God* was released. When asked about the influence of the former film on his movie, Mundruczó replied that the films have "lots of connections."[38]

> [M]y lead trainer, Teresa Ann Miller, her father was Carl Miller who did the Samuel Fuller movie, so it's a huge connection and it was really meaningful for me as well. So I watched the movie after editing mine because it was released in France and was a success, and I thought it was a really strong movie. I'm very proud that we have this connection with the title.[39]

Unlike Fuller's canine character who is largely defined by others as a "White Dog" and lacks an identity that can be separated from this construct, Hagen, the canine protagonist in Kornél Mundruczó's Hungarian film *White God* (2014), has some unique qualities and a sense of belonging. At the beginning of the film the audience is introduced to Hagen and Lili playing in a park. Hagen's individual exuberance is shown as he barks and leaps up to grab the toy (it resembles an animal hide) that Lili is holding. The scene highlights their bond, which is further demonstrated when both Lili and Hagen are both displaced by Lili's mother and forced to go live with her father. It is quite clear through the framing that to Lili and Hagen "home" is each other even when they are placed in unfamiliar spaces. As Lesley Pleasant points out "[d]ogs are often associated with home"[40]; therefore, together Lili and Hagen are able to renegotiate "ways of feeling at home"[41] in places that are unfamiliar. It also serves to highlight her estrangement from her father, Daniel, when he is introduced. Daniel is uncomfortable with Lili coming to live with him from the beginning, and he resents having to take Hagen, often referring to him as "the dog" rather than by his name. Given his occupation as a meat inspector, it is hard to tell if his dislike of Hagen is because of the situation or his desensitized view of animals. His ability to watch with cold detachment as a cow is disemboweled and exsanguinated is quite shocking; Daniel is presented as someone who lacks empathy and compassion. The scene reinforces how human beings can desensitized themselves to the death of animals in certain situations (when animals become a source of food, or inconvenient or undesirable). This part of the film could be Mundruczó's way of introducing a distancing technique or "Verfremdungseffekt."[42] He presents something that may be unfamiliar to many viewers, yet true. No matter how much the audience wants to deny the truth that animals need to be slaughtered for the consumer, the scene suggests that people should become aware of where their meat comes from, even though they would rather pretend that it does not have a face. The scene appears to be shot with a handheld camera and is composed of fragmented sequences, consisting of some third-person limited point of view shots of the workers in the slaughterhouse, shots of the meat being sliced, and some point of view shots from the perspective of the inspector, Lili's father who appears in different sections of the frame over the course of this scene. He declares that the slice of meat is fit for consumption and stamps the meat with a seal of approval. The matter of fact way that the handling and slicing of the meat are presented normalizes the action, which disturbs the complacency of the film's viewers and forces them to acknowledge the connection between animals, food, processing, and future consumption. The audience sees this disruption again after Daniel leaves the plant parking lot with Lili and Hagen just as two cows are casually led across a crosswalk to their deaths. It is such a bizarre transition between scenes that is made stranger through the casual presentation of the action. That said, it demonstrates how animals are often displaced for human consumption as these farm animals are depicted in an urban space, and that juxtaposition of images emphasizes "another human construction of animality, because all of them are based on the idea of human dominance"[43]—the "White God" that decides what lives and what dies according to their need. The linking of Hagen's departure in the vehicle with the cow being led across the street suggests that both animals will become sacrificed in some way.

When Daniel arrives home with Lili and Hagen, the audience is given their first clue that there is something unusual about the image of Hungarian society presented in the film when a neighbor confronts them on their way into the apartment, asking, "'what [that] mutt'" was doing there and that "it" cannot stay as "they've posted a ruling. Mutts have to be reported."[44] While it is not explicitly clear who "they" are, the nosy neighbor does reveal that they are making a "list." Surprisingly, Daniel seems to feign ignorance by stating that he was not aware of the report. This scene provides foreshadowing of the appearance of the canine control officer appearing at their door claiming that someone had been bitten by Hagen, which was not true. The shot shows the neighbor moving toward the center of the screen in the background. She is framed by the window of a door; the audience then knows that she must have filed the false report. The viewer learns that the ruling is just against mixed-breed dogs and that Hungarian breeds, purebred dogs, are exempt. It is revealed that street and mixed-breed dogs are subject to a tax and the need for registration; if it is not paid, then the dog is impounded.[45] According to Mundroczó, this presentation of a dog tax in the film was inspired by "'the extreme right' and its effort to pass a law that would have levied a heavy tax against mixed dogs, a lesser tax for pedigrees and no tax for Hungarian pedigrees."[46] Lili watches as Daniel tells the officer that he will not pay and that the dog will not be there tomorrow, implying that he will be surrendering Hagen. While Lili does not comment, it is apparent that she does not trust her dad to not drop Hagen off at a shelter, so she leaves with Hagen while he is showering. The discrimination being depicted in these scenes is not unlike Breed Specific Legislation that has been adopted by many jurisdictions in North America.[47] All of this is due to basic breedism—a practice that does not improve public safety. New legislation that promotes responsible dog ownership has proven to be much more effective by focusing on individual dogs and owners, rather than villainizing certain breeds. It actually provides another way that dog characters represent displacement and marginalization by representing the underrepresented. It should be noted that in Hungary, BSL is not employed as legally, "euthanasia is prohibited according to Hungarian national law."[48] The exception is in the "mercy killing of animals in order to avoid or prevent the unnecessary prolongation of their suffering"[49] or if they are deemed aggressive[50] and are a danger to public safety. That said, *White God*'s allusion to BSL draws attention to not only its ineffectiveness but also comments on how governmental legislation can be used to control minority populations, further marginalizing them within the system. It emphasizes class distinctions, which Elizabeth Young suggests "is an organizing frame; anyone masterless — human dog thieves as well as stray dogs — threatened social order."[51] Mundruczó intended the film to be "a dog movie, [that is] not about dogs." [52] His focus was to use canine characters to represent "a caste-system [which] has become more sharply defined [in Europe] . . . parallel to the questionable advantages of globalization."[53] In doing so, he uses animals, in this case dogs, to illustrate how "Eastern Europe exists in the midst of massive chaos, mutability, and instability"[54] in order to "create a new Budapest, which expresses a current relationship to the city's history"[55] by allowing "a glimpse [into humanity's] . . . detestable self-confidence, full of lies and lopsided truths, set on domesticating the minorities while actually wishing only to destroy them, hypocritically denying inequalities, not believing in either peace or in peaceful cohabitation."[56] Therefore, the canine characters function as a way to metaphorically navigate the sensitive issues concerning displacement of minorities; the terms "mixed-breed," "stray," and "street dog" highlight the racism and discrimination of minority groups within these spaces. The stray/street dog is the "eternal outcast"[57] that critiques the idea of "belonging" as they "belong" on the street strictly because they do not "belong" anywhere else.[58] Hagen further complicates this idea because he was a domesticated dog that "belonged" somewhere and to someone before becoming homeless. While Hagen is not a "street" dog in the sense that he had a home and was part of a family, he cannot escape his mixed-breed heritage and in a way, it becomes a self-fulfilling prophecy when Lili is forced to abandon him on the side of the road. In Lili's mind, he would stand a better chance on his own than at a shelter, where he would most certainly be euthanized. By being abandoned, Hagen is displaced and becomes a "street dog" but without the experience or survival instinct that most strays/street dogs have. As we discuss below, this also parallels the rise of forced evictions among minority groups in society. Ultimately, Hagen's abrupt abandonment is the beginning of his odyssey and the beginning of a deteriorating relationship with people. The mistreatment of canine characters in the film serves as the fantastic premise for the idea that "man's best friend," might not remain unconditionally loyal to people, but could rise up in an organized way against humanity.

Hagen's new life as a stray demonstrates how his identity shifts from that of a beloved companion to a marginalized creature that can pose a threat to human beings. Unlike the horror elements in *White Dog*, in *White God*, the "horror" element is not the idea of man's best friend turning on humanity so much as it is what humanity does to dogs, specifically Hagen, that becomes horrifying. In *White Dog* it is always clear that the dog was a victim of human violence, but the audience was just told about what was done to him, and not shown the abuse. In *White God,* on the other hand, the audience is exposed to all the horrific detail and has to watch this trusting animal change fundamentally who he is in order to survive. When he is first left out on the street, the audience witnesses his confusion. People noticed Hagen when he was in a domestic space due to his mixed-breed status; however, when he is displaced and forced on the street he almost becomes invisible, which is depicted from his perspective when traffic does not acknowledge him and he is almost hit numerous times. There is no mournful music to guide the audience here; instead, there is almost a silence before the diegetic sounds of the street begin to filter in and almost become overwhelming in order to emphasize Hagen's disorientation. He is used to being seen and acknowledged but by becoming a stray, the homeless dog seems to be hidden under a cloak of invisibility. As a result, he has lost his identity, which determined his individuality or separation from other dogs simply because the system does not recognize him unless he is registered or has some formal proof of ownership. While the audience knows his name, in the film, once on the street, his identity is stripped away, and now he is just one of the many stray dogs that people can easily ignore. This mirrors aspects of homelessness within human contexts as well due to the anonymity that exists within displaced minorities within urban environments. While homeless people have names and individual stories/identities, they are deprived of them, and these unique characteristics are replaced with generic labels that further marginalize them by creating a compromised space that allows them to exist within society without really being a part of it. This reinforces the canine characters' dual function as Hagen's ability to slip between animal and societal representations showcases Mundruczó's intent to highlight how "minorities mirror the way society works," thereby providing a "huge social criticism" of Europe's, specifically, Budapest and Hungary's fear of immigration."[59] The Roma, in particular, have disproportionately suffered due to rising prices, which has caused "armies of homelessness"[60] and "forced evictions."[61] As a result, their access to the primary labor market is restricted and many turned to the black economy (black market) to survive.[62] As a representation of homelessness, the canine character is interesting because it highlights the interchangeable space between invisible and visible. Every society suffers from some degree of homelessness but the reality that certain groups are overrepresented among the homeless and underemployed is important. Hagen's mobility through the spaces of marginalized groups (whether they are the streets occupied by homeless people, a restaurant owned by an immigrant, or the world of a Roma dog trainer called a "Gypo" [the term is related to "gypsy"] by a dog fight organizer) forces the viewer to see the larger fissures within society and acknowledge the discrimination and racism that exists all around them. While caution should be used when drawing parallels between homeless humans and homeless dogs, Christopher Lloyd points out that "the 'structure of subjectivization' that is paralleled in the killing [and marginalization] of various species is vitally important for understanding the ways in which certain populations are perceived and treated."[63] In this case, homeless populations are often dehumanized and Hagen actually provides a way to not only see the unseen but to encourage the viewer of the film to empathize as he struggles to survive day to day and shows us how "mankind and beasts share the same universe."[64] Mundruczó's states directly that the main reason for using a canine character was to make the audience care: "You cannot do such a hero with a human anymore . . . you don't care. It's immediately pathetic. But you can do it with a dog."[65] Aligning Hagen's as well as the other mixed-breed dogs' displacement and marginalization with minorities thus creates a connection that forces the audience to assess the causes and impact of homelessness, and in a way, to question why it is easier to sympathize/empathize with homeless dogs than with homeless humans.

While trying to escape dog control, the first time, Hagen is assisted by a homeless man who hides him from the authorities. Hagen views his action as a reason to trust him even when the first words out of his mouth are "you'll work for me. We're both hungry dogs,"[66] which suggests that he is going to use Hagen for his own benefit. The homeless man's statement that they are both "hungry dogs"[67] directs the audience to the parallel between homeless dogs and people. When animal control is looking for Hagen, they either do not see or do not ask the homeless man if he has seen a dog. They just continue on, which again suggests that in the case of the displaced, society ignores their existence. What is interesting about this scene is that once animal control gives up their search, the seemingly empty street all of a sudden fills with numerous street dogs, providing an indication to the audience just how large the stray dog population is within the city, and if interpreted allegorically, the displaced minority populations even if they are not initially visible. Unfortunately for Hagen, he is still too trusting of people and the homeless man soon sells him to a restaurant owner who is connected with a dogfighting ring that is a part of an underground market. The brief exchange between the immigrant or visible minority restaurant owner and a man looking to buy dogs provides some context about a black market underground economy that is running on the fringe of society. Hagen is then sold to the man who bought him because "he still has a heart."[68] It turns out that the man is actually a dog "trainer" of Romani descent who proceeds to abuse, drug, and mutilate Hagen by filing his teeth to use him for dog fighting. Besides the beating that Hagen endures in these scenes (which may be difficult for viewers to stomach), the systematic dismantling of his innocence and the shattering of his "heart" are even more disturbing and demonstrates yet another way that humans use each other and other living beings for profit. The one thing that is slightly confusing about these scenes is that Mundruczó uses minorities to physically and emotionally change and abuse Hagen, which under the guise that all humans have cruelty in them would be understandable; however, his indication that Hagen's role is to draw attention to displaced minorities groups and their treatment by society loses its focus slightly here because it is the members of those minority groups that are harming him. Having a displaced, mixed-breed dog being beaten and abused by displaced humans seems somewhat problematic other than to suggest that they have both been placed in the situation where they have to do whatever it takes to survive. In that sense, while Hagen loses his innocence, the trainer illustrates the loss of his humanity by forcing Hagen to become a monstrous canine, much like the White German Shepherd in *White Dog*. By effectively treating Hagen as a tool, an object, he is actually dehumanizing himself. Hagen does manage to escape the trainer but his freedom is short-lived as he is soon captured by dog control. At this point, Hagen has had enough of humans altogether. After witnessing the euthanasia of a dog, for the simple reason of being a stray, he stops eating and snaps at a girl's fingers when she seeks to pet him. The shelter director places him on the list to be euthanized, thus transforming him into a victim again. However, as they begin to move him, he resists, slips the leash and attacks, leading to the climax of the film: a mixed-breed dog revolution.

After quite literally ripping the throat out of the dog control officer, and assuming the role of the monstrous canine, Hagen proceeds to release the dogs at the shelter and leads a call to arms among the stray population. At this point in the narrative he may be seen as a hero or savior figure. However, because he and other dogs attack humanity, the term anti-hero may be more appropriate because some would consider them to be monsters for attacking humans who did not directly cause them harm or degrade them. The audience now gets to see the grand scope of the stray population within Budapest as they swarm the city and punish humanity as a whole. By populating the screen with the sheer number of displaced and marginalized dogs running through the streets, Mundruczó is illustrating how a "dispossessed species that was once man's best friend . . . [has] revolted against their former masters and companions in order to validate their existence."[69] As the dogs wreak havoc and vengeance against "members of this privileged mass,"[70] it is not without cause. Hagen seeks out and kills those who wronged him including the homeless man, the trainer, and the nosey neighbor whose lie started the chain of events. Hagen has fully shaken his domestic origins and has become something other, but unlike the White Dog, he is not framed as a typical monster; if anything he is presented as "less 'doglike' and more 'human,'"[71] which is interesting in that humans often define a descent into the primitive or the loss of humanity as animality.[72] That said, Hagen is also framed as an animal revolutionary, "that emphasizes its status as animal"[73] that is "not subsumed under a generalized human term."[74] In this way, the canine character has the agency that the White Dog character did not. Hagen is not dependent on humans to "fix" him; if anything, he is cognizant that they in fact created him, and he is making them acknowledge their role. This is reinforced when Hagen and Lili find each other again, and she tries to command him to "fetch,"[75] which fails miserably, and she is forced to "see" Hagen on his terms instead of according to how she defines him. In doing so, it forces her to renegotiate their relationship in her mind and find a new way to communicate with him on an equal level rather than returning to the master–subordinate relationship they had previously. Lili has gone through her own metamorphosis of sorts, and it is through her growth that the possibility of human understanding is communicated. Unlike *White Dog*, where the ending is ambiguous and somewhat tragic, *White God*'s ending provides the possibility of introspection and finding common ground. The final scene where Lili plays her music in order to reconnect with Hagen shows their ability to recognize in each other the capacity to listen. While Hagen does not come to Lili, he changes his confrontational stance by sitting and then by lying down, effectively defusing the conflict and calming the pack behind him who proceed to follow his lead and "lay down [their] arms."[76] It is a stalemate of sorts, but it is Lili's action of lying down in the same position as Hagen and their shared look that provide more meaning than dialogue. Lili looks at Hagen with tears in her eyes, while Hagen stares back with anguish in his, and it is in that willingness to show vulnerability that they are able to truly communicate and "hear" each other. While the ending is still ambiguous in the sense that it is not clear what will happen to Hagen and the dogs, it is more hopeful than *White Dog* in that it clearly provides a place to start. The rather negative image of Lili's father, Daniel, in the slaughterhouse near the beginning of the film is counterbalanced by the father's transformation at the end. Mundroczó indicates that the father visually and psychologically changes his position: "The story of Lily is also important for me, as is the story of the father, and at the end he can switch and when everybody is on the ground, it means, 'I believe in equality.'"[77] The final shot in the film is a cut to a high-angle shot that shows Hagen and the dogs in the formation of a heart-like image, and perhaps that is the final message that the canine characters are meant to convey—that regardless of species, race, or place, we all have the capacity for love or compassion at the core of our being and that core is the same "color" regardless of species.

CONCLUSION

Ultimately, Samuel Fuller's *White Dog*'s (1982) and Kornél Mundruczó's *White God*'s (2014) use of canine characters provides a way for viewers to examine not only what they see on screen but also what it represents beyond the scope of the screen. Fuller's *White Dog*, while underappreciated at the time, highlights how canine characters are able to function in various spaces in order to critique humanity by existing within society and outside of it. The White Dog character is both the poisoned victim and the monstrous manifestation of human hatred, creating a compromised figure that subverts the viewers' expectations in order to force them see that the real problem is not just a few "sick" individuals who perpetuate racism; racism is systemic and exists within the fundamental structures of society. His marginalization provides the space with which to see what human characters cannot; in other words, it is not about "curing" the dog; it is about curing the system that created this dog. Therefore, *White Dog*'s final image of the canine character with a frozen snarl is quite apt because even through the destruction of the dog, there is no peace; racism still exists. The dog was never the problem; he was the result of the problem. He remains frozen in that state because until humanity can focus on the cause of destructive actions rather than the outcome, there can be no progression. Unlike the dog in *White Dog*, Hagen attains some agency by fighting back by the end of the film. *White God* uses the canine character, Hagen, to amplify what it means to be displaced or marginalized. Hagen makes visible the invisible magnitude of displaced minority groups within Europe, specifically Budapest, in order to comment on the inequity and racism that exists within society. The displaced stray dog has lost his home and has to reinvent himself to survive in the White God's world. It is a world that hates him due to his mixed-breed status, which is used to illustrate the ambivalence that humans have toward issues that do not impact them directly. However, unlike *White Dog*, Hagen does not need to be "fixed"; his ability to navigate the roles of companion, victim, monster, hero, anti-hero, and revolutionary allows him to create his own identity that is not dependent on humanity. It is important to note that even though Mundruczó acknowledges that the dogs in the film correspond to different minorities ("the gypsies," "poor people," "the homeless," "All the minorities"), he does not wish to diminish the importance of the dogs as dogs: "We did the movie with the dogs—so, the movie is about dogs."[78] This may help explain why the stalemate at the end between Hagen and Lili is a dialogue without dialogue. Lili has to concede that Hagen is no longer "hers," and she has to acknowledge the change in their relationship. Lili must relate to him in a new way; she does so by physically placing herself on his level. Through this action, some progress is made visible as the human "masters" strip themselves of their dominance by giving up their superiority in the moment. The problems are still there, but in that moment, human and canine really see one another as equals, which provides a place to start. The canine–human relationship is dynamic and evolving, but there is no denying the dog's impact on society and culture. They are the mirror that often shows humanity who they really are. Sometimes what is reflected back is ugly, but it cannot be ignored. Thus, beyond making the invisible visible, canine characters more importantly function as a way to hold humanity accountable for its actions by connecting with the viewer in a way that forces them to not look away from the truth that has always been there.

NOTES

1. *White Dog*, directed by Samuel Fuller (Paramount Pictures, 1982), DVD. 84 minutes.

2. Eric Ortiz Garcia, "Morelia 2014 Interview: *White God* Director Kornél Mundruczó," *ScreenAnarchy*, October 24, 2014. https://screenanarchy.com/2014/10/morelia-2014-interview-white-god.html

3. Caleb Chodosh, "Good Boy: Canine Representation in Cinema," *Momentum* 5, no. 1 (2018): 9–10.

4. Chodosh, "Good Boy," 10.

5. Chodosh, "Good Boy," 10.

6. Katarina Gregersdotter, Johan Höglund, and Nicklas Hållén, eds., *Animal Horror Cinema* (London: Palgrave Macmillan, 2015), 7.

7. Lisa Dombrowski, "Every Dog Has Its Day." *Film Comment* 44, no. 6 (2008): 48.

8. Lisa Dombrowski, "Every Dog Has Its Day," 48.

9. Lisa Dombrowski, "Every Dog Has Its Day," 48.

10. Lisa Dombrowski, "Every Dog Has Its Day," 48.

11. Dombrowski, "Every Dog Has Its Day," 48.

12. Anne Rogers Clark and Andrew H. Brace, eds. *The International Encyclopedia of Dogs* (New York: Miracle Books, 1995). "Saint Bernard," 381.

13. Josh Doble, "Can Dogs Be Racist? The Colonial Legacies of Racialized Dogs in Kenya and Zambia." *History Workshop Journal* 89 (2020): 9.

14. Doble, "Can Dogs Be Racist?," 9.

15. Aaron Skabelund. "Breeding Racism: The Imperial Battlefields of the 'German' Shepherd Dog." *Society & Animals* 16, no. 4 (2008), 355.

16. Skabelund. "Breeding Racism," 357.

17. Skabelund. "Breeding Racism," 357.

18. Skabelund. "Breeding Racism," 357.

19. Skabelund. "Breeding Racism," 358.

20. Skabelund. "Breeding Racism," 358.

21. "Official Standard of the German Shepherd Dog, American Kennel Club. http://images.akc.org/pdf/breeds/standards/GermanShepherdDog.pdf, 3. https:/www.akc.org

22. Susanne Schwertfeger. "Re-Education as Exorcism: How a White Dog Challenges the Strategies for Dealing with Racism," in *Animal Horror Cinema* (London: Palgrave Macmillan, 2015), 131.

23. Christian Parenti cited in Khalil Saucier. "Traces of the Slave Patrol: Notes on Breed-Specific Legislation." *Drexel L. Rev.* 10 (2017): 680.

24. Chodosh, "Good Boy," 7.

25. Chodosh, "Good Boy," 7.

26. *White Dog,* directed by Samuel Fuller (Paramount Pictures, 1982), DVD. 84 minutes.

27. *White Dog*, 1982.

28. *White Dog*, 1982.

29. *White Dog*, 1982.

30. Alexandra Horowitz, *Inside of a Dog: What Dogs See, Smell, and Know* (New York: Simon and Schuster, 2010), 128.

31. Horowitz, *Inside of a Dog,* 128.

32. *White Dog*, 1982.

33. *White Dog*, 1982.

34. *White Dog*, 1982.

35. *White Dog*, 1982.
36. *White Dog*, 1982.
37. Donna Haraway. *The Companion Species Manifesto: Dogs, People, and Significant Otherness*. (Chicago: Prickly Paradigm Press, 2003), 5.
38. Edward Douglas, "White God Director Kornel Mundruczó on His Less Family-Friendly Dog Movie," March 26, 2015. https://www.comingsoon.net/movies/features/422899-white-god-director-kornel-mundruczo-on-his-less-family-friendly-dog-movie#/slide/1
39. Douglas, "White God Director."
40. Lesley Pleasant, "Seeing Beings: 'Dog' Looks Back at 'God': Unfixing Canis Familiaris in Kornél Mundruczó's Film Fehér isten/White God (2014)." *Humanities* 6, no. 4 (2017): 4.
41. Pleasant, "Seeing Beings," 4.
42. The "Verfremdungseffekt," often translated as alienation effect, is a concept developed by German writer Bertolt Brecht to be able to engage with the material of a play in a critical way instead of simply identifying with a character or situation without any critical perspective. His "intention was to jolt the sensibilities of all concerned in order to sharpen their objectivity and awareness" (Jonathan Law, ed., *The Methuen Drama Dictionary of the Theatre,* London: Bloomsbury, 2011), 12.
43. Pleasant, "Seeing Beings," 1.
44. *White God (Fehér isten)*, directed by Kornél Mundruczó (Proton Cinema, 2014) DVD (Magnolia Home Entertainment, 2015), 121 minutes.
45. *White God*, 2014.
46. *White God* 2014, *New Zealand International Film Festival*. NZIFF 2014 Archives. https://www.nziff.co.nz/2014/archive/white-god/
47. Typically, BSL restricts the ownership of "pit bull" type breeds and often comes down to visual comparisons. If the owner wants to dispute a seizure, they have to pay for a DNA test and contest it in court. Even then, there is no guarantee that the dog will be released and instead will face three options: euthanasia, transport out of the area, or to laboratories for animal testing.
48. Pleasant, "Seeing Beings," 14.
49. Zoltan J. Toth. "Animal Protection and Animal 'Rights' in Hungary." *Jogelméleti Szemle* 4 (2012), 170.
50. Louisa Tasker. *Stray Animal Control Practices (Europe) An Investigation of Stray Dog and Cat Population Control Practices Across Europe* (London: WSPCA and RSPCA International, 2006), 9.
51. Young reviews Philip Howell's *At Home and Astray: The Domestic Dog in Victorian Britain* (Charlottesvile VA: University Press of Virginia, 2015) in her article. Elizabeth Young, "Canine Uncanny Zone," *Humanimalia* 7, no. 2 (2016): 139.
52. Steve Dollar, "Brando Revisited at New Directors/New Films festival." *Wall Street Journal Online*, March 24, 2015, https://www.wsj.com/articles/brando-revisited-at-new-directors-new-films-festival-1427241527 (accessed on January 1, 2022).
53. "*White God*: a Film by Kornél Mundruczó." Interview with the Director. Film /Press / Plus, 2014. https://www.the-match-factory.com/catalogue/films/white

-god.html?file=files/downloads-public/films/w/white-god/White_God_Pressbook_Screen.pdf

54. "*White God*: a Film by Kornél Mundruczó."
55. "*White God*: a Film by Kornél Mundruczó." Interview with the Director.
56. "*White God*: a Film by Kornél Mundruczó." Interview with the Director.
57. "*White God*: a Film by Kornél Mundruczó." Interview with the Director.
58. "*White God*: a Film by Kornél Mundruczó." Interview with the Director.
59. Thompson, Anne. "Why Director Kornél Mundruczó Goes to the Dogs on 'White God' (Trailer)," *IndieWire,* March 20, 2015, https://www.indiewire.com/2015/03/why-director-kornel-mundruczo-goes-to-the-dogs-on-white-god-trailer-188398/
60. Malcolm Langford, "Hungary: Social Rights or Market Redivivus," in *Social Rights Jurisprudence: Emerging Trends in International and Comparative Law,* ed. Malcolm Langford (New York: Cambridge University Press, 2008), 261.
61. Malcolm Langford, "Hungary," 261.
62. Monika Mária Váradi, "Increasingly Fossilised Labour Market Structures and Strategies of Livelihood: Chances of Disadvantaged Groups in the Labour Market," in *Hungarian Spaces and Places: Patterns of Transition*, eds. Györgyi Barta et al, (Pécs, Hungary: Centre for Regional Studies, 2005), 295.
63. Lloyd, Christopher. "Creaturely, Throwaway Life after Katrina: Salvage the Bones and Beasts of the Southern Wild," *South: a Scholarly Journal* 48, no. 2 (2016): 251.
64. Kornél Mundruczó cited in Pleasant, "Seeing Beings," 4.
65. Thompson, Anne. "Why Director Kornél Mundruczó Goes to the Dogs on 'White God' (TRAILER)," *IndieWire,* March 20, 2015, https://www.indiewire.com/2015/03/why-director-kornel-mundruczo-goes-to-the-dogs-on-white-god-trailer-188398/
66. *White God*, 2014.
67. *White God*, 2014.
68. *White God,* 2014.
69. "*White God*: a Film by Kornél Mundruczó." Interview with the Director.
70. "*White God*: a Film by Kornél Mundruczó." Interview with the Director.
71. Pleasant, "Seeing Beings," 9.
72. Una Chaudhuri, "Animal Geographies: Zooësis and the Space of Modern Drama." *Modern Drama* 46, no. 4 (2003): 654.
73. Erica Fudge, *Pets* (New York: Routledge, 2014), 39.
74. Pleasant, "Seeing Beings," 4.
75. *White God.* 2014.
76. "*White God*: a Film by Kornél Mundruczó." Interview with the Director. https://www.the-match-factory.com/catalogue/films/white-god.html?file=files/downloads-public/films/w/white-god/White_God_Pressbook_Screen.pdf
77. *White God* 2014, "New Zealand International Film Festival." NZIFF 2014 Archives. https://www.nziff.co.nz/2014/archive/white-god/
78. Anya Jaremko-Greenwold, "Kornél Mundruczó: Wild Dogs, Revolution, and Humanism," *Bomb* April 2, 2015. https://bombmagazine.org/articles/korn%C3%A9l-mundrucz%C3%B3/

BIBLIOGRAPHY

American Kennel Club. "Official Standard of the German Shepherd Dog." *American Kennel Club*, February 11, 1978. http://images.akc.org/pdf/breeds/standards/GermanShepherdDog.pdf, 3; https:/www.akc.org.
Barta, Györgyi, ed. *Hungarian Spaces and Places: Patterns of Transition.* No. 26. Hungary: Centre for Regional Studies, 2005.
Chaudhuri, Una. "Animal Geographies: Zooësis and the Space of Modern Drama." *Modern Drama* 46, no. 4 (2003): 646–662.
Chodosh, Caleb. "Good Boy: Canine Representation in Cinema." *Momentum* 5, no. 1 (2018): 8–17.
Clark, Anne Rogers, and Andrew H. Brace, eds. *The International Encyclopedia of Dogs.* New York: Miracle Books, 1995. "Saint Bernard," 381–383.
Doble, Josh. "Can Dogs Be Racist? The Colonial Legacies of Racialized Dogs in Kenya and Zambia." *History Workshop Journal* 89 (2020): 68–89.
Dollar, Steve. "Brando Revisited at New Directors/New Films festival." *Wall Street Journal Online*, March 24, 2015. https://www.wsj.com/articles/brando-revisited-at-new-directors-new-films-festival-1427241527 (Accessed on January 1, 2022).
Dombrowski, Lisa. "Every Dog Has Its Day." *Film Comment* 44, no. 6 (2008): 46–49.
Douglas, Edward. "White God Director Kornel Mundruczó on His Less Family-Friendly Dog Movie." March 26, 2015. https://www.comingsoon.net/movies/features/422899-white-god-director-kornel-mundruczo-on-his-less-family-friendly-dog-movie#/slide/1.
Fudge, Erica. *Pets.* New York: Routledge, 2014.
Garcia, Eric Ortiz. "Morelia 2014 Interview: *White God* Director Kornél Mundruczó." *ScreenAnarchy*, October 24, 2014. https://screenanarchy.com/2014/10/morelia-2014-interview-white-god.html.
Gregersdotter, Katarina, Johan Höglund, and Nicklas Hållén, eds. *Animal Horror Cinema.* London: Palgrave Macmillan, 2015.
Haraway, Donna J. *The Companion Species Manifesto: Dogs, People, and Significant Otherness.* Chicago: Prickly Paradigm Press, 2003.
———. *When Species Meet.* Vol. 3. Minneapolis: University of Minnesota Press, 2013.
Horowitz, Alexandra. *Inside of a Dog: What Dogs See, Smell, and Know.* New York: Simon and Schuster, 2010.
Jaremko-Greenwold, Anya. "Kornél Mundruczó: Wild Dogs, Revolution, and Humanism." *Bomb*, April 2, 2015. https://bombmagazine.org/articles/korn%C3%A9l-mundrucz%C3%B3/.
Langford, Malcolm. "Hungary: Social Rights or Market Redivivus." In *Social Rights Jurisprudence: Emerging Trends in International and Comparative Law*, edited by Malcolm Langford, 250–266. New York: Cambridge University Press, 2008.
Law, Jonathan, ed. *The Methuen Drama Dictionary of the Theatre.* London: Bloomsbury, 2011.

Lloyd, Christopher. "Creaturely, Throwaway Life After Katrina: Salvage the Bones and Beasts of the Southern Wild." *South: A Scholarly Journal* 48, no. 2 (2016): 246–264.

McLean, Adrienne L, ed. *Cinematic Canines: Dogs and Their Work in the Fiction Film*. New Jersey: Rutgers University Press, 2014.

Pleasant, Lesley C. "Seeing Beings: 'Dog' Looks Back at 'God': Unfixing Canis familiaris in Kornél Mundruczó's Film Fehér isten/White God (2014)." *Humanities* 6, no. 4 (2017): 82.

Saucier, P. Khalil. "Traces of the Slave Patrol: Notes on Breed-Specific Legislation." *Drexel Law Review* 10 (2017): 673.

Schwertfeger, Susanne. "Re-Education as Exorcism: How a White Dog Challenges the Strategies for Dealing With Racism." In *Animal Horror Cinema*, edited by Katarina Gregersdotter, 126–145. London: Palgrave Macmillan, 2015.

Skabelund, Aaron. "Breeding Racism: The Imperial Battlefields of the 'German' Shepherd Dog." *Society & Animals* 16, no. 4 (2008): 354–371.

Tasker, Louisa. *Stray Animal Control Practices (Europe) an Investigation of Stray Dog and Cat Population Control Practices Across Europe*. London: WSPCA and RSPCA International, 2006.

Thompson, Anne. "Why Director Kornél Mundruczó Goes to the Dogs on 'White God'." *Indie Wire,* March 20, 2015. https://www.indiewire.com/2015/03/why-director-kornel-mundruczo-goes-to-the-dogs-on-white-god-trailer-188398/.

Toth, Zoltan J. "Animal Protection and Animal 'Rights' in Hungary." *Jogelméleti Szemle* 4 (2012): 166–175.

Váradi, Monika Mária. "Increasingly Fossilised Labour Market Structures and Strategies of Livelihood: Chances of Disadvantaged Groups in the Labour Market." In *Hungarian Spaces and Places: Patterns of Transition*, edited by Györgyi Barta, 289–306. Hungary: Centre for Regional Studies, 2005.

White Dog, director Samuel Fuller. 1982, Paramount Pictures. Criterion, 2008. DVD. 84 minutes.

White God (Fehér isten), director. Kornél Mundruczó, 2014, Proton Cinema. Magnolia Home Entertainment, 2015. DVD. 121 minutes.

White God 2014. *New Zealand International Film Festival*. NZIFF 2014 Archives. https://www.nziff.co.nz/2014/archive/white-god/.

"*White God*: Interview With the Director." *Film Press Plus*, May 2014. https://www.the-match-factory.com/catalogue/films/white-god.html?file=files/downloads-public/films/w/white-god/White_God_Pressbook_Screen.pdf.

Young, Elizabeth. "Canine Uncanny Zone," Review of *Cinematic Canines: Dogs and Their Work in the Fiction Film* by Adrienne L. McLean, ed.; *Seeing Ourselves: Vintage American Photographs* by Ann-Janine Morey, *At Home and Astray: The Domestic Dog in Victorian* by Philip Howell." *Humanimalia* 7, no. 2 (2016): 131–140.

Part II

ANIMALS AND NARRATIVE FUNCTIONS

MONSTERS/VICTIMS/HEROES

Chapter 5

Worse than Their Bite

Dogs and Horror

Catherine Pugh

The domestic dog (or *Canis familiaris*) has special status as the first domesticated animal and enduring human companion, developing alongside humans from nomadic hunters to settled, agricultural communities throughout the Ice Age.[1] The co-dependent relationship of dogs and humans is therefore interwoven into the evolution of both species. Horror traditionally casts dogs as tools used by the villain to intimidate or attack their victims (*The Omen* [1976]) or as savage beasts let loose on the world (*Cujo* [1983],[2] *Resident Evil* [2002][3] and its successors, *Wilderness* [2006][4]). However, dogs are associated with both aggression and victimization, able to exist simultaneously as hero, victim, and monster, prone to outbursts of external (violence) and internal (emotional) trauma. In films such as *I Am Legend* (2007)[5] and *The Hills Have Eyes* (1977/2006)[6], dogs sometimes replace female or child victims in horror tropes for emotional impact, as well as offering a significant threat for the antagonist to overcome. Companion dogs are increasingly utilized in screen horror, although their relationship with the protagonist suggests a gender and age divide. The companion dog's role as a humanization or emotional influence for adult male characters (*The Walking Dead* [2010–present][7]) and protection and assistance to female characters and children (*Game of Thrones* [2011–2019][8]) suggest a balancing between gender stereotypes via a canine proxy that is simultaneously natural and symbolic.[9]

Carol J. Clover proposes that female characters in horror simultaneously embody three roles—that of the hero, the victim, and the monster.[10] This model can also be applied to dogs in film or television, particularly in cases where they inhabit the companion role. For example, *I Am Legend* features a German Shepherd called Sam who is protagonist Neville's only companion in a post-apocalyptic world filled with vampire-like creatures. However, Sam is bitten while protecting Neville from an attack by feral dogs infected by the vampiric virus, and despite Neville's best efforts, she succumbs to the infection and becomes aggressive. At the beginning of the sequence, she is a hero, protecting Neville from attack by the rabid dogs; however this leads to her becoming a victim through injury and infection, until she mutates into a monster and Neville is forced to kill her. A similar model that runs parallel to this is the real/symbolic/transformed model. This proposes that in horror narratives—again particularly those with companion dogs—the dog is simultaneously real, symbolic, and transformed. For example, Sam is a real, non-supernatural dog, but she is symbolic of Neville's family (although in other cases the symbolic dog may represent the beast within and so on) and is later physically transformed by the virus.

Dogs, therefore, have a naturally adaptive role in horror, in part due to their interconnection with the evolution of humankind, as well as their status as an extremely transgressive animal. Symbolically, they are ideal conduits for themes of liminality and transgression, particularly in mythology and folklore. As Alby Stone notes:

> They exhibit a halfway state between domestic and the feral . . . the dog's existence in the in-between, liminal place allows it access to other worlds and to sense the inhabitants of those realms . . . The dog is perfectly suited to this role—it is the quintessential domestic animal, the tamed carnivore that stands midway between beast and human, the wild and the civilised.[11]

It is the dog's position as an in-between creature that endures, contributing to the canine's popularity as in horror texts. As well as allowing them to inhabit the paradoxical role of hero/victim/monster, they also bring together other conflicting themes into one creature, such as life/death/afterlife. At once familiar and Other, wild and domesticated, natural and supernatural, and—especially with a heavy dose of anthropomorphism—strange and understood, the literary dog becomes more than animal, if not quite human.

TRANSGRESSIVE DOGS

Horror's fascination with death and the undead naturally borrows from folklore and mythology across the world. Rituals of death, and the development of folklore that accompanies them, have influenced essential horror (particularly Gothic) archetypes such as the vampire, the zombie, and the ghost, as well as the spectral dog. Traditionally, dogs were and continue to be associated with death, from dog sacrifices alongside interred bodies, representations on tombs and monuments, as well as stories about grieving pets (including Greyfriars Bobby and Hachiko) and public memorials to specific dogs.[12] Furthermore, Susan McHugh notes that the bones of dogs interred with human skeletons "suggest that dogs were present within human cultures throughout this archaeological significant period of transition, from the palaeolithic to the neolithic periods."[13]

Mythological dogs are agents of transition; protecting travelers as well as guarding thresholds and crossroads, particularly those between the worlds of the living and the dead.[14] These dogs are harbingers of death or psychopomps, guardians of the dead themselves. The Egyptians had Anubis, the jackal-headed god of the afterlife; the giant, three-headed Cerberus patrols the underworld in both Greek and Roman mythology; Garmr is the bloodstained hound from Norse mythology who guards the gates of Hel; St Christopher, the patron saint of travel (among other things) in the Christian religion, is often depicted in paintings as having the head of a dog. It is often the head that is notable in these narratives. In his work on fairy-tales, Bruno Bettelheim writes that when a child is born as an animal/human hybrid, "the upper part of the body including the head is usually animal-like, while the lower part is of a normal human form. This indicates that things are wrong with the head—that is, mind—of the child, and not his body."[15] Using this theory, it can be argued that the human bodies adorned with the heads of both domestic and wild dogs in ancient mythology can also represent problems with the mind, whether this is in relation to the fear of primal behavior or "beast within," the "Black Dog" associated with mental illness, or whether to reinforce images of liminality and the otherworld.

The phantom dogs of folklore (notably the ghostly Black Dogs of British and Irish folklore) are typically found in liminal spaces—ley lines, crossroads, gates, and bridges—as well as near water. When benevolent, they accompany travelers on their journeys as a companion or guide, even protecting their charges from robbers and "suspicious looking men."[16] However, when aggressive, they can attack, cause accidents, or even explode,[17] although it should be noted that in most cases the dog only does so when threatened. These black dogs can also be a warning of danger to come, usually the death of either the witness or a member of their family. Typical accounts of otherworldly dogs in Britain and Ireland speak of a huge, shaggy black dog appearing shortly before death; a creature as "big as a calf"[18] with fiery, saucer-like eyes[19] and an eerie howl. The image of an intimidating black hound that signifies death is a potent one, and one that has prevailed throughout different modes of storytelling. In the titular novel, Dracula briefly masquerades as an "immense dog ... evidently a fierce brute,"[20] an image that is revisited in both film (*Bram Stoker's Dracula*, [1992],[21] Dracula's vampire dogs in *Dracula's Dog/Zoltan ... Hound of Dracula* [1977],[22] and *Blade: Trinity* [2004][23]) and television (including a notable scene in the BBC 2020 adaptation where Dracula arrives at a convent in the form of a black wolf, later emerging from its skin[24]). The archetypal Black Dog is able to transgress all worlds, walking the line between reality and the supernatural, life and death. Furthermore, black dogs are linked with mental illness, particular depression in both sociological and (now outdated) medical terminology. As Megan McKinlay explains, "Early medical writers documented a phenomenon they dubbed *melancholia canina* [a possible precursor of lycanthropy] in which sufferers were observed to go out howling at night, and a number of early texts make explicit associations between the dog and a state of melancholy."[25]

Perhaps conversely, dogs in folklore are also associated with healing. Consuming dogs and their products has been associated with healing in numerous cultures, from folk remedies such as ingesting dog hair to help a bite (leading to the euphemism "hair of the dog that bit you" for consuming alcohol as a cure for a hangover), or indeed, transferring human illness to the dog, to dog meat, to hair and excrement being used in medicine.[26] As explored in more detail below, the dog's capacity for healing is transformed in literary texts into a balm or catalyst for psychological recovery; while they help to protect the body from attack, their presence also supports the mind against trauma, whether that means encouraging the protagonist to indulge in their primal urges or to re-engage with community (such as people, nature, emotions, or compassion). The Black Dog, then, is an early indicator of the dog's role in horror storytelling, from the ancient guardians to the dead to the enigmatic Black Dogs of folklore.

DOG EAT DOG

For many, the primary fear of aggressive dogs is of being attacked and killed, or, more disturbingly, the threat of being eaten. If the horror of the domestic dog as enemy is unnerving, then the idea of being eaten by a once-beloved family pet seems almost taboo. Katarina Gregersdotter, Nicklas Hållén, and Johan Höglund suggest that animals as consumers of human meat speaks to "the fear of finding ourselves in a situation where our position as the apex predator is challenged; that we as a species are no longer the consumer but the consumed."[27] The consumption of dog meat that is still practiced across the world is controversial (and often disturbing), particularly to a Western audience because of "the tremendous range of feelings stirred even by representations of dogs in Western industrialized cultures."[28] In Western cultures, dogs are generally seen as pets, companions, and working partners, inhabiting a social position above those kept only to be consumed. However, McHugh explains:

> Part of the reason is that dogs defy conventional standards about what counts as food—greedily consuming the carrion, rubbish, excrement and poison reviled by other animals—as well as how to eat, often begging (even stealing), drooling over and dragging about their food. But these different attitudes also signal

profound cultural differences. For people all over the world, historically dogs serve as food containers or converters, consuming excess food during rich months and themselves becoming food sources for humans in lean ones. For their role in this unequal exchange of energy resources, in many cultures dogs have become sacrificial objects and religious symbols.[29]

Gregersdotter, Hållén, and Höglund go on to suggest that the fear of being eaten by the animal, though possibly universal, is particularly prevalent in Western animal horror, drawing a parallel between colonialism that was "eating up the non-European world and the many societies it had designated as animal rather than as human. Thus, when animals begin to eat people, this signals a profoundly disturbing reversal of an order on which the notion of the West is premised."[30] Notably, cultures where dogmeat was traditionally eaten (and, in some cases, still is) are from Eastern and Southern counties, prime locations for colonizers throughout history. Social contempt for dogs is particularly prevalent in Middle Eastern cultures, with cursing frequently including phrases such as "Your father/mother was a dog."[31] Donna Haraway notes that "Generally speaking, one does not eat one's companion animals (nor get eaten by them); and one has a hard time shaking colonialist, ethnocentric, ahistorical attitudes towards those who do (eat or get eaten)";[32] dogs eating humans not only disrupts the so-called "natural" order of consumer and consumed, but also perceived superiors and subordinates, self and Other. In the *Game of Thrones* (2011–2019) episode "Battle of the Bastards"[33] villainous Ramsey Bolton, who has a history of using his dogs to hunt, kill, and eat his human "playthings," is locked in a room with his hungry animals. Although he insists that the dogs will not harm their master, he is reminded by a vengeful Sansa Stark that he has purposefully starved them for seven days before he is promptly devoured. Survival trumps loyalty; the faithful and obedient hounds quickly reverse the master/subordinate and feeder/food dynamics when they are hungry and abused. In this case, Ramsey's death is deemed justified because he is a villain. Generally, however, the dog consuming the human is thought of as so "unnatural" that it usually takes the influence of a monstrous infection before the dog will turn on a human in this way. The man-eating dogs of *The Breed* (2006),[34] *Zoo* (2015-2017),[35] and the *Resident Evil* franchise have all been physically altered by viruses or genetic enhancements; the dogs must be made Other before it is acceptable for them to commit so heinous an act.

German Shepherds

Many different breeds of dog are used in horror films; however, there is a definite preference for German Shepherds. Although the breed is notoriously intelligent and strong (which for practical reasons makes them ideal dogs for the genre), there is an underlying symbolism at work in the enduring popularity of this breed of dog in horror texts. Visually, German Shepherds are reminders of the horror aspects of the wolf: big and powerful with bushy tails, long muzzles, erect ears, thick fur, and strong jaws. When the name was temporarily changed after World War I in order to maintain the popularity of the breed, it was changed to Alsatian Wolf Dog (later shortened to simply Alsatian, again in order to limit negative connotations, this time with wolves). In Western culture, German Shepherds are inextricably linked with militarism, both as a tool for intimidation and as a symbol of the trauma of (particularly military) violence. For example, McHugh discusses 1970s television dramas (*Run, Joe, Run* [1974–1976] and *The Bionic Woman* [1976–1978]) where, "Even more directly than Lassie before them, these [German Shepherds] are aimed to heal war wounds, and in the process reveal deeper questions about the conflicts of identity and culture."[36]

Historically, however, German Shepherds are associated with intimidation and torture, being not only the breed admired by Adolf Hitler (who also liked to favorably compare himself to the wolf)[37] but used at concentration camps such as Auschwitz, by the guards at Guantanamo Bay and to threaten the American Civil Rights movement. Their powerful barks, snapping jaws, and aggressive appearance make them ideal tools for intimidation. The constant images of barking German Shepherds lunging at unarmed people, "secure a historically specific meaning, the identification of this breed as a special kind of weapon that defends dominant political systems with brute force."[38] Along with Rottweilers and Staffordshire Bull Terriers, German Shepherds have been claimed by hysterics as "killer dogs," appearing on numerous dangerous dog lists. However, the internationally renowned Kennel Club in the United Kingdom describes the German Shepherd as a "Versatile working and service dog noted for its bravery and intelligence,"[39] with the breed standard (ideal qualities of the dog) listed as "Steady of nerve, loyal, self-assured, courageous and tractable. Never nervous, over-aggressive or shy."[40] This is not to suggest that German Shepherds are the only breeds of dog used in horror, but the frequency of their appearance as both aggressor and companion over the years, in films as disparate as *Halloween* (1978),[41] *The Lost Boys* (1987),[42] *Signs* (2002),[43] *Dreamcatcher* (2003),[44] *The Hills Have Eyes* (both versions), *Wilderness*, *I Am Legend*, and *Paranormal Activity 2* (2010),[45] is suggestive of a deep cultural or psychoanalytical symbolism.

ON THE ATTACK: AGGRESSIVE DOGS

It is no coincidence that the vast majority of antagonistic or aggressive dogs in horror have either been trained or mutated to become that way. Rarely is this violence the result of the dog's original nature; instead it is almost exclusively the fault of humans. Aggression can be due to human experiments (*Resident Evil* franchise; *Man's Best Friend* [1993][46]; *The Breed* [2006]) or training (*White Dog* [1982][47]; *Don't Breathe* and its sequel [2016[48]; 2021[49]]). Alternatively, aggression can be the result of abuse or neglect (*The Pack* [1977][50]; *Cujo*; *Gerald's Game* [2017][51]) or eco-horror/animal horror revenge narratives against humankind as a whole (*Dogs* [1976][52] and *Zoo* both feature dogs becoming violent after human actions indirectly alter their pheromones, while in *The Pack* [2015, not to be confused with the 1977 film][53] there is no explanation why the feral dogs attack). In film and literature, antagonistic dogs are usually "real," in that they are normal domestic dogs, albeit sometimes genetically enhanced or infected, rather than something supernatural (although this is not impossible).[54] Noël Carroll speaks of the horrors of fusion figures, a "composite that unites attributes held to be categorically distinct and/or at odds in the cultural scheme of things in *unambiguously* one, spatio-temporally discrete entity."[55] These aggressive dogs are at once domesticated/feral, familiar/alien, inside/outside and, in some cases, living/dead or real/unreal.

In texts such as *Wilderness*, *The Pack* (1977 version), *The Breed*, *Cujo*, and *Zoo*, domestic dogs turn feral, violently attacking humans. This plays on numerous societal as well as personal fears, such as the fear of bringing the wild animal into the home, the mundane and domestic turning violent, a return to primitive and uncivilized instincts in a similar way to the werewolf. These are the blood-soaked hellhounds that leap off the screen or the page with their teeth bared. Black Dog iconography plays a significant role here. The posters for these films all make use of the image of the violent (usually black) dog, with red eyes and teeth bared in a snarl as they get ready to lunge, reminiscent of the fiery-eyed brutes associated with phantom dogs. These dogs are savage in the way many predators are considered savage, with an innate, uncontrollable violence nestled deep within them that the rest of the civilized population is able to keep in check. This is because, as Mary Midgley writes, "The unconscious part of the mind was regularly associated with the bestial, instinctive life of the natural, material world as opposed to the rational, cultured world of the conscious mind. In this sense, the unconscious became strongly linked with a notion of a 'beast within.'"[56] Despite the tradition of animals being associated with darker, primal urges, it is Freud's work that firmly collated the iconography of the beast and the unconscious. Freud was heavily influenced by Thomas Hobbes's aphorism *homo homini lupus* ("man is wolf to man"),[57] meaning that humankind behaves more like an animal than a so-called "civilized" creature. It states that humans are more capable of the stereotypical negative associations of the savage or wolf (deceptive, violent, predatory) than civilized societies would like to believe: acting generously to those in their "pack" while being cruel to those not deemed worthy, using the Other to satisfy aggressive and selfish impulses.

Anthropomorphism is common in depictions of both aggressive and companion dogs in horror narratives, with dangerous animals assigned human desires such as revenge. Paradoxically, however, animals in these texts are also seen as naturally savage, forcing the human to regress to a devolved state in order to survive. Gregersdotter, Hållén, and Höglund write that:

> In animal horror cinema, the animal [. . .] typically exists beyond the ethical, as do other familiar characters in horror cinema, such as zombies, monsters and psychopathic killers. The animal is hardwired to be a relentless predator, unable to show remorse or pity. Therefore, the only way for humans to protect themselves against the ferociousness of the animal is to respond to it by becoming as ferocious as the animal, and to kill it.[58]

However, this does not negate humans' ethical responsibility toward animals and nature, with transgressions quickly and viciously punished. While the animal may be continually placed beyond ethics, it continues to function as "an agent who upholds ethical frameworks and metes out punishment."[59] Incidentally, the werewolf has the potential to subvert these ethical concerns, with transgressions against the creatures seemingly forgiven because the werewolf is neither fully innocent animal (often referred to as "beasts" rather than wolves or dogs), nor fully human. During an army training exercise at the beginning of *Dog Soldiers* (2002),[60] soldier Private Cooper is berated for his unwillingness to shoot a dog (a German Shepherd) in cold blood during an army training exercise, with his superior officer asking "What use are you to my team if you can't even kill a dog?" Despite the officer insisting that it is "just" a dog and ultimately shooting it himself, Cooper is adamant that, while capable, he "will not kill *that* dog for no reason." Shortly afterward, the tables are violently turned when Cooper's team are pitted against werewolves who viciously tear them apart. Notably, however, the family of werewolves also own a friendly Border Collie (traditionally a working, herding dog) called Sam, who is adopted by the soldiers and ultimately survives in the film. The earlier scene foreshadows the fate of both men; while Cooper saves the dog and eventually survives the werewolf attack along with Sam, the officer is bitten and turned into a werewolf, to be later destroyed by Cooper. Here placing domestic dogs against werewolves highlights the innocence of the domestic animal, while sounding a warning that they have the potential to be wild.

Much like the werewolf, the typical aggressive horror hound will stalk its victims. Ôrît Kāmîr writes about the importance of stalking in a horror film: "The stalking monster's target is its closest kin; its other self; its creator, the man who represents the monster's abandonment and rejection. It is from him that the monster demands what it considers justice: acknowledgement, acceptance, and painful sacrifice."[61] A common technique used in animal horror (or any horror that involves stalking) is the point-of-view (POV) shot, allowing the spectator to see through the eyes of the subject, to build tension, and to demonstrate the animal's consciousness. Another notable shot that anthropomorphizes the animal is a close-up of the animal's eye as it watches the human, creating a connection between the two: "close ups of the animal eye are a reminder of the simultaneous closeness and remoteness of the world of the animal's psyche [. . .] it meets the look across the narrow abyss that separates the world of humans and the world of animals."[62]

There are, of course, times when the dog is associated with villainy through its connection with the antagonist rather than its own actions. In *The Silence of the Lambs* (1991),[63] for example, the murderous Buffalo Bill owns a Bichon Frise called Precious. Although Precious does nothing to hurt Bill's captive (and, in fact, is threatened at knifepoint by her), she is nevertheless seen as an indication of his antagonistic character. Bill is a problematic character, a serial killer who, after being denied gender-reassignment surgery, begins to kill women in order to make a suit from their skin. It is Bill's sexual identity, rather than his desire to kill, that is demonized in the film, with his supposed sexual deviancy "supported" by the presence of the "effeminate" Precious. Lapdogs or toy breeds, as McHugh explores in more detail, have typically been associated with women and sex since the Middle Ages,[64] with the image of a defiant, childless, older, or wealthy woman and her small dog "bringing together such disparate ideas of sex perversion, sociopathy and wastefulness."[65] She goes on to note that this contempt is still widespread, with homosexuals (and presumably other non-heteronormative people) now added to the list of stereotypes who use small dogs as replacements for humans as objects of affection. In this derogatory framework, rather than a cisgender, masculine-presenting man experiencing a heteronormative, socially acceptable relationship, Bill is only capable of showing affection toward a spoiled, useless, and frivolous effeminate dog, signaling that he has a "deviant" relationship with sexuality and gender. Therefore, although Bill does not have a big, aggressive, and powerful-looking dog typical of the masculine horror villain, Precious is still used to "disturb" the audience by inverting the social and literary norms of the time.

KEEP YOU SAFE: VICTIMS AND COMPANIONS

Companion dogs are loyal to their charges, offering protection, guidance, and a link to family. Horror texts have an unfortunate tendency to "kill off" a dog in place of a person—which arguably has a bigger impact—putting them in the role of victim, innocent or "damsel in distress." In some texts, such as *Rear Window* (1954),[66] *Alien³* (1992),[67] *Ginger Snaps* (2000),[68] or *Secret Window* (2004),[69] the death of the dog indicates that something is amiss, that something horrific has occurred not yet obvious to the protagonist(s). However, dogs can also be the victims themselves, such as in French horror film *Eyes Without a Face* [*Les yeux sans visage*] (1960),[70] where several dogs (primarily German Shepherds) are cruelly experimented on and eventually brutally attack and disfigure the evil doctor who tortured them. In this case they act as an extension of the female protagonist Christine, able to extract revenge for her while her characterization is left intact and she exits serenely into the woods holding a dove. In essence she is a type of Final Girl and the end of the film is a (metaphorical) rape-revenge film; she cannot be seen to be violent nor androgynous. Instead, the dogs act as her revenge—her "hand"—while she remains unsullied and virginal as the innocent, waif-like victim.

A similar dynamic occurs in the aforementioned *Game of Thrones* episode "Battle of the Bastards" where Sansa releases Ramsey's ravenous dogs upon him to avenge his many crimes, including her rape. Like Christine, Sansa's use of a canine proxy allows her to commit a violent act while keeping her hands clean, both figuratively and literally. However, the image of virtue here is reversed; the innocent and naïve Sansa from earlier seasons has developed into a steely and pragmatic woman who smiles as she listens to her tormentor's death. The irony of Ramsey being devoured by his own killer dogs aside, there is a kinship between the dogs and Sansa in that they have all been abused by the same person. The dogs have been a symbol of Ramsey's power and a tool for his violently and overtly masculine cruelty,[71] used to hunt and kill people on command, including a newborn baby. Here, however, they represent Sansa's power over Ramsey (perhaps even becoming a flesh-and-blood domestic version of the direwolf used in the Stark vigil), his cruelty turned back on him as a snarling embodiment of feminine revenge and justice.

While the vast majority of aggressive dogs in horror are ultimately killed, the companion dog is constantly under threat of death. Unlike the typical aggressive dog, an emotional relationship is fostered with the companion dog, provoking an emotional response when the dog dies to the point where there are websites devoted to forewarning the audience (such as www.doesthedogdie.com/).[72] Even if the companion dog does not have what could be termed a hero moment (protecting their charge from attack, rescuing them from being trapped, injured, or killed, or even saving them through sacrifice), these dogs are cared for and usually an attempt is made to protect them. The dogs in *Poltergeist* (1982),[73] *Dog Soldiers*, and *Crawl* (2019),[74] for example, do not have a narrative role so much as a symbolic one. *Poltergeist*'s E Buzz is associated with the children of the film; like them, he is particularly sensitive to early supernatural events, initially has a somewhat innocent reaction to the spirits (bringing toys to play with them) and is sent away to safety with the remaining children before the climactic final scenes. Sam and Sugar, the dogs from *Dog Soldiers* and *Crawl* respectively, are tamed and trained versions of the savage threats of the uncontrollable wild, domestic counterpoints to the feral beasts of the werewolf or the eco-horror animal revenge narrative. They do not protect their charges nor are they left behind and, crucially, they survive.

Dogs can also represent the need for the protagonist to get in touch with their darker instincts. Even in the dog world, survival in horror depends upon accessing a more primitive, darker nature. For example, in both versions of *The Hills Have Eyes* there are two German Shepherds, called Beauty and Beast. In the same fairy-tale tradition of vulnerable girls wandering off the path, early in the film Beauty runs into the hills alone and is killed and eaten by the mutants hiding there. Beast, on the other hand, as his name suggests, follows his primal instincts and kills in order to protect his pack. Beauty's fate foreshadows the decimation of the family, whereas Beast acts aggressively, tearing out the throat of a mutant who is spying on them. This parallels the development of the protagonist Doug, who begins the film as mild-mannered and "soft" (read: "feminine") but by the end storms the mutants' home, killing almost all of them in order to rescue his infant daughter, led, of course, by Beast.

For the most part, however, these dogs are essential for both the physical and emotional survival of the protagonists. As well as offering physical protection and practical assistance (such as the dog, Chips, who carries messages and food between groups of survivors in the *Dawn of the Dead* remake [2004][75]), they encourage a nurturing or humanizing element through comfort and healing. The dog's capacity for healing appears in literary texts—particularly more sentimental texts—as an ability to (re)connect people: reuniting unhappy families, soothing traumas, and allowing unsociable or isolated characters a pathway to community. Jonathan Burt discusses the role of the "all-knowing animal healing a loss within the family,"[76] noting that these texts "have a similar moral purpose to sentimental instructional tales for children with regard to outlining how one should behave and the manner in which animal and human relations are supposed to mirror each other."[77] Although Burt explores this in relation to children, the animal (and dog in particular) offers a healing balm for all those dealing with death or trauma. Traits such as compassion, loyalty, care, and strength are nurtured through the dog's simultaneous status as a vulnerable/comforting yet powerful/protective creature; it is through contact with the dog that the "recalcitrant or unhappy"[78] are transformed.

Companion dogs appear in various horror media as both a practical and healing entity, becoming their own character rather than being simply a pet or asset (weapon or hunting tool). However, the gender of the protagonist can affect the emotional role of the dog in these games. While, as noted above, female protagonists tend to primarily rely on the dog for protection and defense, for male protagonists, dogs tend to abate the protagonist's loneliness or even add a humanizing element; canines become family, giving the protagonist something to protect. These animals are simultaneously pastoral or war dogs that will attack enemies, and companions that allow for a softer side of the male protagonist to be seen as they protect and interact with their canine partners.[79] Dog, the canine companion to Daryl Dixon in *The Walking Dead*, is a useful working dog, able to track and hunt people and food as well as killing human and zombie enemies alike. However, he provides significant emotional and healing support to Daryl, first encountering him when a grieving Daryl is at his most isolated. Dog also (re)engages Daryl's bond with others by leading him (figuratively and literally) to people multiple times, notably Connie, Judith, and Leah. Both Dog and Daryl embody the hero-victim-monster model; both have committed heroic acts (that can equally be seen as monstrous depending on the perspective) while suffering through immense traumas and peril. During the episode "Find Me" (10.18),[80] more of Dog and Daryl's backstories are revealed, underlining their bond while tying their character development together.

This healing capacity is prominent in films such as *I Am Legend*, where the dynamic between protagonist Neville and his German Shepherd, Sam, is arguably the most important relationship in the film. Neville, ostensibly the last person alive after a virus wipes out humankind, talks to and treats Sam as human. Sam is the only living contact Neville has, to the point where he can no longer interact appropriately with other humans when they actually appear. Sam's death, after being bitten by infected dogs, is heart-breaking. Neville desperately tries to stop the infection, but unfortunately fails and Sam begins to show signs of the aggression associated with the infected mutants left behind after the virus. Neville is forced to kill Sam, the camera providing a close-up on his tearful but empty face as he breaks her neck.

CONCLUSION

The versatility of dogs in horror means that they can comfortably represent both good and evil, hero and villain, thus inhabiting both a moral and symbolic gray area. In the 2021 film sequel *Don't Breathe 2*, dogs are employed to complicate the hero/villain binary. In the previous film, *Don't Breathe*, a group of thieves attempt to rob the home of a blind man, only to learn that he is a veteran with formidable fighting skills. However, this supposed victim or possible anti-hero, Norman Nordstrom, is revealed to have kidnapped and impregnated the young woman who killed his daughter in a hit-and-run. The audience is aligned with one of the thieves as she fights to escape Nordstrom after he kills her friends and attempts to use her to replace the young woman when she is accidentally shot. Nordstrom and his unnamed Rottweiler are clearly positioned as the antagonists in this film. However, in the sequel, both the dog (now with a name: Shadow) and Nordstrom are on the side of the protagonist, a young girl called Phoenix. The film opens with Phoenix, seemingly terrified, being chased by Shadow, who is revealed to be friendly and affectionate as they play their game. Later, Phoenix's biological father kidnaps her to be an unwilling organ donor with the help of his aggressive dog. Shadow is killed in the fight and Nordstrom eventually wins the trust of the other dog to track down and rescue Phoenix. The changing roles of the two dogs reflect the murky ideas of hero and villain across the two films: dogs are simultaneously aggressive, unnamed, and belong to the antagonist as well as protective, abused, and aligned with the protagonist. Both dogs initially appear murderous but are later revealed to be affectionate; both are used as an aggressive tool but are ultimately shown to be victims. Furthermore, how people respond to the dogs indicates their morality. In *Don't Breathe 2*, for example, one of the antagonist's henchmen protests that the dog has been left behind to die in a fire; this same henchman later assists Nordstrom as he does not want to be complicit in murdering a child. Nordstrom is given the opportunity to kill the attacking dog, instead choosing to trap it and ultimately braving the fire to save its life, for which he is rewarded with the dog leading him to Phoenix. Despite Nordstrom's heinous acts in the first film, he is granted an avenging, anti-hero role while acknowledging his crimes. His is not a redemptive arc as he never quite becomes the hero, but his behavior toward the two dogs—and, more importantly, the dogs' behavior toward him—assists in altering the hero/villain dynamic of the first film to the victim-monster-hero framework of the second.

A similar dynamic occurs in the post-apocalyptic video game *The Last of Us Part II* (2021),[81] where protagonist Ellie is forced to defend herself against a militant paramilitary organization known as Wolves and their German Shepherds, usually by killing them. The dogs are given names and their handlers show great distress when they are killed. The game later switches perspective, flashing back to a few days previously with the player now controlling Wolf member Abby and her German Shepherd, Alice. Not only does Alice help to protect Abby during combat, but the player is given opportunities to pet and play with her. Ultimately, the player realizes that a dog Ellie killed earlier in the game with particular brutality (and the player's assistance) was Alice. The switch from enemy to ally reinforces the game's exploration of morality and revenge; whereas the human characters can commit both heroic and horrific actions, resulting in a moral ambiguity, Alice remains "beyond ethics," without desire for violence despite the ability to commit it. The difference with a video game format is that the player is ultimately complicit in the death of several dogs such as Alice. While from Ellie's point of view these killings are seen as collateral damage, Abby's perspective condemns the player for their actions. The inclusion of dogs in the video game not only complicates the morality of the characters, but also serves as a way to question the player by allowing (later forcing) them to kill animals with whom they are able to bond retroactively.

As McHugh explains in detail, the development of humankind and *Canis familiaris* are inextricably intertwined, to the point where different peoples across the world trace their ancestry back to both real and mythical dogs, as spouses and "primal parents."[82] In these stories and frameworks, dogs exist before humans, displacing the human from the central narrative. Depending on the culture, the dog may nurture or produce human offspring, disrupting the idea of humans domesticating animals as a "paradigmatic act of masculine, single-parent, self-birthing, whereby man makes himself repetitively as he invents (creates) his tools."[83] Here, it is the acknowledgment and cooperation of the animal that makes civilization possible, not their domestication, something that is echoed centuries later in the relationship between service or working dogs and their handlers.

Yet, in history, myth, literature, film, and television, and even in contemporary parlance, dogs are referred to in derogatory descriptions of the Other. They are connected to representations of different cultures or serve as symbols of political and social ridicule. They may also be used to highlight "discrimination and social power imbalances"[84] in the contexts of gender, race, sexuality, class, or disability (consider the various connotations of the word "bitch" when used as an insult, for example). In these cases, dog terminology dehumanizes the Other, although, as McHugh suggests, "the cross-cultural mythological use of dogs specifically to signify people who are 'not us' suggests a universal human history not of understanding the world so much as of misunderstanding it."[85] Historically, culturally, and literarily, the dog remains an oddly controversial figure, constantly considered as hero, villain, and monster.

Despite this insidious derogatory language, the dog remains an unstable Other—an uncanny creature at once alien and familiar, at once loyal and feral, family and beast. While Haraway argues that dogs are, and should remain, simply dogs rather than metaphor, projection or theory,[86] it is natural that their close and enduring connection with humans (whether positive or negative) feeds into our stories, and perhaps inevitable that so much wonder, fear, and symbology can be found in the horror hound tropes of savage beasts, otherworldly phantoms, and loyal companions. McHugh suggests that mythological dogs assist in the hero's transformation, that through their relationship with the dog, the hero is able to "internalize—and thereby accept responsibility for negotiating—the borderlands defining human identity and society."[87] Similarly, Gregersdotter, Hållén, and Höglund argue that the role of the animal in horror film is to "simultaneously subvert and re-inscribe the basic conceptual separation of the human and non-human animal."[88] No matter where on the victim/hero/monster spectrum they land, the horror dog is simultaneously Other and "one of us," offering the possibility of uncomfortable commentary on the behavior of humankind.

Mary Midgley suggests that *"man has always been unwilling to admit his own ferocity, and has tried to deflect attention from it by making animals out to be more ferocious than they are."*[89] Perhaps this goes some way to untangling why these vicious dogs continue to appear, despite the dog's status as the original companion animal and "man's best friend." The dog is a complacent, safe, and furry companion—but one that can pose a very serious threat in certain circumstances. Some of this anxiety certainly comes from the dog's own version of feral madness (rabies) which can transform a beloved pet into a frightening and dangerous adversary. The horror hound helps to balance this complicated relationship. Ally to some, antagonist to others, these dogs continue to haunt our landscapes and our stories, one paw on either side of the threshold between fighting our monsters and being a part of them.

NOTES

1. Susan McHugh, *Dog* (London: Reaktion Books, 2004), 16. See also, Donna Haraway, *The Companion Species Manifesto: Dogs, People and Significant Otherness* (Chicago: Prickly Paradigm Press, 2003).

2. *Cujo*, directed by Lewis Teague (Warner Brothers; PSO International, 1983).

3. *Resident Evil*, directed by Paul W.S. Anderson (Constantin Film Produktion, 2002).

4. *Wilderness*, directed by Michael J. Bassett (Momentum Pictures, 2006).

5. *I Am Legend*, directed by Francis Lawrence (Warner Bros., 2007).

6. *The Hills Have Eyes*, directed by Wes Craven (Vanguard, 1977); *The Hills Have Eyes*, directed by Alexandre Aja (Fox Searchlight Pictures, 2006).

7. *The Walking Dead*, created by Robert Kirkland, Tony Moore, and Charlie Adlard, aired October 31 2010 to present on AMC.

8. *Game of Thrones*, season 1, episode 2, "The Kingsroad," directed by Tim Van Patten, written by David Benioff and D.B. Weiss, aired April 24, 2011 on HBO. Although the direwolves of the series are generally wild, the ones that protect young Bran and Arya are domesticated and treated as pets.

9. This divide is more noticeable in video games; however, that is beyond the scope of this current work.

10. Carol J. Clover, *Men, Women and Chainsaws: Gender in the Modern Horror Film* (New Jersey: Princeton University Press, 1992), 4.

11. Alby Stone, "Infernal Watchdogs," in *Explore Phantom Black Dogs*, ed. Bob Trubshaw (Loughborough: Heart of Albion Press, 2005), 56.

12. See McHugh, *Dog*; Mark Norman, *Black Dog Folklore* (London: Troy Books, 2015); Bob Trubshaw, *Explore Phantom Black Dogs*.

13. McHugh, *Dog*, 16.

14. For a detailed history, see McHugh, *Dog*, 39–43; Stone, "Infernal Watchdogs," 36–56; Norman 127–144.

15. Bruno Bettelheim, *The Uses of Enchantment: The Meaning and Importance of Fairytales* (London: Penguin Books, 1991), 70.

16. Jeremy Harte, "Black Dog Studies," in *Explore Phantom Black Dogs*, ed. Bob Trubshaw (Loughborough: Heart of Albion Press, 2005), 18.

17. Harte, "Black Dog Studies," 12.

18. Harte, "Black Dog Studies," 7.

19. Harte, "Black Dog Studies," 7, 9.

20. Bram Stoker, *Dracula* (London: Penguin Books, 1994 [1897]), 99.

21. *Bram Stoker's Dracula*, directed by Francis Ford Coppola (Columbia Pictures, 1992).

22. *Dracula's Dog* or *Zoltan . . . Hound of Dracula*, directed by Albert Band (Vic Productions, 1977).

23. *Blade: Trinity*, directed by David S. Goyer (New Line Cinema, 2004).

24. *Dracula*, series 1, episode 1, "The Rules of the Beast," directed by Jonny Campbell, written by Mark Gatiss and Stephen Moffat, aired January 1, 2020 on BBC One.

25. Megan McKinlay, "Churchill's Black Dog?: The History of the 'Black Dog' as a Metaphor for Depression" Black Dog Institute [PDF], 2005, http://www.blackdoginstitute.org.au/docs/McKinlay.pdf, 13.

26. McHugh, 33. See also Patricia Dale-Green, *Lore of the Dog* (Boston: Houghton Mifflin, 1967).

27. Katarina Gregersdotter, and Johan Höglund and Nicklas Hållén, eds. *Animal Horror Cinema: Genre, History and Criticism* (London: Palgrave Macmillan, 2015), 9.

28. McHugh, *Dog*, 31.

29. McHugh, *Dog*, 31.

30. Gregersdotter, Hållén and Höglund, *Animal Horror Cinema*, 9–10.

31. Thank you to Stan Beeler for the observation.

32. Donna Haraway, *The Companion Species Manifesto: Dogs, People and Significant Otherness* (Chicago: Prickly Paradigm Press, 2003), 14.

33. *Game of Thrones*, season 6, episode 9, "Battle of the Bastards," directed by Miguel Sapochnik, written by David Benioff and D.B. Weiss, aired June 19, 2016 on HBO.

34. *The Breed*, directed by Nicholas Mastandrea (TriStar Pictures, 2006).

35. *Zoo*, created by James Patterson and Michael Ledwidge, aired June 30, 2015 to September 21 2017 on CBS.

36. McHugh, *Dog*, 121.

37. Robert G.L Waite, *The Psychopathic God: Adolf Hitler* (New York: Basic Books, 1977), 26–27.
38. McHugh, *Dog*, 119.
39. The Kennel Club, "German Shepherd Dog," The Kennel Club, August 2016, https://www.thekennelclub.org.uk/search/breeds-a-to-z/breeds/pastoral/german-shepherd-dog/
40. The Kennel Club, "Breed Standards: German Shepherd Dog," The Kennel Club, August 2016, https://www.thekennelclub.org.uk/breed-standards/pastoral/german-shepherd-dog/
41. *Halloween*, directed by John Carpenter (Compass International Pictures, 1978).
42. *The Lost Boys*, directed by Joel Schumacher (Warner Bros., 1987).
43. *Signs*, directed by M. Night Shyamalan (Buena Vista Pictures, 2002).
44. *Dreamcatcher*, directed by Lawrence Kasdan (Warner Bros. Pictures, 2003).
45. *Paranormal Activity 2*, directed by Tod Williams (Paramount Pictures, 2010).
46. *Man's Best Friend*, directed by John Lafia (New Line Cinema, 1993).
47. *White Dog*, directed by Samuel Fuller (Paramount Pictures, 1982).
48. *Don't Breathe*, directed by Fede Álvarez (Sony Pictures, 2016).
49. *Don't Breathe 2*, directed by Rodo Sayagues (Sony Pictures, 2021).
50. *The Pack*, directed by Robert Clouse (Warner Bros. 1977).
51. *Gerald's Game*, directed by Mike Flanagan (Netflix, 2017). In the original 1992 Stephen King novel, the German Shepherd, Prince, who eats the deceased Gerald is an abandoned pet. Stephen King novels offer alternative views to the reader that the main characters may not be aware of, explaining why seemingly vicious dogs act the way they do (such as Cujo's rabies and Prince's cruel abandonment and starvation), reinforcing that these animals, while committing sometimes monstrous acts, are actually victims.
52. *Dogs*, directed by Burt Brinckerhoff (R.C. Riddell and Associates, 1976).
53. *The Pack*, directed by Nick Robertson (IFC Midnight, 2015).
54. Incidentally, there appears to be an interesting relationship between the dogs of Italian horror, disability and the supernatural that warrants more investigation, with the German Shepherd Guide Dogs of both *Suspiria* (1977) and *The Beyond* (1981) moving very swiftly between hero and villain by attacking otherworldly enemies before fatally turning on their visually-impaired owners.
55. Noël Carroll, *The Philosophy of Horror, or, Paradoxes of the Heart* (London: Routledge, 1990), 43.
56. Chantal Bourgault du Coudray, *Curse of the Werewolf: Fantasy, Horror and the Beast Within* (London and New York: I.B. Tauris & Co. Ltd, 2006), 66.
57. The source for the saying *homo homini lupus* is given as the Roman playwright Platus in his play *Asinaria*.
58. Gregersdotter, Hållén and Höglund, "Introduction," in *Animal Horror Cinema*, 7.
59. Gregersdotter, Hållén and Höglund, "Introduction," in *Animal Horror Cinema*, 8.

60. *Dog Soldiers*, directed by Neil Marshall (Pathé, 2002).

61. Ôrît Kāmîr, "What Makes Stalking Monsters So Monstrous, and How to Survive Them?" in Caroline Joan S. Picart and John Edgar Browning, eds., *Speaking of Monsters: A Teratological Anthology* (London: Palgrave Macmillan, 2012), 164.

62. Katarina Gregersdotter and Nicklas Hållén, "Anthropomorphism and the Representation of Animals as Adversaries," in Katarina Gregersdotter, and Johan Höglund and Nicklas Hållén, eds. *Animal Horror Cinema: Genre, History and Criticism* (London: Palgrave Macmillan, 2015), 219.

63. *The Silence of the Lambs*, directed by Jonathan Demme (Orion Pictures, 1991). 118 minutes.

64. See McHugh, *Dog*, 82–88, 134.

65. McHugh, *Dog*, 87.

66. *Rear Window*, directed by Alfred Hitchcock (Paramount Pictures, 1954).

67. *Alien³*, directed by David Fincher (Twentieth Century Fox Film Corporation, 1992).

68. *Ginger Snaps*, directed by John Fawcett (Motion International, 2000).

69. *Secret Window*, directed by David Koepp (Sony Pictures, 2004).

70. *Eyes Without a Face [Les yeux sans visage]*, directed by Georges Franju (Lux Compagnie Cinématographique de France, 1960).

71. As well as killing tactically to enhance his status, Ramsey enjoys debasing and dehumanizing people as much as he does physically hurting them, including rape, castration and flaying people alive.

72. Various, "Does the Dog Die? Crowdsourced, emotional spoilers for movies, tv, books, and more" Does the Dog Die? N/A, https://www.doesthedogdie.com/

73. *Poltergeist*, directed by Tobe Hooper (MGM, 1982).

74. *Crawl*, directed by Alexandre Aja (Paramount Pictures, 2019).

75. *Dawn of the Dead*, directed by Zack Snyder (Universal Pictures, 2004).

76. Jonathan Burt, *Animals in Film* (London: Reaktion Books, 2002), 115.

77. Burt, *Animals in Film*, 187.

78. Burt, *Animals in Film*, 187.

79. A dynamic particularly persistent in video games.

80. *The Walking Dead*, season 10, episode 18, "Find Me," directed by David Boyd, written by Nicole Mirante-Matthews, aired March 5 2021, on AMC+.

81. *The Last of Us Part II*, directed by Neil Druckmann, Anthony Newman and Kurt Margenau (Naughty Dog, 2021).

82. McHugh, *Dog*, 38. See 38–39 for more details.

83. Haraway, *Companion Species*, 27.

84. McHugh, *Dog*, 52. See also 192–195 for how this symbolism can be used politically.

85. McHugh, *Dog*, 52.

86. Haraway, *Companion Species*, 5, 11–12.

87. McHugh, *Dog*, 48.

88. Gregersdotter, Hållén and Höglund, "Introduction," in *Animal Horror Cinema*, 5.

89. Mary Midgley, *Beast and Man: The Roots of Human Nature* (Sussex: The Harvester Press Ltd, 1978), 31. Italics in original.

BIBLIOGRAPHY

Aja, Alexandre, director. *Crawl*. Paramount Pictures, 2019. 87 minutes.
Aja, Alexandre, director. *The Hills Have Eyes*. Fox Searchlight Pictures, 2006. 106 minutes.
Álvarez, Fede, director. *Don't Breathe*. Sony Pictures, 2016. 88 minutes.
Anderson, W. S., director. *Resident Evil*. Constantin Film Produktion, 2002. 100 minutes.
Argento, Dario, director. *Suspiria*. Seda Spettacoli, 1977. 99 minutes.
Band, Albert, director. *Dracula's Dog* or *Zoltan . . . Hound of Dracula*. Vic Productions, 1977. 90 minutes.
Bassett, Michael J., director. *Wilderness*. Momentum Pictures, 2006. 110 minutes.
Bettelheim, Bruno. *The Uses of Enchantment: The Meaning and Importance of Fairytales*. London: Penguin Books, 1991.
Bourgault du Coudray, Chantal. *Curse of the Werewolf: Fantasy, Horror and the Beast Within*. London & New York: I. B. Tauris & Co. Ltd, 2006.
Boyd, David, director. *The Walking Dead*. Season 10, Episode 18, "Find Me." Aired March 5, 2021, on AMC+.
Brinckerhoff, Burt, director. *Dogs*. R. C. Riddell and Associates, 1976. 90 minutes.
Burt, Jonathan. *Animals in Film*. London: Reaktion Books Ltd, 2002.
Campbell, Jonny, director. *Dracula*. Series 1, Episode 1, "The Rules of the Beast." Aired January 1, 2020, on BBC One.
Carpenter, John, director. *Halloween*. Compass International Pictures, 1978. 91 minutes.
Carroll, Noël. *The Philosophy of Horror, or, Paradoxes of the Heart*. London: Routledge, 1990.
Clouse, Robert, director. *The Pack*. Warner Bros., 1977. 95 minutes.
Clover, Carol J. *Men, Women and Chainsaws: Gender in the Modern Horror Film*. New Jersey: Princeton University Press, 1992.
Coppola, Francis Ford, director. *Bram Stoker's Dracula*. Columbia Pictures, 1992. 128 minutes.
Craven, Wes, director. *The Hills Have Eyes*. Vanguard, 1977. 89 minutes.
Dale-Green, Patricia. *Lore of the Dog*. Boston: Houghton Mifflin, 1967.
Demme, Jonathan, director. *The Silence of the Lambs*. Orion Pictures Corporation, 1991. 118 minutes.
Druckmann, Neil, Anthony Newman, and Kurt Margenau, directors. *The Last of Us Part II*. Naughty Dog, 2020.
Fawcett, John, director. *Ginger Snaps*. Motion International, 2000. 108 minutes.
Fincher, David, director. *Alien³*. Twentieth Century Fox Film Corporation, 1992. 114 minutes.

Flanagan, Mike, director. *Gerald's Game*. Nexflix, 2017. 103 minutes.
Franju, Georges, director. *Eyes Without a Face [Les yeux sans visage]*. Lux Compagnie Cinématographique de France, 1960. 90 minutes.
Fulci, Lucio, *The Beyond* [. . .*E tu vivrai nel terrore! L'aldilà*]. Fulvia Film, 1981. 87 minutes.
Fuller, Samuel, director. *White Dog*. Paramount Pictures, 1982. 90 minutes.
Goyer, David S., director. *Blade: Trinity*. New Line Cinema, 2004. 113 minutes.
Gregersdotter, Katarina, Johan Höglund, and Nicklas Hållén, eds. *Animal Horror Cinema: Genre, History and Criticism*. London: Palgrave Macmillan, 2015.
Gregersdotter, Katarina, and Nicklas Hållén. "Anthropomorphism and the Representation of Animals as Adversaries." In *Animal Horror Cinema: Genre, History and Criticism*, edited by Katarina Gregersdotter, Johan Höglund, and Nicklas Hållén, 206–223. London: Palgrave Macmillan, 2015.
Gregersdotter, Katarina, Nicklas Hållén, and Johan Höglund. "A History of Animal Horror Cinema." In *Animal Horror Cinema: Genre, History and Criticism*, edited by Katarina Gregersdotter, Johan Höglund, and Nicklas Hållén, 18–36. London: Palgrave Macmillan, 2015.
Haraway, Donna. *The Companion Species Manifesto: Dogs, People and Significant Otherness*. Chicago: Prickly Paradigm Press, 2003.
Harte, Jeremy, "Black Dog Studies." In *Explore Phantom Black Dogs*, edited by Bob Trubshaw, 5–21. Loughborough: Heart of Albion Press, 2005.
Hitchcock, Alfred, director. *Rear Window*. Paramount Pictures, 1954. 112 minutes.
Hooper, Tobe, director. *Poltergeist*. MGM Entertainment, 1982. 114 minutes.
Kāmîr, Ôrît, "What Makes Stalking Monsters So Monstrous, and How to Survive Them?." In *Speaking of Monsters: A Teratological Anthology*, edited by Caroline Joan S. Picart and John Edgar Browning, 161–171. London: Palgrave Macmillan, 2012.
Kasdan, Lawrence, director. *Dreamcatcher*. Warner Bros. Pictures, 2003. 134 minutes.
Kirkland, Robert, Tony Moore, and Charlie Adlard, creators. *The Walking Dead*. First Aired October 31 2010 on AMC.
Koepp, David, director. *Secret Window*. Sony Pictures, 2004. 96 minutes.
Lafia, John, director. *Man's Best Friend*. New Line Cinema, 1993. 87 minutes.
Lawrence, Francis, director. *I Am Legend*. Warner Bros., 2007. 110 minutes.
Marshall, Neil, director. *Dog Soldiers*. Pathé, 2002. 105 minutes.
Mastandrea, Nicholas, director. *The Breed*. TriStar Pictures, 2006. 101 minutes.
McHugh, Susan. *Dog*. London: Reaktion Books, 2004.
McKinlay, Megan. "Churchill's Black Dog?: The History of the 'Black Dog' as a Metaphor for Depression." Black Dog Institute, 2005. http://www.blackdoginstitute.org.au/docs/McKinlay.pdf.
Midgley, Mary. *Beast and Man: The Roots of Human Nature*. Sussex: The Harvester Press Ltd, 1978.
Norman, Mark. *Black Dog Folklore*. London: Troy Books, 2015.
Patterson, James, and Michael Ledwidge, creators. *Zoo*. First Aired June 30, 2015 on CBS.

Robertson, Nick, director. *The Pack*. IFC Midnight, 2015. 90 minutes.
Sapochnik, Miguel, director. *Game of Thrones*. Season 6, Episode 9, "Battle of the Bastards." Aired June 19, 2016 on HBO.
Sayagues, Rodo, director. *Don't Breathe 2*. Sony Pictures, 2021. 99 minutes.
Schumacher, Joel, director. *The Lost Boys*. Warner Bros., 1987. 98 minutes.
Shyamalan, M. Night, director. *Signs*. Buena Vista Pictures, 2002. 106 minutes.
Snyder, Zack, director. *Dawn of the Dead*. Universal Pictures, 2004. 110 minutes.
Stoker, Bram. *Dracula*. London: Penguin Books, 1994 [1897].
Stone, Alby. "Infernal Watchdogs." In *Explore Phantom Black Dogs*, edited by Bob Trubshaw, 36–56. Loughborough: Heart of Albion Press, 2005.
Teague, Lewis, director. *Cujo*. Warner Brothers: PSO International, 1983. 93 minutes.
The Kennel Club. "Breed Standards: German Shepherd Dog." *The Kennel Club*, August 2016. https://www.thekennelclub.org.uk/breed-standards/pastoral/german-shepherd-dog/.
———. "German Shepherd Dog." *The Kennel Club*, August 2016. https://www.thekennelclub.org.uk/search/breeds-a-to-z/breeds/pastoral/german-shepherd-dog/.
Trubshaw, Bob. "Phantom Black Dogs: An Introduction." In *Explore Phantom Black Dogs*, edited by Bob Trubshaw, 1–4. Loughborough: Heart of Albion Press, 2005.
Van Patten, Tim, director. *Game of Thrones*. Season 1, Episode 2, "The Kingsroad." Aired April 24, 2011 on HBO.
Various. "Does the Dog Die? Crowdsourced Emotional Spoilers for Movies, TV, Books, and More." N/A. https://www.doesthedogdie.com.
Waite, Robert G. L. *The Psychopathic God: Adolf Hitler*. New York: Basic Books, 1977.
Williams, Tod, director. *Paranormal Activity 2*. Paramount Pictures, 2010. 91 minutes.

Chapter 6

The Bad Habits of Rabbits

An Ecocritical Examination of Rabbits as Antagonists in Film

MK Pinder

"The Beast of Caerbannog" from the film *Monty Python and the Holy Grail*[1] is possibly the best-known killer rabbit in cinema. As the ordinary-looking white rabbit emerges from the prophesied cave, it becomes apparent that this is the terrible beast of legend that King Arthur and his men have been seeking. What follows is the ludicrous spectacle of an animatronic rabbit flinging itself at the brave knights, ripping at their throats, covered in the blood of the human interlopers. *Monty Python and the Holy Grail* subverts the pastoral use of rabbits as symbols of innocence, childishness, and passivity, making them amusing machines of war and deliberately unconvincing monstrous cryptids. But not all depictions of monstrous rabbits are intended to elicit laughter; some of these rabbit antagonists are designed to prey on our fears and anxieties about the nonhuman and the uncanny. In this chapter I will examine the role of the rabbit as antagonist in film to establish the relationship between ecological anxieties and cultural representations of rabbits.

In 1972, two very different manifestations of the rabbit antagonist entered the cultural consciousness. One was a novel by Richard Adams entitled *Watership Down*[2] which would go on to become an iconic animated film[3] which subverted pastoral ideas of the innocence and benignity of rabbits. The antagonist Woundwort has been interpreted as a savage and thoughtful critique of corrupt political systems. The other rabbit antagonists that emerged from their burrows and into cinemas were those at the center of the sci-fi horror film *Night of the Lepus*.[4] By contrast these rabbits appear to be a mindless plague, made monstrously large by scientific hubris.

The rabbits under discussion are symptomatic of the human understanding of rabbits as part of the broader ecology. This understanding is linked to cultural engagement with rabbits as a species stretching across centuries and beyond continental borders. While some cultural manifestations of rabbits are deeply entrenched in human spaces, they communicate cultural understandings of the relative role of rabbits and humans in the broader ecology. The ecological connotations attributed to rabbits inform their use as allegory, symbol, and antagonist. The characterization of rabbits varies considerably geographically and according to unique cultural and historical associations with rabbit species. This variation can have a profound impact on interpretation of rabbits in texts as we see in the adaptational decay of *Night of the Lepus*. By contrast, the association of the rabbit with the bucolic ideal of the British countryside heightens the terror and monstrosity of *Watership Down* antagonist Woundwort.

It is important to also consider less uniformly leporine antagonists and the convention of the bipedal *human-in-a-rabbit-suit* antagonists. Commonly found in horror films these entities still draw upon cultural associations with rabbits, with one of their primary technologies of fear being the blurring of the boundaries between the human and the nonhuman. *Bunny the Killer Thing*[5] is humanoid enough to be a legitimate predatory threat to humans, Frank of *Donnie Darko*[6] poses a more psychological threat to the human concept of self, and David Lynch's *Rabbits*[7] directly threatens the comfort and predictability of domestic and mainstream media conventions. These bipedal, humanoid rabbits call into question human supremacy and specificity highlighting the artificiality of the established barriers between humans and the greater ecosystem.

ECOCRITICISM AND RABBITS

Ecocriticism as a framework for considering ecologies within texts examines how the human is situated within those ecologies.[8] Ecocriticism in its infancy primarily focused on the examination of explicitly ecocritical texts, those that explicitly commented on, or advocated for environmental interests. As the discipline evolved scholars began to recognize the value of interrogating non-ecocritical texts to better understand the cultural conception and construction of the environment. Ivakhiv emphasizes the necessity of exploring texts outside those that explicitly advocate for, or explore, ecological issues in order to answer important ecocritical questions such as "How do films generate meanings and affects ... especially those related to our understandings of the 'human' and the 'natural'?"[9]

The need to look beyond explicit environmental discourse and into the realms of fantasy, science fiction, and horror informs this exploration of monstrous nature. EcoGothic and ecohorror as genres, themes, or modes of ecocritical discourse may define an entire text, or isolated elements within that text. In simplified terms, *ecoGothic* refers to representations of the ecology invoke the monstrous, sublime, and uncanny,[10] whereas *ecohorror* is the use of the ecology as a technology of fear. Tidwell and Soles note that "contemporary ecohorror narratives can be read as a response to real-world environmental fears,"[11] meaning that the nonhuman animals of the ecology that frighten us are a response to fears about phenomena such as *invasive species* and *disease*. Both ecoGothic and ecohorror rely on our anxieties about the nonhuman and the broader ecology to induce extreme emotions such as fear and despair. Essential to understanding these anxieties is the concept of *ecophobia*, a term Simon Estok uses to describe the fear and hatred exhibited toward the environment in texts.[12] This fear of the nonhuman is intrinsic in forming an understanding of these rabbits and the methods by which they provoke fear in audiences.[13] Halberstam argues that the monster is a construct that contains multitudes: "The monster itself is an economic form in that it condenses various racial and sexual threats to nation, capitalism and the bourgeois in one body."[14] When we bring Estok's work on ecophobia into discussions of Halberstam's work on monstrosity it follows that ecological threats should be considered in conjunction with racial and sexual threats when analyzing the technologies of the monstrous.

The rabbit as an opportunistic herbivore does not pose a direct physical threat to humans, thus making their positioning as monstrous all the uncannier and unsettling. While rabbits are known for the ferocity of their attacks against other rabbits, humans are rarely exposed to this aspect of the rabbit's demeanor until texts like *Watership Down* use it as a focal point of their narrative. The main threat that rabbits pose to humans is food scarcity. They are, however, a food source for predators such as foxes and coyotes, and depending on the location, these predators are instrumental in keeping rabbit numbers manageable. When rabbits are introduced into an ecology without major predators there is a risk of overpopulation.[15] As a result, the space rabbits occupy in the ecologies varies considerably according to their status as an invasive or endemic species. Ideally these labels are deployed for the benefit of protecting native Indigenous ecologies, but they are also illustrative of the human perception of a species. For example, the perception of the rabbit as a part of the bucolic countryside of Britain stands in stark contrast to the perception of rabbits as invasive pests in Australia. This invasion discourse is intrinsic in analyzing *The Night of the Lepus*.

The Revenge of Nature

An uneasy part of the Australian ecological narrative is the transportation of rabbits to Australia by Europeans, creating one of the greatest ecological disasters of the twentieth century.[16] The decimation of the land and the resulting extinction of native species have made rabbits synonymous with invasion and overpopulation. Their impact mirrors the devastating impact of colonization on the Aboriginal population of Australia. In Marsden and Tan's 1998 picture book *The Rabbits*[17] invading rabbits represent the colonization and the invasion of Indigenous Australian lands by Europeans. The rabbits take everything, change everything, and exploit the Indigenous population until almost nothing is left. This allegory reflects the stark reality of the introduction of rabbits to Australia from 1859.[18] The rabbit population grew until MYXV (myxoma virus) was released in Australia in 1950 in an effort to cull the population: "MYXV circulates naturally in American cottontail rabbits (*Sylvilagus* spp.), where it causes benign skin tumors, but in European rabbits it causes the highly lethal systemic disease myxomatosis."[19]

The hemorrhages and lesions caused by myxomatosis[20] caused the deaths of an estimated half a billion rabbits.[21] Images of plagues of rabbits flooding through paddocks were now replaced with macabre images of rabbit corpses. The depiction of rabbit populations as a formidable plague in the 1964 book *The Year of the Angry* Rabbit by Russell Braddon[22] suggests that the rabbit plague and gruesome cull did not quickly fade from the Australian public consciousness. Not only had the rabbits posed a serious threat to ecosystems and livelihoods, but the subsequent spectacle of their slaughter seemed to be inviting repercussions from the natural world. Could this many creatures die without consequence?

In 1972 *The Year of the Angry Rabbit* was adapted into *The Night of the Lepus*. Despite acknowledging the Australian origins of the anxieties expressed in the film, the rabbit plague was relocated to Arizona and many of the geopolitical themes and science fiction plot points were removed. While Arizona does have a wild antelope jackrabbit and desert cottontail rabbit population,[23] they form part of a complex ecosystem in which predators like coyotes keep the rabbit population in check. Perhaps in an effort to evoke some of the anxieties associated with the Australian plague and cull, the film opens with a news broadcast detailing the rabbit infestation in Australia. The relocation of the plague of rabbits to Arizona meant taking the story out of the context of the Australian relationship with rabbits, misaligning with the pre-existing anxieties of the audience.

The monstrous rabbits of *Night of the Lepus* were originally laboratory rabbits, which in their mutated state have become enormous, but are otherwise identical to their pre-experimentation form. In an attempt to subvert audience expectations and transform the rabbits into a formidable plague, they were depicted as omnivorous predators. The "lepus" attack all flora and fauna indiscriminately, as evidenced by blood smeared across their mouths and scenes of carnage and murder left in their wake. The technology of the horror that is the fictional horde or plague has been effectively used to create ecohorror and Gothic affect. *The Birds*[24] (Hitchcock 1963) utilizes the unsettling strangeness of large numbers of birds to create an eerie atmosphere that suggests an immediate threat to humans, whereas threats to food security and the unchecked reproduction of rabbit populations pose a long-term threat; they are slow burning anxieties that are difficult to convey with the urgency required to induce immediate terror. This coupled with their unimposing appearance and vegetarianism makes this horde of average live rabbits, unconvincingly made to look gigantic, less than compelling antagonists.[25]

Despite the ineffectiveness of the "Lepus" as a monstrous antagonist, *Night of the Lepus* tapped into some of the most effective ecohorror themes associated with rabbits: abnormal size, rampant reproduction, and the role of scientific hubris in creating monstrosity. The "mutants" as they were billed in the promotional material for the film were transformed through experimentation with methods of biological control of rabbit populations. Researchers Roy and Gerry Bennett were endeavoring to find a means of stopping the animals from reproducing without the means of poisons, guns and explosives. These attempts allude to the introduction of myxomatous into the Australian rabbit population as an alternative to conventional culling practices such as hunting and trapping. Roy injects a rabbit with an untested serum and this rabbit is accidently released into the general rabbit population. The rabbit's monstrous offspring and the scientific process that created them serve as a warning to modern science not to meddle with things they do not understand. This narrative of scientific hubris highlights a fear of scientific intervention and a victory for traditional methods of animal population control. In the end it is the culling of the animals with an electrified barrier that brings them down—brute strength and transparent human ingenuity that are tangible and not reliant on knowledge obscured by education and experimentation.

The Worst of Us

The rabbits of *Night of the Lepus* manifest as an almost shapeless threat, a mass of monsters without any individuation. In stark contrast, the rabbits of the film *Watership Down* are humanized and afforded hopes, ambitions, and spirituality. *Watership Down* is as much a quest for a new Eden as it is a story about leadership and ideology. Fiver's premonition of fields covered in blood foreshadows the destruction and violence that humans are about to inflict on the colony. Driven out of their safety of home, the quest for a new paradise begins. Informed by rabbit theology and ideology, Hazel the benevolent leader of the Watership Down colony deftly navigates various threats posed by humanity and the group develops goals distinctly independent of humans. Central to this lack of anthropocentrism is the categorization of humans as just another predator. There is certainly a demonstrable impact from the cruelty and greed of the human world. For example, Captain Holly relays horrific images of the burrows being filled in and the rabbits suffocating. However, this was an avoidable tragedy that could have been prevented through a truly democratic approach to governance. As evidenced by the upper echelons of the burrow refusing to listen to the prophecies of Fiverr and the advice of Hazel, the societal tension and conflict comes from the societal constructs enforced by rabbits themselves. In *Watership Down*, morality and the social responsibility of the individual are at the core of the film's message; it is not rabbits in general that are evil, but individual rabbits that have sinister motivations. The key antagonist General Woundwort is as complex as he is terrifying, representing authority, corrupted idealism, and a need for dominance and control.

Despite Adams's professed respect, affection, and sympathy for rabbits as creatures in their own right, the 1978 film *Watership Down* and its literary antecedent are primarily read as allegories, a fate that Hadas notes is commonly attributed to texts with nonhuman protagonists.[26] This often means that the unique qualities of the animal themselves are neglected in favor of those that are demonstrative of anthropomorphic qualities. *Watership Down* conveys the experience of the rabbits through the frame of human experience but also pays attention to those qualities that lie outside the human experience. For example, the rabbit belief system provides insight into the experience of being on the lower end of the food chain: of being a food source. The mythical introduction to the film explains not only the complexity of rabbit belief systems but the key to rabbit survival in the face of predators. It depicts rabbits as being perpetually on the run and threatened constantly, but they are equipped with speed, agility, and cunningness to get away from other species that would prey on them. This does not prepare them for General Woundwort, a predator and dictator from within their own species.

In Woundwort's role as a fictional rabbit rather than allegorical figure, he transgresses culturally accepted qualities of the anthropomorphized rabbit characters. Notably, he refuses to let rabbits leave the warren to form new warrens and hierarchies. Through this unnatural act of tyranny, Adams uses real-world rabbit social organization and biology to demonstrate Woundwort's physical and psychological violence. When the doe pleads with Woundwort to let them leave as the does are not able to deliver litters, she is referring to the ability that does have to reabsorb the fetal tissue of unborn litters if their warren is overcrowded. As these are anthropomorphized rabbits, there is a tone of sadness and despair associated with this process, further solidifying Woundwort's status as an evil villain. As a monstrous spectacle, Woundwort has many features that challenge the image of the adorable quaint figure of the wild rabbit, an idyllic image that until this point the film had done very little to contradict. His battle scars and damaged eye show him to be a formidable fighter, something which he proves in the final scenes of the film. The blood smeared across his face and paws and the saliva frothing from his mouth create a spectacle of a ferocious creature evoking feelings of fear and revulsion that we would not typically associate with a rabbit. He is scarred, battle hardened, and predatory, transgressing the cultural construction and ecological positioning of the passive herbivorous rabbit.

Woundwort's allegorical role as the fascist dictator or tyrant allows him to stand in opposition to the leadership of Hazel who represents more democratic or egalitarian values. Hazel takes advice from his colony and builds comradery, whereas Woundwort has complete authoritarian rule over the burrow. Woundwort also demonstrates corruption and total control over his colony through his use of the does as currency, blithely offering Big Wig his choice of the female rabbits as a perk of being a guard. The allegorical use of a large brutish rabbit to convey the ills of a society demonstrates the monstrous potential of a relatively leporine rabbit. He is not humanoid like some of the other rabbit antagonists under discussion, and yet he is capable of conveying the worst of human nature.

Unnatural Predators

As Hazel navigates the dangers that lie in wait in the wilderness, he must wrestle with external threats that challenge his courage and capacity to lead. But ultimately the threat posed by Woundwort of *Watership Down* is external and tangible. However, the threats posed by his monstrous lepine successors are less easy to define and more difficult to overcome. Soles, referring to the evolution of ecological threats in horror (or ecohorror) that occurred between *The Birds* and *The Night of the Living Dead*, observes the shifting of the locus of fear from the exterior to the interior.[27] *The Birds*, like *Night of the Lepus* and *Watership Down*, deals with a threat outside the human body, whereas *The Night of the Living Dead* depicts a threat that manifests within the human body. The mutation or zombification of the human form through contagion in Romero's film provokes human anxieties about the invasion and contamination of the body. Similarly, the ecological threat in *Bunny the Killer Thing* occurs within the corporeal form. Nordsploitation[28] film *Bunny the Killer Thing* continues the narrative preoccupation with scientific hubris and the rabbit form as the uncanny monster through the depiction of a man who is kidnapped and transformed into a monstrous hybrid rabbit / human creature. When the man who would become the *Bunny* of the title is tied down in a dingy makeshift laboratory the camera pans across caged rabbits from which the audience is to infer that the injection Bunny is about to receive involves rabbit DNA. Where Romero's zombies were purportedly infected by radiation from a returning space satellite (there are multiple theories surrounding the cause of the outbreak), Bunny the Killer Thing is genetically altered by scientists to create hybrid rabbit / human creatures. These narratives that focus on interior threats rather than the exterior are still stories of the revenge of nature, of humans experiencing the consequences of cruelty, greed, and hubris. But unlike plague and horde narratives, the fear is not the invasion of our country, our town, or our home, but the invasion of our bodies.

Through the act of hybridizing human and rabbit DNA, the "scientists" have created a being who is neither. The ordinary rabbits in the lab are not the monsters that Bunny would become; instead, it is the compromising and mutating of the human form that makes Bunny a monstrous spectacle and informs his devious and murderous behavior. The film quickly makes clear the quality of rabbits that it is most interested in, and that is the drive to reproduce. Despite the cultural perception of rabbits as possessing an uncontrolled drive for reproduction, this does not manifest as a rampage of rape as depicted in *Bunny the Killer Thing*. Davis and DeMello describe the mating ritual of Wild European rabbits as primarily consensual or non-violent, with the female accepting or rejecting male advances.[29] This is a stark contrast to the violent spectacle of Bunny chasing down people in the forest and violently tearing apart their genitals.

Bunny's comically enlarged penis is symbolic of that excess of sexual energy that has been inferred from the aforementioned cultural associations with rampant reproduction. This refers to, not only the purpose for which Bunny was created but also the threat he poses to human reproduction. The animalistic nature of his murder and rape spree is seen as being a direct result of his change from human to rabbit. This violence and insatiability are definitively categorized as being the result of the mutation, his regression into animality. In a less eloquent fashion than the anxieties expressed by H. G. Wells in response to Darwinism,[30] *Bunny the Killer Thing* represents concerns about the regression of the human into animalism.

Bunny the Killer Thing is unique among the films referred to in this chapter in terms of its conflation of sex and extreme violence. Scientific experimentation is being used to bridge the gap between rabbits and humans for the purposes of bestiality and sexual gratification. He is restrained and forcibly subjected to an injection which mutates him into a rabbit man. The severity of the effects on Bunny, including the impairment of his intellect and reasoning, indicates that the other subjects that we meet later have also been unable to give any form of reliable consent.

The Manipulated Dead

While Bunny of *Bunny the Killer Thing* is an animalistic creature governed by sexual gratification and violence, Frank of *Donnie Darko* is concerned with the abstract and the metaphysical. Donnie Darko offers a succinct summary of some of these cultural connotations of rabbits in his rejection of the allegoric significance of *Watership Down*:

> The rabbit's not like us. It has no history books, no photographs, no knowledge of sorrow or regret. . . . They're cute and they're horny. And if you're cute and you're horny, then you're probably happy that you don't know who you are or why you're even alive. You just wanna have sex as many times as possible before you die. I just don't see the point in crying over a dead rabbit, you know, who never even feared death to begin with.[31]

These associations uncannily echo the rudimentary thinking behind *Bunny the Killer Thing*. Donnie's rejection of allegory is almost a statement of intention for the character of Frank in *Donnie Darko*. Frank is not intended to be an animal allegory; he is a man in a rabbit suit, an artifact from a disruption of space and time. However, in invoking the image of a monstrous rabbit as Donnie's metaphysical guide through his messianic journey to save the world, Kelly is engaging with cultural perceptions and anxieties of the rabbit as a species.

The implication that species or identity is performative in *Donnie Darko* makes Frank perhaps the most ambiguous of the rabbit antagonists in this chapter. In fact, depending on which version of the film one watches, he may not be an antagonist at all. My analysis focuses on the original release and the director's cut of *Donnie Darko* as the discrepancies give greater context to Frank, the man in a rabbit costume, and his role in the narrative. The rabbit Halloween costume that Frank wears is unsettling and monstrous, with its shiny silver disfigured skeletal face being juxtaposed against the bunny suit that surrounds it. Designed to be scary, even before it is taken out of the context of a Halloween party, when it appears out of the darkness with a bullet wound in one eye it is absolutely terrifying. In the original version of the film Frank was depicted as a hallucination, a manifestation of Donnie's implied paranoid schizophrenia. He appears and talks to Donnie initially when he is asleep, telling him to commit acts of destruction. In this interpretation Frank the rabbit is a manifestation of his dark desires. Therefore, the important events that happen after Donnie's crimes are mere coincidence with the connections being drawn by a delusional mind. But the director's cut invites a different interpretation, one that sees Frank the rabbit as a kind of time traveling echo that is directing Donnie set in motion a series of events that will result in his death, but ultimately save the lives of others. In this interpretation Frank exists in two places at once. He exists both in his role as a conventional auxiliary character and in his role as the "manipulated dead," an entity designed to correct errors and anomalies in the timeline.

Frank is an allusion to Harvey, the 6-foot-tall invisible rabbit of the film of the same name.[32] Harvey is hardly an antagonist, but he certainly causes a great deal of trouble for Elwood P. Dowd. Harvey embodies the trickster archetype, similar to the Algonquin symbolic use of the rabbit as outlined by Carroll.[33] Harvey is referred to as a pooka or puca. The puca has an entity of obscure origins which has associations with Puck in Celtic cultural traditions and goblin through the word puca's Germanic etymological roots.[34] The puca is variously a playful troublemaker, an elusive protector, and impish bogeyman. Harvey fits the role of both the elusive protector and the playful troublemaker.[35] This entity that only Elwood can see becomes more corporeal as the film progresses, beginning to manipulate items and appearing to others, indicating that he is not just a figment of a troubled psyche. This is perhaps the most meaningful debt the film *Donnie Darko* owes to the relationship between Elwood and Harvey: the film illustrates how drastically our understanding of the narrative and the protagonist hinges on the identity of a 6-foot-tall rabbit.

Eldritch Leporidae

Harvey and Frank are notable, and clearly articulated, examples of rabbits that act as mediators between humans and the metaphysical. Frank is a transdimensional being guiding Donnie through a complex journey of martyrdom and Harvey is a supernatural creature from a folkloric tradition who destabilizes ideas of normality. However, the role of uncanny rabbits in film is not always as simple to define. The symbolic role of rabbits and hares (in this section there will be some conflation of the two, hence the family title Leporidae) in rituals and sacred imagery is believed to go back to the cultural practices of Ancient Rome, Greece, and the British Isles.[36] These ritual and cultural uses of rabbits associated them with love and fertility for much the same reason as contemporary cultural representations of the rabbit conflate high rates of reproduction with an aggressive libido. Beyond the rabbit's association with entities like Aphrodite in ancient pantheons of gods, the association between rabbits, hares, and the supernatural also has its origins in Nordic folklore and the folklore of the British Isles. Witches could purportedly transform into hares and conjure up creatures often called milk-hares by imbuing crude effigies with animation through a pact with the devil.[37] The folkloric witch of European tradition (and indeed many other traditions) is a profoundly ecoGothic figure, not just associated with the supernatural, but the nonhuman ecology.[38] Often lacking a fixed form and shifting between the human and the nonhuman, the witch shares a natural kinship with the rabbit and the hare as the trickster or associate of the devil. While the tricksters belong to the realm of the Harveys, Bugs Bunnies, and

Brer Rabbits of the cinematic world, the rabbits' cultural association with the ancient dark magic and their uncanny duality can be found in David Lynch's *Rabbits*.[39]

Rabbits uses humanoid rabbits with featureless faces to invoke the conflation of the supernatural and psychological in a far more sinister and subversive way than *Donnie Darko*'s Frank. *Rabbits* was released as a web series and was also embedded in the film *Inland Empire*[40] as a surreal television show being watched by the traumatized auxiliary character known as the Lost Girl. This uncanny faux sitcom starring anthropomorphic rabbits makes the domestic strange through temporal disruption and disjointed cycles of displaced dialogue. The three rabbits, Suzie, Jack, and Jane are terrified of an unseen threat from outside their home. The threat known as "the man in the green suit" is referred to in vague terms, and the clearest signifier of an actual threat from the outside to the rabbits is a sequence of screams and flashing lights that seem to come from the outside, engulfing the entire room. Through surrealist narrative sequences, the viewer is drawn back into the complex portrait of the rabbit as both antagonist and victim, as found in *Watership Down*.

In one of the more uncanny and unsettling spectacles, Suzie holds torches aloft, appearing to distort time. This summons an Eldritch horror which has been referred to as the "red rabbit." The rabbits' faces are featureless, "the man in the green suit" that they are scared of is unseen and formless, but the "red rabbit" is almost entirely composed of features suspended in a red amorphous haze. The connection to otherworldliness is already established by the ambiguous hybridity of the rabbits themselves as a distorted nonhuman incursion into a human space. The use of the unsettling soundscape, slow meditative actions, and disjointed speech makes clear that we are not watching a sitcom, despite what the setting and audience laugh track might lead us to believe. Once again, we are witness to rabbits in a state of fear. As in *Watership Down*, the rabbits are scared of the threat from the outside; meanwhile the threat from within the house is looming and ambiguous.

The strange monologues delivered by Suzie and Jack at different stages in the series echo some of the experiences of disease from the spread of the myxoma virus and the experiences of the rabbits navigating the human world in *Watership Down*: "The socket drips. Disease. Hot electricity . . . Barbed wire, sharp, tearing open red and wiggling wet dogs. Running, swollen blue feet. Tearing, scraping. Black old blood. Yellow. Saliva."[41] This monologue is grotesque and eerily familiar when compared to Evan's gruesome description of the myxoma virus: "Once a rabbit is infected with the myxoma virus... after about a week of incubation, its eyes begin to shed a watery discharge. This thickens, and the eyelids also swell, blinding the animal behind lesions encrusted with hardened yellow matter. The genitals, nose and ears erupt in the same way, and jelly-like bulges appear on other parts of the body."[42]

The corporeality and visceral imagery of Lynch's monologue is ambiguous enough that a variety of associations can be drawn, including the above interpretation that it reflects experiences of the wild rabbit. Lynch has a history of deploying animals to convey human qualities and experiences such as the predatory and otherworldly owls of Twin Peaks.[43] It is possible that the writhing animalistic suffering of the monologue is being deployed in much the same way as the featureless rabbits with deadpan line delivery of disjointed lines to remove the human experience from its context through the use of the nonhuman. Lynch uses this unsettling fusion of the human and nonhuman to emphasize the distorted personal horror of *Inland Empire* and the protagonist's subsequent disconnection from reality.

CONCLUSION

Due to the multifaceted nature of rabbits as cultural symbols and as part of the biosphere it is impossible to determine a neat formula for the monstrous rabbit. Perhaps the most meaningful commonality between these antagonists and pseudo-antagonists is that they are out of context. This is what makes "The Beast of Caerbannog," the giant Lepus, and maybe even Bunny in his own morbid way amusing. But it is also what makes Woundwort, Frank, and Lynch's *Rabbits* so deeply upsetting. As a means of making the comfortable domestic, uncomfortable and strange, the surprising presence of rabbits is disarming, thus allowing directors such as Lynch and Kelly to disturb audiences and disrupt meaning making. These rabbits are inhabiting human spaces and playing human, discussing the rain in lounge rooms, and running fascist regimes. They are invaders, bringing their esoteric and eldritch horrors with them. Even this attempted binary of terrifying and ridiculous is inherently flawed as any one of these rabbit antagonists could be interpreted as transgressing that binary. And perhaps that is the point. These rabbits, the oft-underestimated tricksters of the animal world, defy easy cultural categorization, and we attempt to redefine their context at our peril.

NOTES

1. Terry Gilliam and Terry Jones. *Monty Python and the Holy Grail* (EMI Films, 1975).
2. Richard Adams. *Watership Down* (London: Bloomsbury, 2018).
3. Martin Rosen and John Hubley. *Watership Down* (Nepenthe Films, 1978).
4. William F. Claxton. *Night of the Lepus* (Beverly Hills, CA: Metro-Goldwyn-Mayer, 1972).

5. Joonas Makkonen. *Bunny the Killer Thing* (Finland: Raven Banner, 2015).

6. Richard Kelly. *Donnie Darko* (Los Angeles, CA: Newmarket Films, 2001).

7. David Lynch. *Rabbits* (Online, 2002).

8. Greg Garrard ed. *The Oxford Handbook of Ecocriticism* (Oxford: Oxford University Press, 2013).

9. Adrian Ivakhiv. "Teaching Ecocriticism and Cinema." In *Teaching Ecocriticism and Green Cultural Studies* (Springer, 2012), 144–55.

10. Andrew Smith, William Hughes, and Manchester University Press. *EcoGothic* (Manchester: Manchester University Press, 2015). http://ezproxy.st-andrews.ac.uk/login?url=https://dx.doi.org/10.7765/9781526102911.

11. Christy Tidwell and Carter Soles. *Fear and Nature: Ecohorror Studies in the Anthropocene* (New York: Penn State Press, 2021), Vol. 8.

12. Simon C. Estok. *The Ecophobia Hypothesis* (New York: Routledge, 2018). https://www.taylorfrancis.com/books/9781315144689.

13. Jack Halberstam. *Skin Shows* (Durham, NC: Duke University Press, 1995).

14. Halberstam, *Skin Shows*, 3.

15. Susan E. Davis and Margo DeMello. *Stories Rabbits Tell: A Natural and Cultural History of a Misunderstood Creature* (New York: Lantern Books, 2003), 23.

16. Richard Evans. *Disasters That Changed Australia* (Australia: Melbourne University Publishing, 2009). http://ebookcentral.proquest.com/lib/deakin/detail.action?docID=5718730, 45.

17. John Marsden and Shaun Tan. *The Rabbits* (Australia: Lothian Books, 1999).

18. Joel M. Alves, Miguel Carneiro, Jade Y. Cheng, Ana Lemos de Matos, Masmudur M. Rahman, Liisa Loog, Paula F. Campos et al. "Parallel Adaptation of Rabbit Populations to Myxoma Virus." *Science* 363, no. 6433 (2019), 1319–26. doi: 10.1126/science.aau7285.

19. Alves Joel M. et al., "Next Step in the Ongoing Arms Race between Myxoma Virus and Wild Rabbits in Australia Is a Novel Disease Phenotype."

20. Peter J. Kerr, Isabella M. Cattadori, June Liu, Derek G. Sim, Jeff W. Dodds, Jason W. Brooks, Mary J. Kennett, Edward C. Holmes, and Andrew F. Read. "Next Step in the Ongoing Arms Race between Myxoma Virus and Wild Rabbits in Australia Is a Novel Disease Phenotype." *Proceedings of the National Academy of Sciences* 114, no. 35 (2017). doi: 10.1073/pnas.1710336114.

21. Lee, Tim. "'It Was Unprecedented': The Virus That Wiped out Feral Rabbits Was Almost a Bust." *ABC News*, August 7, 2020. https://www.abc.net.au/news/2020-08-08/biological-control-weapon-myxomatosis-almost-failed/12529702.

22. Russell Braddon. *The Year of the Angry Rabbit* (London: Pan Books, 1967).

23. Andrew T. Smith, Charlotte H. Johnston, Paulo C. Alves, and Klaus Hackländer. *Lagomorphs : Pikas, Rabbits, and Hares of the World* (Baltimore: Johns Hopkins University Press, 2017), 120–22, 159–63.

24. Alfred Hitchcock. *The Birds* (Universal-International Pictures, 1963).

25. Winston Wheeler Dixon. "When Animals Take Over: The Post-Pandemic Backlash." *Quarterly Review of Film and Video* 38, no. 4 (2021): 303–309. doi: 10.1080/10509208.2020.1772005.

26. Marcus Hadas. "An Ecocritical Approach to Cruelty in the Laboratory." *Journal of Animal Ethics* 6, no. 2 (2016): 223–33. doi: 10.5406/janimalethics.6.2.0223.

27. Carter Soles. "'And No Birds Sing': Discourses of Environmental Apocalypse in 'The Birds' and 'Night of the Living Dead.'" *Interdisciplinary Studies in Literature and Environment* 21, no. 3 (2014): 526–37.

28. Nordsploitation is defined as a style of film from Nordic nations such as Norway, Denmark, Sweden and Finland that contains transgressive content. Pietari Kääpä and Tommy Gustafsson, *The Politics of Nordsploitation: History, Industry, Audiences* (New York: Bloomsbury Publishing, 2021), 10–13.

29. Susan E. Davis and Margo DeMello. *Stories Rabbits Tell: A Natural and Cultural History of a Misunderstood Creature*, 36–37.

30. Kelly Hurley. *The Gothic Body: Sexuality, Materialism, and Degeneration at the Fin de Siècle* (Cambridge: Cambridge University Press, 2004), 65.

31. Kelly, *Donnie Darko*.

32. Henry Koster. *Harvey* (Universal Pictures, 1950).

33. Michael P. Carroll. "Lévi-Strauss, Freud, and the Trickster: A New Perspective upon an Old Problem." *American Ethnologist* 8 no. 2 (1981).

34. Erin Sebo. "Does OE Puca Have an Irish Origin?" *Studia Neophilologica*, 89, no. 2 (2017):165. doi: 10.1080/00393274.2017.1314773.

35. Deasún Breatnach. 1993. "The Púca: A Multi-Functional Irish Supernatural Entity." *Folklore* 104 (1993): 105–10.

36. Davis and DeMello, *Stories Rabbits Tell: A Natural and Cultural History of a Misunderstood Creature*, 134.

37. Bodil Nildin-Wall and Jan Wall. "The Witch as Hare or the Witch's Hare: Popular Legends and Beliefs in Nordic Tradition." *Folklore* 104 (1993): 67.

38. Elizabeth Parker. 2020. *The Forest and the EcoGothic : The Deep Dark Woods in the Popular Imagination* (Switzerland: Springer International Publishing, 2020). http://ebookcentral.proquest.com/lib/deakin/detail.action?docID=6109822.

39. Lynch, *Rabbits*.

40. David Lynch. *Inland Empire* (France: Studio Canal 2006).

41. Lynch, *Rabbits*.

42. Evans, *Disasters That Changed Australia*, 49.

43. David Lynch and Mark Frost. *Twin Peaks: Complete Series* (Showtime, 2017).

BIBLIOGRAPHY

Adams, Richard. *Watership Down*. London: Bloomsbury Publishing UK, 2018.

Alves Joel M., Miguel Carneiro, Jade Y. Cheng, Ana Lemos de Matos, Masmudur M. Rahman, Liisa Loog, Paula F. Campos, N. Wales, A. Eriksson, A. Manica, and T. Strive. "Parallel Adaptation of Rabbit Populations to Myxoma Virus." *Science* 363, no. 6433 (2019): 1319–1326. https://doi.org/10.1126/science.aau7285.

Braddon, Russell. *The Year of the Angry Rabbit*. London: Pan Books, 2018.

Breatnach, Deasún. "The Púca: A Multi-Functional Irish Supernatural Entity." *Folklore* 104 (1993): 105–110.

Carroll, Michael P. "Lévi-Strauss, Freud, and the Trickster: A New Perspective Upon an Old Problem." *American Ethnologist* 8, no. 2 (1981): 301–313.

Chew, Matthew K. "Symposium 19 Good Ideas at the Time: Historians Look at Ecology." *Bulletin of the Ecological Society of America* 90, no. 1 (2009): 142–152.

Claxton, William F. *Night of the Lepus*. Metro-Goldwyn-Mayer, 1972.

Davis, Susan E., and Margo DeMello. *Stories Rabbits Tell: A Natural and Cultural History of a Misunderstood Creature*. New York: Lantern Books, 2003.

Dixon, Wheeler Winston. "When Animals Take Over: The Post-Pandemic Backlash." *Quarterly Review of Film and Video* 38, no. 4 (2021): 303–309. https://doi.org/10.1080/10509208.2020.1772005.

Dodd, Kevin. "Donnie Darko and the Messianic Motif." *Journal of Religion and Film* 13, no. 2 (2009). https://link.gale.com/apps/doc/A242454079/AONE?u=deakin&sid=bookmark-AONE&xid=19e3c571.

Estok, Simon C. *The Ecophobia Hypothesis*. New York: Routledge, 2018. https://www.taylorfrancis.com/books/9781315144689.

Evans, Richard. *Disasters That Changed Australia*. Australia: Melbourne University Publishing, 2009. http://ebookcentral.proquest.com/lib/deakin/detail.action?docID=5718730.

Garrard, Greg, ed. *The Oxford Handbook of Ecocriticism*. Oxford: Oxford University Press, 2013. https://doi.org/10.1093/oxfordhb/9780199742929.001.0001.

Gilliam, Terry, and Terry Jones. *Monty Python and the Holy Grail*. EMI Films, 1975.

Hadas, Marcus. "An Ecocritical Approach to Cruelty in the Laboratory." *Journal of Animal Ethics* 6, no. 2 (2016): 223–233. https://doi.org/10.5406/janimalethics.6.2.0223.

Halberstam, Jack. *Skin Shows*. Durham, NC: Duke University Press, 1995.

Hitchcock, Alfred. *The Birds*. Universal-International Pictures, 1963.

Hurley, Kelly. *The Gothic Body: Sexuality, Materialism, and Degeneration at the Fin de Siècle*. Cambridge: Cambridge University Press, 2004.

Ivakhiv, Adrian. "Teaching Ecocriticism and Cinema." In *Teaching Ecocriticism and Green Cultural Studies*. London and New York: Springer, 2012, 144–155.

Kääpä, Pietari, and Tommy Gustafsson. *The Politics of Nordsploitation: History, Industry, Audiences*. New York: Bloomsbury Publishing, 2021.

Kelly, Richard. *Donnie Darko*. Newmarket Films, 2001.

Kerr, Peter J., Isabella M. Cattadori, June Liu, Derek G. Sim, Jeff W. Dodds, Jason W. Brooks, Mary J. Kennett, Edward C. Holmes, and Andrew F. Read. "Next Step in the Ongoing Arms Race Between Myxoma Virus and Wild Rabbits in Australia is a Novel Disease Phenotype." *Proceedings of the National Academy of Sciences* 114, no. 35 (2017): 9397. https://doi.org/10.1073/pnas.1710336114.

Koster, Henry. *Harvey*. Universal Pictures, 1950.

Lee, Tim. "'It Was Unprecedented': The Virus That Wiped Out Feral Rabbits Was Almost a Bust." *ABC News*, August 7, 2020. https://www.abc.net.au/news/2020-08-08/biological-control-weapon-myxomatosis-almost-failed/12529702.

Lynch, David. *Rabbits*. Online, 2002.

Lynch, David. *Inland Empire*. Absurda, 2019.

———. *Twin Peaks: Complete Series*. Showtime, 2017.

Makkonen, Joonas. *Bunny the Killer Thing*. Raven Banner, 2015.
Marsden, John, and Shaun Tan. *The Rabbits*. Hawthorn East: Lothian Books, 1999.
Menozzi, Filippo. "Invasive Species and the Territorial Machine: Shifting Interfaces Between Ecology and the Postcolonial." *Ariel: A Review of International English Literature* 44, no. 4 (2013): 181–204. https://doi.org/10.1353/ari.2013.0038.
Nildin-Wall, Bodil, and Jan Wall. "The Witch as Hare or the Witch's Hare: Popular Legends and Beliefs in Nordic Tradition." *Folklore* 104 (1993): 67–76.
Parker, Elizabeth. *The Forest and the EcoGothic: The Deep Dark Woods in the Popular Imagination*. Switzerland: Springer International Publishing AG, 2020. http://ebookcentral.proquest.com/lib/deakin/detail.action?docID=6109822.
Pennington, John. "From Peter Rabbit to 'Watership Down': There and Back Again to the Arcadian Ideal." *Journal of the Fantastic in the Arts* 3, no. 2 (1991): 66–80.
Radley, Emma. "Where is Donnie? Psychosis and Agency in Richard Kelly's Donnie Darko." *Psychoanalysis, Culture & Society* 17, no. 4 (2012): 392–409.
Rosen, Martin, and John Hubley. *Watership Down*. Nepenthe Films, 1978.
Sebo, Erin. "Does OE Puca Have an Irish Origin?" *Studia Neophilologica* 89, no. 2 (2017): 167–175. https://doi.org/10.1080/00393274.2017.1314773.
Smith, Andrew, and William Hughes. *EcoGothic*. Manchester: Manchester University Press, 2015. http://ezproxy.st-andrews.ac.uk/login?url=https://dx.doi.org/10.7765/9781526102911.
Smith, Andrew T., Charlotte H. Johnston, Paulo C. Alves, and Klaus Hackländer. *Lagomorphs: Pikas, Rabbits, and Hares of the World*. Baltimore: Johns Hopkins University Press, 2018. https://search.ebscohost.com/login.aspx?direct=true&db=e000xww&AN=1501160&site=eds-live&scope=site.
Soles, Carter. "'And No Birds Sing': Discourses of Environmental Apocalypse in 'The Birds' and 'Night of the Living Dead'." *Interdisciplinary Studies in Literature and Environment* 21, no. 3 (2014): 526–537.
Tidwell, Christy. "Monstrous Natures Within: Posthuman and New Materialist Ecohorror in Mira Grant's 'Parasite'." *Interdisciplinary Studies in Literature and Environment* 21, no. 3 (2014): 538–549.
Tidwell, Christy, and Carter Soles. *Fear and Nature: Ecohorror Studies in the Anthropocene*. New York: Penn State Press, 2021.

Chapter 7

Of Animals and Aliens

Identifying with the Nonhuman Other in Guardians of the Galaxy

Jessica Bay and Jonathan Osborn

Disney's *Guardians of the Galaxy* franchise (2014, 2017, 2023 expected) constellates around a figure characterized by juvenile, dismissive, and reckless masculinity deeply invested in nostalgia that thrives within the universe the films depict and explore. Here, Peter Quill (Chris Pratt) exists as the only "human" character, and his Terran/Earth heritage marks him as distinctly alien. Because of this, the (Terran) audience is encouraged to both identify with and situate him as both an individual immersed in a galaxy of Otherness and as the leader of a group of flawed "others." This positionality encourages a conversation constellating around the concepts of human and alien in which the "human" is defined through the actions, sentiments, and belongings of Peter Quill and the "alien" exists as almost anything else. With this in mind, the earthly and problematic dichotomy between human and animal is extended out into the galaxy so that the term "animal," as with geographer Yi-Fu Tuan's conception of "pet," incorporates multiple forms of aliens—women, animals, and plants.[1]

In this chapter, we will discuss the portrayal of significant *nonhuman* characters within the *Guardians of the Galaxy* franchise (hereafter *GotGV.1* and *GotGV.2*) with a focus on three aliens from Star-Lord's menagerie: the warrior woman, Gamora (Zoe Saldana); the laboratory animal, Rocket Raccoon (Bradley Cooper, voice); and the sentient plant, Groot (Vin Diesel, voice), in relation to their status as Quill's "pets" and companions. These characterizations will be discussed through their changing relationships with the objects, individuals, and collectives present within the morally gray constructed galaxy that they inhabit and in relation to archetypal animal figures with Northrop Frye's Romance Mythos.

Alien Pets

In *Dominance and Affection: The Making of Pets*, Yi-Fu Tuan investigates "our tendency to dissociate power and domination from the world of pleasure, play, and art"[2] and the "inescapable" human need to civilize through collecting, organizing, and cultivating living things in particular ways.[3] Interested in exploring the application of power, Tuan differentiates between two different modes: "Dominance may be cruel and exploitative, with no hint of affection in it. What it produces is the victim. On the other hand, dominance may be combined with affection, and what it produces is the pet."[4] Tuan describes "the pet" as not an animal but rather the outcome of a "relationship of inequality" where "affection mitigates domination."[5] Tuan examines the social histories of particular "pets" including plants, animals, and women,[6] and his historical survey creates correlations between the form of zoos, the structure of formal gardens, and the organization of domestic households with all being interpreted as spaces where particular forms of life (or ways of being) are cultivated by humans according to values and aesthetics related to power. In Tuan's history, all roads lead toward the different iterations of the "menagerie," a "discriminative trait of high civilization, combining as it does the desire for order with the desire to accommodate the heterogeneous and the exotic."[7]

Within the universe of *GotG*, Quill can be interpreted as a "civilizing" force whose "naïve" human values (predominantly drawn from his interpretation of 1980s American popular culture) are translated into actions which surprisingly save a planet inhabited by an advanced culture from destruction—thus indicating that despite visual evidence that this culture possesses technology far beyond the complexity and sophistication of contemporary Earth, Quill's "crude" American masculine values are in fact transcendent and not to be underestimated. Quill's values also collect, organize, and cultivate his alien crew of misfits—changing them from a gang of damaged criminals to a menagerie or family force fighting for "good." While Quill is the central protagonist of the film, he is joined in his escapades by a crew of near sociopathic conspirators/companions who are all survivors of trauma, and with whom the audience is encouraged to identify shortly after they all bond in a maximum-security prison. Included in this motley crew are Gamora, a green-skinned, technologically enhanced former henchman of a genocidal extremist and daughter of a totalitarian overlord; Drax, a humorless single-minded and literal tattooed killer intent on avenging the deaths of his wife and daughter;[8] Rocket, a genetically modified raccoon-like creature and survivor of laboratory experiments with a lack of impulse control and a predilection for creating weapons of destruction; and Groot, a sentient and animate tree with a surprising talent for violence and an incredibly small vocabulary.

It is only through interacting with Quill (vis-à-vis his individualistic American social values, emotional associations, and cultural artifacts/practices) that the audience witnesses the Guardians transform from alien "animals" to companions as they begin to develop complex identities, reveal their complicated and tragic pasts, and "grow." Over the course of the film, Quill's display of emotion and sentiment (depicted through his words, musical taste, and movement/dancing), while initially dismissed by his co-conspirators as ridiculous, petty, or pathetic, is actually the means by which this motley crew are able to bond with one another in different ways, cooperate in a cohesive manner, and work toward the uncharacteristically altruistic goal of stopping a genocidal warlord and then become, by the end of the film, *his* animal menagerie. Although it may seem that the characters become more individualized, what occurs is the opposite as their individualities are sublimated to the needs of a group modeled on a dysfunctional human (Terran) family. This sublimation occurs through the interpellation of seemingly foreign human values of trust, respect, and love as typified within the 1970s and 1980s nostalgia that Quill has constructed his identity with and around.

Throughout the *GotG* films, the extent of Quill's "civilizing" of his crew with American values can be seen most clearly through his popular culture references. Stuck as he is in his own past, Quill filters the world through the movies and music of the White America of his childhood. He has purposely placed all of his acquaintances into the roles of popular culture characters so that he can better relate to them, and then he teaches them their role in his universe by continuously evoking the "legends" of these characters. In *GotGV.1*, Quill teaches Gamora that dancing is an important part of his personality and a trait that he strongly desires in a romantic partner by telling her the "legend" of *Footloose* (1984) and the town of people who had "sticks up their butts," until a hero came along and taught them how to dance.[9] By *GotGV. 2*, Gamora has hesitantly begun to adopt this role and is seen dancing with him.[10] By the time the Guardians meet up with the Avengers in *Avengers: Infinity War* (2018), this legend has cemented itself in the minds of Quill's companions as they are able to repeat the tale with enough clarity for the human Avengers to recognize it as the original film.[11] While these moments provide comedic and nostalgic purposes for the film-viewing audience, they also work to tame, domesticate, and enculture the Guardians to Quill's particular views on the world and create expectations for their actions as members of his "menagerie."

Peter Quill as Hero

To better understand the roles of Quill's "pets" in the *GotG* films, it is imperative to consider the character around whom they assemble. Depicted as a dancing, casual, free-spirited rascal who thinks quickly under pressure, Peter is a narcissistic rogue who treats the world around him and its inhabitants as objects of a game to which only he knows the rules. Our introduction to the adult character occurs in the first film, *GotGV.1*, on an alien planet.[12] He initially appears to be an alien creature as he walks through a desolate rain-soaked and fog-filled landscape wearing what we later learn to be a metallic mask with glowing, red eye lenses. With his determined movement accompanied by a soundscape suggesting a dark, dangerous journey, it is a surprise when once out of the rain, Quill retracts his mask in order to put on headphones connected to a Sony Walkman and begins to dance through the ruined landscape to the diegetic sounds of Redbone's "Come and Get Your Love" (1974). In this particular scene Quill overtly uses animals for his own enjoyment, kicking the small rat-like creatures (known as "orloni") in sync with the music in his headphones. At one point, Quill grabs an orloni and pretends to use it as a microphone. Thus, his character is presented to the audience as a contrast to the conventional stoic science fiction character that was suggested by the expressionless metallic mask and non-diegetic soundtrack; Quill instead is seen as a light-hearted trickster who is playing everything by ear.

As the film progresses, it is revealed through his words and actions that he also uses property and living beings, particularly women, in a similar fashion. He has built his self-image around this sentiment, unironically maintaining the title "Star-Lord"—a name which alludes to his self-appointed yet delusional dominion over anything that enters the field of his juvenile vision.[13] In addition to establishing Quill as the main character of the film, this sequence also introduces us to a contemporary representation of White male sociability and violent masculinity that is dismissive, reckless, irresponsible, and remorseless while simultaneously deeply invested in nostalgia and the seduction of the spectacular.

Guardian Mythos

As they unfold, the *GotG* films present the audience with a clear hero narrative that centers on Peter Quill while relegating the rest of the Guardians to supporting cast or sidekicks in his (heroic) journey of personal discovery. As magical/valuable animal (Rocket), woman (Gamora), and element of nature (Groot), Quill's crew ferry him from "[c]all to [a]dventure"[14] through "the crucial struggle"[15] to "[a]tonement with the [f]ather."[16] Through consideration of the very closely linked concepts of Northrop Frye's Romance Mythos and Joseph Campbell's Monomyth, we can trace ways that this ensemble cast is reorganized to center a deluded, White, human man's narrative of self(ish)-discovery.

Fantasy has often been linked with myth and legend, but while the genre certainly has its roots in those types of stories, it differs most noticeably, as suggested by Joan Aiken, in that "myth is universal [while] fantasy is personal."[17] In using myth-based narrative structures within a space-based superhero story, *GotGV.1* and *GotGV.2* offer the audience a personal narrative that producers hope will resonate with their intended audience—young human (White) men. The link between myth and fantasy can be seen in Northrop Frye's Romance Mythos. This mythos presents a quest narrative, featuring a traditional hero, that follows the hero's life from his childhood (often as an orphan) through multiple challenges and stunning deeds to a major battle that may or may not result in the hero's death (or redemption).[18] Similarly, Joseph Campbell's Monomyth discusses the universality of the narratives of human myth.[19] Campbell's structure also begins with a young man and follows his journey through many adventures to a major identity-defining battle.[20] These basic descriptions can also be seen to resonate with the structures of many fantasy tales, particularly those sub-genres of high fantasy, sword and sorcery, and, of course, superhero narrative. Modern superhero narratives, in particular, have been connected with mythical storytelling in their ability "to bring a costumed superhero to genuine, if fictional, life, surrounded by a universe that makes believable sense."[21] It is this grounding in the real, if fictionalized, world that makes these stories myths rather than fairy tales. The space of the fairy tale is "an unreal world without definite locality or definite characters" while the mythopoeic tale occurs in and is concerned with the world of the real.[22]

In addition to the general description of the hero's journey, Frye's and Campbell's myth narratives are populated with a number of helpful characters. These characters can be "old crone[s],"[23] helpful, magical animals, or personifications of nature itself who appear to bend to his will in order to advance his, often divine, if violent, quest.[24] Margery Hourihan points out that the hero's "human companions are frequently subordinates removed from their own cultural or social group and his animals are often wild creatures who voluntarily leave the wilderness to serve him, recognizing him as their master."[25] In the *GotG* films, we can see Hourihan's observations in action; since Quill is the only technically "human" character and the point of identification for the audience, he becomes the superior figure within the story. The rest of his crew, while perhaps also "removed from their own cultural or social group" are, as we shall see later, more readily identified by the audience as "wild animals who [have] voluntarily [left] the wilderness to serve him."[26]

It should be mentioned here that myth narratives tend to have a very clear sense of morality with strong divides between the divine and demonic or good and evil. This is definitely not the case with the *GotG* films. *GotGV.1* ends with Quill asking his crew if, as the newly named Guardians of the Galaxy, they should now do something that is "[s]omething good? Something bad? Bit of both?" When Gamora assures him that the crew will "follow your lead," Quill decides that means "Bit of both," ensuring they end the first film in a state of ambiguous morality.[27] Similarly, *GotGV.2* ends with an epic yet sentimental funeral celebration for a murderous space pirate. The Guardians are very clearly willing to risk their lives to save the galaxy when absolutely necessary, but they are also very clearly interested in profiting in any way that they can and are more than likely to be "a little bad" when in pursuit of some fun. It is in this way that this narrative expands upon the myth narratives. However, while the Guardians' motives may be ambiguous, their demonstrated desire and commitment to save the galaxy ensures they appear to have a moral compass that is similar to that of characters in Frye's Romance Mythos where "[c]haracters tend to be either for or against the quest."[28] They may not be characterized as wholly good, but Quill's Guardians are fully committed to the quest once the decision has been made to save the galaxy.

Quill, as a character, is forever stuck in one part of the quest journey. He has been called to adventure and has had some success in completing various dangerous tasks to further him on his ultimate journey toward manhood, but he appears forever stalled at the third stage of romance (the quest) and never makes it entirely to the climax that would be signified by a proper death or rebirth (leading to tragedy and irony, respectively). This is an impotent form of the narrative: "The essential element of plot in romance is adventure ... [and at] its most naïve it is an endless form in which a central character who never develops or ages goes through one adventure after another."[29] Despite appearing to almost die and come to a new understanding of his provenance at the end of each of the *GotG* films, we can see how far Quill is from completing his heroic journey when he meets members of the Avengers while fighting Thanos in *Avengers: Infinity War*. At this moment Quill has lost Gamora to Thanos and is, understandably, upset but when confronted with other "genuine" Terrans/humans, he is unable to maintain his standing with his crew as they begin to suspect that he might not be the best hero for them to follow: Tony Stark/Iron Man (Robert Downey Jr.) points out Quill's inability to lead and ignores him completely; Dr. Strange (Benedict Cumberbatch) recognizes him as an obstacle and leaves him entirely out of the planning session; and, Peter Parker/Spider-Man (Tom Holland), an actual teenager and the one Avenger that Quill comes closest to identifying with, dismisses Quill's favorite pop culture icons in front of his crew (who have come to view them as heroic figures from Terran legends).[30] In this moment, not only do we understand that Quill's hero journey has stalled, we also recognize that Quill remains emotionally an adolescent. Quill, like the figure of Peter Pan, is an extreme manifestation of one aspect of the hero's nature: youthful energy and extroversion, but the energy is sterile, expressed only in self-glorification, rebellion and destruction. [Like Pan, he] is an all too appropriate idol for twentieth-century Western civilization which fetishizes youth but provides few guides for the second half of life's journey which should be a progress towards wisdom and self-integration.[31]

With Quill as the focus of the narrative and thus the only character that can be considered to be on a conventional heroic journey, the remaining members of the Guardians *serve*—narratively and practically—to further his journey of self-discovery by fulfilling the role of submissive companions. As the narrative unfolds, these aspects of the character of Quill become fleshed out through his escapades and interactions with other characters in the film. Like Peter Quill, whose behavior is naturalized and partially explained due to our knowledge of his abduction by and apprenticeship with mercenaries, the other Guardians of the Galaxy are rendered faultless through their characterizations as victims of experiment, genocide, and brainwashing—facets of their life which they all quickly and candidly reveal at different moments. As victims of past trauma, all are shielded from judgment by these disclosures. As de facto virtual crewmembers, viewers of the film empathize with these characters.

Quill's Mythic Menagerie

We can examine the roles of three members of Quill's menagerie more closely to further consider both their roles as supporting characters of myth and as domesticated "pets." Our real introduction to the rest of the main Guardian characters occurs when they all find themselves jailed within a maximum-security prison. Their shared goal of escaping (depending on their individual motives) to sell or protect the "orb" (ultimately revealed to contain one of the Infinity Stones), collect the bounty on Quill, and/or get revenge on Ronan the Destroyer (Lee Pace) and Thanos (Josh Brolin) has placed them in a tenuous detente.

Rocket

Rocket Raccoon, while appearing to be (to the audience and Quill) an actual talking raccoon similar to other animated animals in film,[32] is actually self-described as a bizarre alien experiment developed in a lab. As an individual character Rocket is suffering from trauma related to these experiments, but appears to find his place with the newly formed Guardians by the end of *GotGV.1*. During the prison sequence we see that Rocket is definitely the brains of the group as he very quickly produces a plan for the group to escape from this inescapable prison, though we also learn that he feels the need to watch others suffer indecencies for his own amusement; when listing tools he needs in order to engineer their escape, Rocket stipulates that: "That dude there . . . I need his prosthetic leg."[33] During the escape, he reveals that this tool was not a necessary component for the escape and he just "thought it would be funny."[34] At this point in the narrative, Rocket appears as intelligent, capable, very dangerous, and partially unhinged.

During *GotGV.2*, *Avengers: Infinity War*, and *Avengers: Endgame* (2019), we begin to witness Rocket on adventures of his own; most notably in *Endgame* when he is leading his own team while trying to salvage what is left of the galaxy after the "Thanos Snap,"[35] but his role in relation to Quill is generally one of support and conscience. As mentioned above, Rocket acts as Quill's protector in the jail scene in *GotGV.1* that brings all of the Guardians together. Additional "protector" moments specifically directed at Quill occur when Rocket, Drax, and Groot attempt to free Quill from the Ravagers by using the "Hadron Enforcer" weapon that Rocket designed[36] and, in *GotGV.2* Rocket risks the lives of Yondu (Michael Rooker), Groot, and Kraglin (Sean Gunn) by jumping too quickly through space to rush to "rescue Quill" from his father Ego (Kurt Russell) before they all recklessly rush headlong at the planet that is the physical embodiment of Ego.[37]

Rocket's need for a human "master" can be seen more clearly when he abandons Quill in order to "serve" Thor, after he, along with the other Guardians, judges Thor to be the more complete heroic specimen. While all of the Guardians are enamored with Thor's physique, commenting on his deep voice, his "muscles . . . made of Cotati metal fibres," and referring to him as a "pirate angel," Rocket very quickly decides to abandon Quill when Thor praises his intelligence:

THOR: "I assume you're the captain, sir?"
ROCKET: "You're very perceptive."
THOR: "You seem like a noble leader. Will you join me on my quest to Nidavellir?"
ROCKET: "Yeah, I'll go."[38]

Quill's objections to this plan fall on deaf ears as Rocket chooses to leave the group with Thor and Groot to see the legendary Nidavellir and spend some time with the god-like hero, Thor.

Within the structure of the myth narrative, Rocket fulfills the very traditional role of a magical and helpful animal. These figures can be true companions such as the hero's faithful steed or temporary helpers along the journey such as the ants and eagle who directed Psyche in her quest for Cupid[39] or the eagles who helped Gandalf and the rest of the Fellowship in *The Lord of the Rings* trilogy of films (2001, 2002, 2003). These characters play pivotal roles in the myth through both rescuing and guiding the hero when necessary. Rocket, as mentioned above, moves very quickly from the position of bounty hunter to Quill's protector. When attempting to rescue him from the Ravagers, he has completely forgotten that these are the same people who were going to pay him to hand Quill over to them.[40] By this point in the narrative, Rocket is no longer concerned with profiting from his friendship with Quill, he is only trying to protect the one man who has given direction and meaning to his life. His decision to rescue Quill and Gamora here is driven entirely by sentiment as we see when he responds to Groot with "I know they're the only friends we ever had."[41] Rocket has chosen to follow Quill and fulfill the role of faithful animal companion and pet.

Gamora

As the kidnapped and adopted daughter of Thanos and sister of Nebula, Gamora has a complicated history. Both of Thanos's "daughters" were ripped from their respective home worlds as children when Thanos slaughtered their families as part of his pathological desire to cleanse the universe of half of all its inhabitants. Henceforth, Gamora was physically augmented, trained to become the successor to Thanos and, as we learn in later *Avengers* films, was even tasked with the important mission of locating specific Infinity Stones for him. It was during this independent research and travel that Gamora began to realize that it was imperative to keep the stones away from her father for the good of the galaxy. Gamora possesses a very clear goal when we encounter her at the beginning of *GotGV.1—find the orb and bring it to The Collector in Knowhere to keep it safely away from the hands of Ronan and her father*.[42] As the film progresses, her goal becomes integrated with Quill's own goals and slowly, Gamora becomes a vital aspect of Quill's hero quest (so much so that Quill risks his own life for her after her spaceship is destroyed and she is left floating in space).

Gamora performs a dual role for Quill: she provides him with his initial direction/quest narrative and she is one component of his ultimate reward for completing that quest. In Frye's Romance Mythos, "the reward of the quest usually is or includes a bride" who is "often rescued from the unwelcome embraces of another and generally older male, or from giants or bandits or other usurpers."[43] While Gamora is much too skilled an assassin herself to require rescuing from any regular run-of-the-mill "bandits," Quill has, in many ways, "rescued" her from the control of her father Thanos (referred to by an ancillary character as "[t]he most powerful being in the universe"[44]) by providing her with a new "family." Quill's father, Ego, validates this idea when he refers to Gamora as Quill's "girl" and suggests that Quill has given Gamora "freedom."[45]

Frye's myth narrative also highlights the "removal of some stigma from the heroine figures"[46] in preparation for their ultimate role as bride reward. In myths, (as in fairy tales), we see two types of women: the "good" and virtuous woman and the "bad" and dangerous woman.[47] Given the gray moral code practiced by the Guardians, no particular character (with the exception of Quill's fairy godmother-like deceased mother)[48] can ever be seen as wholly one or the other; however, Gamora begins the narrative as a solitary assassin working to doublecross a genocidal maniac and very quickly assumes the role of a domesticated and supportive girlfriend figure who, although skilled in battle, also provides him with confidence and emotional aid. While still a proficient killer when necessary, Gamora becomes more willing to offer a hand to her opponents than the tip of her sword as the narrative progresses. For example, Gamora regularly chooses to save her estranged and confrontational sister Nebula's life during their many fights—despite Nebula's insistence on engaging her in mortal combat.

Through joining Quill's menagerie, Gamora becomes "tamed" and placed in a domesticated role as a potential "bride" figure who helps Quill manage and tend his alien menagerie. At the conclusion of *GotGV.1* this is particularly apparent as Gamora has exchanged her weapons and battle suit for a short skirt and stands behind Quill while he is sitting in the captain's seat. All other members of the Guardians are fitted with a seat and are engaged in tasks in the ship as they prepare to leave, but Gamora's only role appears to be to emotionally support Quill while confirming his dominance. It is Gamora who states to Quill that they (the Guardians) will follow his lead, emphatically cementing his role as the leader of their group while symbolically relinquishing the tactical power that she previously wielded.[49] Through this depiction, Gamora becomes positioned by Quill (and the audience) as a heroic prize rather than a distinct and autonomous individual. In so doing, Quill, (and the audience) surrender to what Tuan states is the "temptation for the powerful to reduce their pets (plants, animals, and humans) to simulacra of lifeless objects and mechanical toys—to the sort of frozen perfection that only the inanimate can attain."[50] Indeed, in *GotGV.2* Quill's behavior is that of negligence and his narcissism leads to near annihilation of his entire menagerie.[51]

Groot

Groot is perhaps the most difficult figure of the Guardians to describe yet is dramatically one of the most interesting as he speaks an "alien" language that is not subtitled for the viewing audience, and thus we must decipher his perspective from hints provided by his actions and the responses and reactions of the other characters. From Quill's perspective, Groot is a walking and talking tree-like being who can only say the words "I am Groot."[52] As Quill and the rest of the Guardians spend time with Groot, they learn his language and eventually we are provided with more characters who can offer translations for the audience. Adult Groot is a loyal partner and companion to Rocket in *GotGV.1* though he appears to be much more concerned with protecting his new companions than Rocket. When Rocket would choose to abandon the other members of the Guardians early in the narrative, Groot reminds him that they are their friends and that Rocket needs friends.[53] Notably, it is also Groot that chooses, without hesitation, to sacrifice himself to ensure the survival of the rest of the team. In many ways, it is this moment that allows the Guardians to emotionally view themselves as a collective and overcome Ronan; Groot's final words to the team in *GotGV.1* are "*We* are Groot," and they resonate as a clear suggestion that the group is a bonded, familial unit, rather than mere individuals.[54]

After Groot's sacrifice, Rocket transplants his remains in a pot and a new, much younger Groot begins to grow and joins them on future adventures in *GotGV.2* and the *Avengers* movies. While being a child in age and form, this Groot does not have the same childlike wonder that prompted the previous iteration of Groot to offer a young pickpocket a flower that was growing from his own palm.[55] However, Groot remains as shockingly violent in his childlike form as he was as an adult. During the final battle of *GotGV.1* on Ronan's ship, the team is faced with combating an overwhelming number of foes but Groot quickly dispatches them by extending his arm branches through all of their chests, lifting them off the ground, and then slapping them against the metal walls of the ship corridor until their bodies are pulverized. He then turns to his companions and smiles a huge and joyful grin.[56] This moment of extreme violence combined with pure joy is mirrored when Baby Groot enacts his revenge on a Ravager who bullied him in *GotGV.2* by growing his arm branches to attack the man and then throwing him off of a gantry before quickly cuddling up on Rocket's shoulder.[57]

In many ways, Groot's ability to combine extreme violence with happiness and love of life situates him in a position of "moral antithesis of heroism and villainy."[58] That is, Groot is neither the hero nor the villain, but instead occupies a position outside of these binary roles—that of an element of nature. As an actual sentient representation of fauna on the Guardian team, Groot clearly represents "the moral neutrality of the intermediate world of nature" and can be seen as similar to "the awkward but faithful giant with unkempt hair [who] has shambled amiably through romance for centuries."[59]

Quill maintains limited control over the animalistic giant iteration of Groot; he has difficulty relating to him because he needs a translator to understand him and Groot always appears to choose to do what he determines is right regardless of the decisions of the team. When reborn as Baby Groot, the audience is introduced to a character who needs discipline and training by Quill and others. Tuan argues that "[a]n infant or a small child is still not thought of as a person in the fullest sense of that word . . . [t]he child, in other words, is a pet and is properly treated as such."[60] Correspondingly, Groot the child is depicted as incapable of understanding language. During *GotGV.2* he needs constant supervision, repetitive instructions, and praise. For instance, in an extended montage on the Ravagers' ship, Groot is repeatedly tasked with fetching Yondu's fin, a very specific and distinctive object, but continually returns with incorrect objects that bear no resemblance to the fin.[61] This game of fetch both alludes to Groot's animal-like capabilities and puts him in the position of a pet displaying the tricks he has learned.

In addition to enlisting Groot to perform certain tasks, Quill also has the opportunity to mold this elemental figure to his needs and paternal expectations. We see the entire team teaching Groot and taking care of him as a child, but it is Quill who has most fully taken on the role of father by the end of *GotGV.2*. As this film, so steeped in motifs of the relationships between fathers and sons, ends, Quill invites Groot onto his lap to join him in listening to "Father and Son" by Cat Stevens (1970)—inviting him into his world of music while also recognizing his role as father figure for Groot.[62] During one of the post-credits sequences of this film, we also see that an adolescent Groot is playing video games in a messy bedroom while Quill reprimands him and states that "now I know how Yondu felt."[63] While continuing the father-son theme of the entire film, this moment also suggests that Quill is successfully raising Groot in his own image—he is playing video games, ignoring his elders, and, as we see in the later *Avengers* films, generally unconcerned with the morality play going on around him. In some ways, Quill has successfully tamed wild "animal" nature to his will through the character of Groot.

CONCLUSION

In this chapter, we have considered how Quill is supported by the aliens of his crew and how they can be considered as analogous to the animal companions or prizes of the Romance Mythos. With a focus on the characters of Rocket, Gamora, and Groot, we have discussed the ways in which Quill, as a representative of failed yet persistent masculinity, is enabled by women, flora, and fauna to further his own development thus rendering them domesticated. Among the films of the Marvel Cinematic Universe (MCU), the *GotG* films exist as those most likely to be described as having an ensemble cast. While the *Avengers* films consist of an increasing number of superheroes, most of those characters have individual hero narratives in other film series or television seasons.[64] This expansion of the characters in what can be considered spin-offs offers insight into the characters as individuals when they are assembled with the larger ensemble. This is not the case with the *GotG* characters. These characters are unknown outside of their roles within the ensemble or team dynamic. For this reason, we can see that their characters are less defined as individual heroes and the narrative, as a structure, needs a defining character to guide the story. Quill, as the representative for the ideal audience, becomes the main hero of the story and we follow his journey through masculinity. In *GotGV2*, Drax speaks with the character Mantis (Pom Klementieff) about her relationship to Peter's monstrous father Ego:

MANTIS: Ego found me in a larva state. Orphaned on my home world. He raised me by hand and kept me as his own.
DRAX: So, you're a pet?
MANTIS: I suppose.[65]

Later, when questioned by Gamora about her presence on Ego, a planet/being otherwise devoid of autonomous life, Mantis describes herself as "[a] flea with a purpose. I help him sleep."[66] Although Ego is depicted as a villain in part because he keeps sentient "pets," Quill avoids becoming like his father because of the work his own "pets" do to save him. All of the Guardians, autonomous beings before encountering Quill, now risk their own lives to save him from losing his autonomy. Like Mantis and the living planet Ego, once under the pull of Quill's planet-like ego the different Guardians have found purpose. The joy that the audience receives from participating vicariously in the team's intergalactic exploits validates the Guardians' chrysalis as they transform from traumatized alien larval individuals and merge into a familial form to collectively excrete a foundation for Quill's fantasy image of American masculinity.

The extent to which the audience is expected to be invested in this image can be ascertained by looking at the tragedy of Gamora's death and the premise for the third installment of the *Guardians* franchise which, presumably, revolves around Quill's search for Gamora.[67] Director James Gunn has suggested that the third film will be a conclusion for this version of the *Guardians of the Galaxy* characters and that the three films will be seen as part of a trilogy.[68] Quill, at the conclusion of the *Avengers* saga, is very focused on finding and "saving" Gamora; as such, his final mythos reward has become solidified and he appears to be embarking on the final stage of his hero's quest. We can only suspect that this means he may mature and recognize what it means to become a man before the ultimate sacrifice that a hero can make—death and/or rebirth.

As Quill navigates this destiny, the films continue to assert the value of stewardship by White masculinity. Despite not actually understanding morality, Quill is still the leader of a group of alien companions who look to him for direction, purpose, and focus. Retaining Quill in this position implicitly devalues the concepts of tolerance, respect for difference, maintenance of order, and the recognition of consequences associated with American nostalgic masculinity despite the potential of the films to explore a more pluralistic vision.

NOTES

1. Yi-Fu Tuan, *Dominance and Affection: The Making of Pets* (New Haven: Yale University Press, 1984), 2–5.
2. Tuan, *Dominance and Affection*, 4.
3. Tuan, *Dominance and Affection*, 6.
4. Tuan, *Dominance and Affection*, 2.
5. Tuan, *Dominance and Affection*, 2.
6. Tuan, *Dominance and Affection*, 5.
7. Tuan, *Dominance and Affection*, 75–76.
8. Within *Dominance and Affection*, Tuan references the "mad man" as another pet of culture but after consideration, we have decided to exclude Drax as representative of this role because he is not "mad" given the context of his alien physiology and culture. That is, Drax truly believes he is indestructible and has a right to avenge the deaths of his wife and daughter against the greatest foes of the galaxy, in part because his alien physiology offers him more protection than most humanoid bodies have and due to the culture of violence and aggression within which he existed prior to meeting Quill.
9. *Guardians of the Galaxy*, directed by James Gunn (Marvel Studios, 2014), 00:51:38-00:53:17, iTunes.
10. *Guardians of the Galaxy Vol 2*, directed by James Gunn (Marvel Studios, 2017), 1:11:25-1:12:55, iTunes.
11. *Avengers: Infinity War*, directed by Anthony Russo and Joe Russo (Marvel Studios, 2018), 1:23:05-1:23:30, iTunes.
12. *GotGV.1*, 00:04:24-00:07:52.
13. It is revealed that Quill was given the title Star-Lord by his deceased mother.
14. Joseph Campbell, *The Hero with a Thousand Faces*, original 1949 (Novato, CA: New World Library, 2008), 28.
15. Northrop Frye, *Anatomy of Criticism: Four Essays* (Princeton, NJ: Princeton University Press, 1957), 187.
16. Campbell, *The Hero with a Thousand Faces*, 28.
17. Joan Aiken quoted in Philip Martin, *A Guide to Fantasy Literature: Thoughts on Stories of Wonder and Enchantment* (Milwaukee, WI: Crispin Books, 2009), 173.
18. Frye, *Anatomy of Criticism*.
19. Campbell, *The Hero with a Thousand Faces*.
20. Campbell, *The Hero with a Thousand Faces*.

21. A.G. Holdier, "On Superhero Stories: The Marvel Cinematic Universe as Tolkienesque Fantasy," *Mythlore: A Journal of J.R.R. Tolkien, C.S. Lewis, Charles Williams, and Mythopoeic Literature* 36, no. 2 (2018): 74.

22. Stith Thompson, *The Folktalke*, 1946 (Berkeley: University of California Press, 1977), 8.

23. Campbell, *The Hero with a Thousand Faces*, 57.

24. Campbell, *The Hero with a Thousand Faces*; Frye, *Anatomy of Criticism*.

25. Margery Hourihan, *Deconstructing the Hero: Literary Theory and Children's Literature* (New York: Routledge, 2005), 76.

26. Hourihan, *Deconstructing the Hero*, 76.

27. *GotGV.1*, 1:52:38-1:53:03.

28. Frye, *Anatomy of Criticism*, 195.

29. Frye, *Anatomy of Criticism*, 186.

30. *Infinity War*, 1:23:05-1:23:30.

31. Hourihan, *Deconstructing the Hero*, 75.

32. As an alien companion to a human protagonist, Rocket joins the ranks of such anthropomorphized characters as: Howard the Duck (who also makes an appearance in *GotGV.1*) (*Howard the Duck*, Willard Huyck, Universal Pictures, 1986); Alvin, Simon, and Theodore (*Alvin and the Chipmunks*, Tim Hill, 20th Century Studios, 2007); Stuart Little (*Stuart Little*, Rob Minkoff, Columbia Pictures, 1999); Pantalaimon and Iorek Byrnison as Lyra's animal companions (*The Golden Compass*, Chris Weitz, New Line Cinema, 2007); Baloo, Bagheera, Raksha, and other animal companions of Mowgli (*The Jungle Book*, Jon Favreau, Walt Disney Pictures, 2016); Scooby-Doo (*Scooby-Doo*, Raja Gosnell, Warner Bros., 2002); and the Cheshire Cat, the Blue Caterpillar, and the White Rabbit (*Alice in Wonderland*, Tim Burton, Walt Disney Pictures, 2010).

33. *GotGV.1*, 00:34:13-00:34:20.

34. *GotGV.1*, 00:39:14-00:39:26.

35. Note that Rocket is one of only two members of the Guardians who survived "The Snap" (the other being Nebula), so he has lost his guide in the form of Quill.

36. *GotGV.1*, 1:14:44-1:15:28.

37. *GotGV.2*, 1:24:16-1:25:51.

38. *Infinity War*, 00:29:27-00:35:48.

39. Campbell, *The Hero with a Thousand Faces*, 82.

40. *GotGV.1*, 1:14:52-1:15:28.

41. *GotGV.1*, 1:09:22-1:11:00.

42. *GotGV.1*, 00:31:19-00:32:01; 00:51:30-00:51:55.

43. Frye, *Anatomy of Criticism*, 193.

44. *GotGV.1*, 1:11:05-1:12:00.

45. *GotGV.2*, 1:18:48-1:21:10.

46. Frye, *Anatomy of Criticism*, 193.

47. Susanne Gruss, "Popular Genres: Sexy Fairy Tales, Feminist Romances, Chick Lit," in *The Pleasure of the Feminist Text: Reading Michèle Roberts and Angela Carter* (New York: Rodopi, 2009), 196–97.

48. Quill's mother bequeaths him letters of love, music recordings, and it is suggested in *GotGv.1* that she aids him in surviving his experience of holding an Infinity Stone.

49. *GotGV.1*, 1:52:35-1:53:00.
50. Tuan, *Dominance and Affection*, 17.
51. Fortunately for Quill, the connections that he has established with them individually ensure they will risk their lives to save him.
52. As the movie progresses, the audience learns that Groot is a complex, aware, and emotionally intelligent being rather than a simple creature—and that it is his emphatic delivery of the words "I am Groot" that differentiates his statements and create meaning.
53. *GotGV.1*, 1:09:22-1:11:00.
54. *GotGV.1*, 1:38:03-1:39:33.
55. *GotGV.1*, 00:49:51-00:50:10.
56. *GotGV.1*, 1:33:30-1:33:55.
57. *GotGV.2*, 1:07:47-1:08:05.
58. Frye, *Anatomy of Criticism*, 196.
59. Frye, *Anatomy of Criticism*, 196.
60. Tuan, *Dominance and Affection*, 115.
61. *GotGV.2*, 1:01:54-1:05:35.
62. *GotGV.2*, 2:03:21-2:04:25.
63. *GotGV.2*, 2:14:03-2:14:29.
64. See, for example, *Iron Man 1, 2,* and *3* (Jon Favreau, 2008, 2010; Shane Black, 2013), *Captain America: The First Avenger* (Joe Johnston, 2011), *Captain America: Civil War* (Anthony Russo and Joe Russo, 2016), *Thor* (Kenneth Branagh, 2011), *Thor: The Dark World* (Alan Taylor, 2013), *Thor: Ragnarok* (Taika Waititi, 2017), and the television shows *WandaVision* (created for television by Jac Schaeffer, 2021-ongoing), and *Hawkeye* (created for television by Jonathan Igla, 2021-ongoing). All produced by Marvel Studios.
65. *GotGV.2*, 00:56:15-00:56:30.
66. *GotGV.2*, 00:58:16-00:58:28.
67. Gamora dies in *Avengers: Infinity War* but in *Avengers: Endgame*, Gamora "returns" from the dead as an iteration of herself as she was before becoming Peter's lover and joining the Guardians.
68. Cooper Hood, "Guardians of the Galaxy 3: Predicting the Fate of Every Character." *ScreenRant*, October 9, 2021. https://screenrant.com/guardians-galaxy-3-characters-team-lives-dies-prediction/.

BIBLIOGRAPHY

Campbell, Joseph. *The Hero With a Thousand Faces*. 1949. 3rd edition. Novato, CA: New World Library, 2008.

Frye, Northrop. *Anatomy of Criticism: Four Essays*. Princeton, NJ: Princeton University Press, 1957.

Gruss, Susanne. "Popular Genres: Sexy Fairy Tales, Feminist Romances, Chick Lit." In *The Pleasure of the Feminist Text: Reading Michèle Roberts and Angela Carter*. New York: Rodopi, 2009: 195–241.

Gunn, James, director. *Guardians of the Galaxy*. Marvel Studios, 2014, 2hr., 1min. iTunes.

Gunn, James, director. *Guardians of the Galaxy, Vol. 2*. Marvel Studios, 2017, 2hr., 16min. iTunes.

Holdier, A. G. "On Superhero Stories: The Marvel Cinematic Universe as Tolkienesque Fantasy." *Mythlore: A Journal of J.R.R. Tolkien, C.S. Lewis, Charles Williams, and Mythopoeic Literature* 36, no. 2 (2018): 73–88. https://dc.swosu.edu/mythlore/vol36/iss2/6/.

Hood, Cooper. "Guardians of the Galaxy 3: Predicting the Fate of Every Character." *ScreenRant*, October 9, 2021. https://screenrant.com/guardians-galaxy-3-characters-team-lives-dies-prediction/.

Hourihan, Margery. *Deconstructing the Hero: Literary Theory and Children's Literature*. New York: Routledge, 2005.

Jackson, Peter, director. *The Lord of the Rings: The Fellowship of the Ring*. Special Extended Edition, New Line Cinema, 2001, 3hrs., 48min. iTunes.

Jackson, Peter, director. *The Lord of the Rings: The Two Towers*. Special Extended Edition, New Line Cinema, 2002, 3hrs., 55min. iTunes.

Jackson, Peter, director. *The Lord of the Rings: The Return of the King*. Special Extended Edition, New Line Cinema, 2003, 4hrs., 23min. iTunes.

Martin, Philip. *A Guide to Fantasy Literature: Thoughts on Stories of Wonder and Enchantment*. Milwaukee, WI: Crispin Books, 2009.

Ross, Herbert, director. *Footloose*. Paramount Pictures, 1984, 1hr., 47min. DVD.

Russo, Anthony, and Joe Russo, directors. *Avengers: Endgame*. Marvel Studios, 2019, 3hrs., 2min. iTunes.

Russo, Anthony, and Joe Russo, directors. *Avengers: Infinity War*. Marvel Studios, 2018, 2hrs., 30min. iTunes.

Thompson, Stith. *The Folktale*. 1946. Berkeley: University of California Press, 1977.

Tuan, Yi-Fu. *Dominance and Affection: The Making of Pets*. New Haven, CT: Yale University Press, 1984.

Part III

ANIMAL/HUMAN HYBRIDS AND OTHER CREATURES

Chapter 8

Hormone Monsters and Animal Antagonists

Animating Teen Horrors and Promoting Eudaimonia in Big Mouth (Netflix, 2017–)

Georgia Aitaki

INTRODUCTION

Netflix's animated show *Big Mouth* (2017–) has received significant popular and critical acclaim for its raw and ludicrous depiction of teen life and struggles, exploring issues such as the changing human body and mental health, as well as friendship, love, sex, and a wide array of emotions that go hand in hand with puberty. Created by Andrew Goldberg, Nick Kroll, Mark Levin, and Jennifer Flacket, the series premiered on Netflix on September 29, 2017, and is currently in its fifth season while the online streaming giant has renewed the series through to a seventh season. *Big Mouth* spotlights the life of a group of seventh graders, including best friends Nick and Andrew, while they go through *puberty*, one of the most defining periods in terms of biological, psychological, and social transitions in a human's life span. In terms of genre, it falls under the category of teen TV, that is television programs "centered around adolescent characters with a focus on cultural milestones and rites of passage—from issues of finding the right romantic partner, rebelling against or conforming to adults rules, choosing a career path, coming to terms with one's parents, and establishing a secure identity."[1] Alongside a diverse constellation of human characters, the show's use of anthropomorphized creatures, such as Hormone Monsters and animal antagonists, constitutes a powerful visual and narrative mechanism that exemplifies the human characters' pubertal (emotional and physical) changes but also gives a pedagogical flavor to entertainment; by using these fantastical creatures, the show manages to tell complex and nuanced stories about teen identity, gender and sexuality, and mental health.

Drawing and expanding on the notion of eudaimonic entertainment, this chapter explores the ways that *Big Mouth* functions as televisual pedagogy, successfully merging pleasure and education, especially when it comes to issues of adolescent development and mental health. More specifically, this chapter focuses on the critical analysis of nonhuman characters in *Big Mouth*, namely the Hormone Monsters that shadow the human characters and stand by their side as they try to navigate early puberty, as well as the animal antagonists that visualize mental health conditions and emotions (such as Depression Kitty, Tito the Anxiety Mosquito, and the Gratitoad). By dissecting the fantastical premises and characters of five seasons of *Big Mouth*, this chapter examines the narrative functions of nonhuman creatures in contemporary animation, investigating how fluctuating hormone levels, physiological changes, and mental health struggles are visualized, encouraging the human characters to work through circumstances that affect a person's broader identity, sense of self, and well-being.

ENTERTAINMENT AND/AS PEDAGOGY

Entertainment, according to Jonathan Gray, is one of the "most automatically moralized concepts"[2] and difficult to define in a value-neutral fashion. As the centerpiece of frequent moral panics and, simultaneously, the victim (often together with the television) of explicit attacks, entertainment and entertaining media content are not by default positively welcome but rather met with suspicion, fear, and even disgust:

> [. . .] entertainment's critics launch three major attacks. First, we see great fear of the incredible powers of television entertainment. Entertainment is posited either as a great ill in and of itself, as capable of masking comparably great ills, or as so completely devoid of content, meaning, and/or value that our culture's love affair with it is seen as the ultimate waste of time and human potential. Second, entertainment is placed in stark and clear opposition to information and education. When writers talk of entertainment "creeping" into information, they employ the imagery of invasion, rival armies, and unlawful occupation. Finally, particularly when metaphors of narcosis are used, entertainment's viewers or "users" are frequently seen as unreliable around such a stimulus, and as slaves to their/our addiction, hence meaning that entertainment plus humans equals a troublesome combination.[3]

As Alan McKee et al. further explain, *entertainment* is an "audience-centred commercial culture. It works as a system driven by audiences, to give them what they want to consume, and it is driven by commercial business models and imperatives."[4] As such, it differentiates from the educational model that gives audiences what they "must" consume and the arts model that gives them what they "should" consume. At the same time, however, it is defined as an aesthetic system characterized by vulgarity, story, seriality and adaptation, happy endings, interactivity, a fast and loud aesthetic, spectacle, emotion, and fun.[5] As a distinct cultural category and reception phenomenon, entertainment is associated with enjoyment and "manifests itself through pleasurable feelings such as exhilaration, laughter, curiosity, excitement, thrill, relief, enjoyable sadness, tenderness, melancholy and/or sensory delight."[6] For the above reasons, entertainment is often discursively positioned, by audiences themselves, but also critics and scholars, in an awkward relation to education, one that emphasizes their antithesis and incompatibility.

Empirical research on entertainment experiences, however, reveals a different story. Entertainment does not only provide fun and enjoyment but also appreciation and meaningfulness.[7] In that sense, to entirely dismiss the multidimensional nature of entertainment would be to consciously strip it of the ability to tell us something meaningful about our world. In an effort to illustrate this complexity, Oliver and Raney have proposed the two-dimensional scale of hedonic (from Greek word hēdonē, meaning "pleasure")—eudaimonic (from the Greek word eudaimonia, meaning "happiness" or "well-being") entertainment motivation together with evidence that audiences consume entertainment not only in the name of pleasure, fun, and suspense but also to receive greater insight into the meaning of human existence.[8] Parsemain argues that while hedonistic entertainment centralizes fun, pleasure, and escapism, eudaimonic entertainment is linked to elaborate thinking, enlightenment, and insight.[9] As such, to allow entertainment a eudaimonic characterization essentially means to describe it as potentially conducive to the Aristotelian idea of happiness and well-being; as Wirth et al. observe, "to be eudaimonically happy, one must live his or her life in accordance with one's daimon, which is the true self (the potentialities and the realizations of each individual)."[10] An additional difference between the hedonistic and the eudaimonic approach to entertainment lies then precisely in their approach to well-being. While hedonic well-being is described as outcome-oriented and is connected to short-term satisfaction and fulfillment of needs, eudaimonic well-being is to be understood as more process-oriented, a way of life rather than a direct outcome of an action or experience.[11]

Through the concept of eudaimonic entertainment, the educational possibilities of entertainment find their way back in the game. Especially when it comes to television content, we know from previous literature that storytelling, narratives, emotions, and engagement can prove to be equally (if not more) efficient pedagogically than formal education strategies and techniques.[12] This pedagogical potential manifests itself in a number of different genres and has been conceptualized in different ways: for example, the "pedagogical invitation" of reality television,[13] the "orientation role" of telenovelas,[14] or the "social education" function of television drama.[15] While the pedagogical dimensions of contemporary teen and youth TV, including animation and particularly the narrative mechanisms activated to design "progressive content"[16] and stories told to woke millennial and Gen Z audiences[17] are yet to be discussed in terms of their unique specificities, (animated) animal representations on television have been theorized as possibilities "to highlight cultural understandings about what it is to be human."[18]

BIG MOUTH AS EUDAIMONIC ENTERTAINMENT

While *Big Mouth* is loosely based on creators (and best friends since childhood) Goldberg's and Kroll's own awkward experiences with puberty, it has been celebrated as a universally relatable series, unapologetically revealing the horrors of one the most formative periods for human beings. By definition, *puberty* is described as:

> The epoch marking transition from child to adolescent and then to adult. The onset of puberty in females is marked by menarche, the first menstrual period; male puberty is less precisely defined, e.g., by growth of axillary and pubic hair, beginning of seminal emissions, and descent and enlargement of testes. In both sexes, puberty is usually preceded by a prepubertal growth spurt.[19]

It is with the help of nonhuman creatures that *Big Mouth* sheds light on the aforementioned themes around physical changes and transitions and, additionally, focuses particularly on the anxieties and delights surrounding the epoch in question. Late-bloomer Nick Birch (Nick Kroll), compulsive masturbator Andrew Glouberman (John Mulaney), sardonic Jessi Glaser (Jessi Klein), hyper/bi-sexual Jay Bilzerian (Jason Mantzoukas), nerdy Missy Foreman-Greenwald (Jenny Slate/Ayo Edebiri), and sassy Matthew MacDell (Andrew Rannells), among other characters, observe their bodies changing, their urges driving their actions and words, their relationships evolving—and occasionally eroding. *Big Mouth* explores topics such as menstruation, masturbation, homosexuality, bisexuality, over-sexualization of girls, transgender identity, shame, depression, and anxiety. As all characters grapple with the same changes in emotions—albeit in different ways—their journey of exploration is accompanied by anthropomorphized fantastical creatures that give emotions, urges, and anxieties a face and a voice. Alongside the main characters, a primary role in the series is played by the Hormone Monsters, freakish but cute creatures who help human beings navigate puberty, and by a number of anthropomorphized animal creatures that animate specific emotions and mental health conditions, such as depression, anxiety, gratitude, love, and hate. As such, it is reminiscent of the iconic edutainment animated series *Il était une fois... la vie* (*Once Upon a Time... Life*, Canal+ & FR3, 1987–1988) since they both make use of the combination of human characters and anthropomorphic representations of constituent elements of the human body, including organs, systems, and defense mechanisms, as well as antagonists such as viruses and bacteria. But while *Il était une fois... la vie* leaned more toward the educational, *Big Mouth* is committed to exploring complex, and often taboo, matters, through powerful educational moments without neglecting to be entertaining.

The series' crude and raunchy humor has been welcomed as a rejuvenating and liberating way to talk about issues that teenagers encounter while having no one to talk about. Even if it could be described as largely silly, "simple gross-out comedy,"[20] the series has above all been hailed for its sensitivity when it comes to depictions of sexual exploration, as well as the equal attention to female characters, throughout its five seasons.[21] What is more, the show has been addressed as a good example of woke comedy not only in terms of the issues it deals with and the refined humor it uses in order to come to grips with complex topics but also in terms of how the creators have been open to criticism and applied a self-reflective approach to their work.[22] Looking at it this way, *Big Mouth* does much more than just entertain; it seems to be committed to a greater endeavor of immersing into a deep and difficult discussion regarding growing up, one that aspires to contribute to increased understanding about the issues talked about on the show. Yet it also facilitates a dialogue between kids and parents. In a conversation with *Salon*, creator Nick Kroll stated:

> [W]e are so dirty, but we're also very conscious of what messaging we're putting out into the world. And I think that is where I sort of will say like, if your kid is around the age of the kids on the show, they're going through it, their friends are, they can see various things like it on the internet, and maybe it'll give you a way to, opportunity to talk to your kids about the things that are happening to them.[23]

More particularly, and in relation to the concept of eudaimonic entertainment, *Big Mouth* is especially sensitized to the dark sides of puberty and committed to initiating an open debate about them. Embarrassment and shame transgress the whole series and are especially tied to the uncontrollable changes and urges motored by hormonal fluctuations. The presence of Hormone Monsters, especially Maury (Nick Kroll) and Connie (Maya Rudolph), provide acute visualizations of the pleasures of satisfying inner, wild, and sometimes inexplicable, desires and of the embarrassments that can accompany them.[24] At the same time, the series features a number of animal antagonists, strategically designed so that the animals' morphology and physiology correspond to the condition they embody. Starting her appearances already in season 2 but holding a primary role in season 4, Depression Kitty (Jean Smart) is a monstrous creature in the form of an oversized cunning cat that antagonizes the well-being of the kids by making them feel sad, unmotivated, and withdrawn. Her friend Tito, the Anxiety Mosquito (Bamford), also holding a major role in season 4, represents anxiety and intrusive thoughts, specifically targeting timid and vulnerable kids. Alongside the ambiguity of the Hormone Monsters and the inherent evil of creatures such as Depression Kitty and Tito the Anxiety Mosquito, there are creatures that represent genuine goodness and positive emotions, namely the Gratitoad (Zach Galifianakis), a laidback toad who embodies the natural predator to mosquitoes and, by extension, self-destructive emotions and intrusive thoughts. In season 5, some additional creatures are added, namely the Lovebugs (Brandon Kyle Goodman and Pamela Adlon) and the Hate Worm (Keke Palmer), whose role is to encourage the kids to get in touch with these emotions while at the same time exploring the side effects they can have on one's mental health.

Big Mouth has been discussed as a continuation of a long tradition of "children's horror" and "dark camp," including literature, film, and television.[25] The argument is that the combination of queer camp aesthetics, such as visual exaggerations and kitsch, and horror conventions, such as ghosts and monsters, allows the series to emerge as a particularly rewarding cultural forum concerned with cultural anxieties about adolescent sexuality—often with a queer twist. Being an animated series, and one that allows for creative intersections between the codes of comedy and fantasy, *Big Mouth* can be said to mitigate the horrific[26] and instead give leeway to less corporeal and more cognitive/reflective ways of experiencing and relating to the series' content. As such, shows like *Big Mouth* have been analyzed as "smart" reflections on popular cultural debates, providing a platform for the vocalization and negotiation of current anxieties, and even tapping into discourses around sex education (and its importance).[27] The remainder of this chapter aims to further contribute to the critical dissection of Netflix's *Big Mouth* as an example of eudaimonic entertainment, with a particular focus on how the codes of animation, including the design of characters such as Hormone Monsters and anthropomorphized animal creatures, visualize not only the horrors of adolescent life, but also the path toward well-being. More specifically, two key ideas are explored. First, the idea of Hormone Monsters as guides to well-being and, by consequence, the notion of eudaimonia as a process is discussed. Second, the pedagogical potential of the animal antagonists and, by extension, the notion of eudaimonia as linked to positive psychology.

MONSTERS R US?: CUTE HORMONE MONSTERS AND THE EXCULPATION OF TEEN SEXUALITY

In their journey through the horrors and pleasures of adolescent life, the human characters are never alone. They are shadowed by their Hormone Monsters, hairy, horned, and—more often than not—horny monstrous creatures whose role is to aid the human characters through their everyday, practical struggles, but also with broader existential questions. Their "job" (they often refer to the kids as their clients) is to facilitate the embracement of inescapable changes brought about by pubertal forces. The two main Hormone Monsters featuring in the show are Maury, a raunchy and sex-crazed male monster, whose main clients include Andrew and Matthew, and Connie, a witty and intense female monster who is primarily responsible for Jessi. The constellation of regularly appearing Hormone Monsters is complemented by Rick, an old, disgusting, and bad at the job monster who works both with adults and kids; Tyler, a young and inexperienced monster who later gets fired; and Mona, a confident, seductive, but also cunning monstress. The help they offer is not always to the kids' best interest; the monsters' advice is almost exclusively driven by urge and desire, and not by rational deliberation or consideration about the consequences of potential actions. Above all, the Hormone Monsters encourage the kids to get in touch with their emotions and explore their sexuality, which usually results in electrifying social encounters, blowing up friendships and relations with family members, as well as landing in feelings of self-loathing. But they mean well.

The presence of Hormone Monsters and the monstrous appearance of these characters are approached in this chapter first as a point of connection with the conventions of the children's horror stories as genre/cultural category, as previously mentioned.[28] It has been argued that "[t]he monster is perhaps one of the most significant creations serving to reflect and critique human existence,"[29] and *Big Mouth* makes use of the monstrous to both visualize and concretize not only the horrors of puberty but also how they can be understood and dealt with. In essence, these horrors have to do with scary, incomprehensible changes that the body and mind of teenagers go through in the process of growing up, including becoming sexually active. Mason argues that the Hormone Monsters in *Big Mouth* particularly animate the feeling of losing bodily control, by embodying these "frightening sensations."[30] A characteristic example of such a scary loss of bodily control is the multiple times Andrew is shown getting aroused and/or pleasuring himself encouraged by Maury—often in inappropriate contexts such as while watching an educational video about the female reproductive organ in the classroom, masturbating next to his best friend, Nick, during a sleep-over, or edging (i.e., the sexual practice of holding off ejaculation) while watching a film with Jessi and Nick in the latter's parents' living room. Another characteristic example is when Connie first reveals herself to Jessi, in episode 2 of season 1, after Jessi gets her first period and tries to cope with mood swings and the general emotional whirlwind caused by changes in the levels of hormones:

Connie: Listen to me! You want to shoplift lipstick, you want to listen to Lana Del Rey on repeat while you cut up all your t-shirts. You want to scream at your mother and then laugh at her tears!
Jessi: But I don't want to scream at my mom.
Connie: She's not your mom anymore. From now on, you call her Shannon.

Interestingly enough, the Hormone Monsters are not scary; if anything, they would be described as funny, likeable, and even cute. Despite their rough appearance and monstrous aura, the Hormone Monsters are one of the primary sources of humor, as the comic effect of the series depends largely on Maury's punchlines, Connie's sassiness, and even Rick's goofiness. A recurring comic mechanism throughout the series is visual exaggeration. For instance, Maury carries around with him a bunch of sentient mini penises that he treats as adorable little pets. Another example is the fact that Maury and Connie often indulge in dirty, rough sexual encounters with each other. It could be argued that the comic aspects of these monsters soothe the horrific and propose instead a more light-hearted approach to everything. In this sense, the Hormone Monsters in *Big Mouth* are reminiscent of creatures seen in *Happy Tree Friends* or the monsters in *Monsters, Inc*; freakish but cute, uncanny but familiar.[31] While they don't really resemble any known living creatures of the animal kingdom, certain features, such as horns, tails, sharp teeth, and hairy bodies, point to some kind of primordial animality, thus allowing for some common characteristics to emerge between the Hormone Monsters and the animal antagonists. However, the defining characteristic of the Hormone Monsters in terms of appearance would have to be their grotesque qualities, their hybrid/unclassifiable morphology, more so than anything else. It could then be argued that the ambivalent intersection between the cute and the grotesque as they are embodied by the Hormone Monsters mirrors the ambiguous and confusing state that the kids are in. As their bodies are changing, the teenagers are turning into a weird hybrid of kid and adult, often exhibiting uncontrollable and unacceptable—by social standards—behaviors.

In addition to the monstrous as appearance, it is worth examining how it works in terms of ideology, here explored as an aspect of the moral framing of puberty and yet another space of ambivalence. As previously mentioned, the Hormone Monsters shadow the kids, being rather omnipresent in their lives. One could argue that the way they relate to the kids' characters reminds us somewhat of the popular shoulder advisors' plot device used frequently in visual entertainment, including animation, to signal a character's inner conflicts and moral dilemmas: the side that encourages the character to be evil, naughty, or succumb to temptation and the side that is more cautious, considerate, and promotes virtue. What is commonly depicted with the help of religious references (i.e., an angel and a devil, often in the form of little versions of the person involved in the ethical dilemma) takes in *Big Mouth* endocrinological dimensions and is therefore purged from any moral assessment. In the shoulder advisor trope, the two conflicting sides are usually depicted visually as "good" and "bad" versions of the self, thus signaling that both sides reside in a human's soul. The fact that the Hormone Monsters are not depicted as neither inherently good nor bad nor as versions of the kids themselves gives an additional dimension to the show's understanding of pubertal shocks and panics. While the Hormone Monsters know the kids inside out, they are not them; they are rather depicted as an outside force that offers a very particular kind of counseling service. This idea is reinforced by the fact that they appear as having a life of their own, that is, relationships, feelings, professional aspirations, among others. In episode 10 of season 2, after Nick, Andrew, and Jessi travel through a magic portal, we witness the Hormone Monsters in their professional setting at the Department of Puberty and the Hormone Division having water cooler chat.

The above observations are particularly relevant when it comes to the question of teen sexuality. Having long been exposed to moral evaluations and panics, childhood and youth—and not least the issue of sexual development and desire—moralizing discourses have prevailed, discussing and representing children and teenagers as "innately innocent" and vulnerable, but at the same time "as a threat, innately programmed for wrongdoing."[32] The aforementioned social anxieties are alleviated in *Big Mouth* through the presence of Hormone Monsters. By externalizing the grossness and the impulsivity of puberty, by shedding light on the hormonal forces and the difficulty to manage them, this innateness is relativized. As such, *Big Mouth*'s monsters "both embody and deflate anxieties surrounding young people and (queer) sexuality."[33] They function as counterweight to dominant moralized narratives about teen sexuality and, instead, promote a messier, more realistic, understanding of puberty, one that liberates teens from morally based anxieties and focuses on the immersion in the process and the pleasures that accompany it. At the same time, the Hormone Monsters do not appear to be particularly concerned with dominant cisheteronormative ways of thinking; both Jay's bisexuality and Matthew's homosexuality, for instance, are completely normalized through the monsters' encouragement to act upon their desires without being too concerned with questions about social norms and social control. In this sense, the Hormone Monsters also function as narrative catalysts, encouraging the human characters to keep going, embrace the changes, explore the urges, even flirt with trouble, thus suggesting that puberty is to a large extent a process based on exploring and experiencing that eventually leads toward better connections with one's emotions, promoting acceptance, self-worth, and—ultimately—well-being.

ANIMAL ANTAGONISTS AND THE SHAPE OF TEEN MENTAL HEALTH

During their journey through puberty, the human protagonists are not only accompanied by the omnipresent Hormone Monsters, they also encounter other hybrid creatures that in one way or another intervene in their mental health. Some of these creatures are called to play the role of the antagonist, a plot device used to create conflicts, problems, obstacles, and challenges "in the way of the protagonist's achievement of his or her goal."[34] Two such antagonists that appear in *Big Mouth*, in the form of anthropomorphized animals, are Depression Kitty and Tito, the Anxiety Mosquito. Both creatures, separately but also in collaboration with each other, get in the way of the kids' well-being and the process of getting through puberty without irreversible traumas. Precisely like the Hormone Monsters, the animal antagonists are thoughtfully animated and externalized in a way that creates a meaningful distance between the human character and the mental condition; the two are not one and the same.

By taking these big, complicated, intimidating, and value-laden concepts, such as depression and anxiety, and turning them into tangible creatures, *Big Mouth* not only defines and gives shape to mental health conditions but also educates about how to live and cope with them. The codes of animation are particularly relevant here; animated animals have long functioned as "semiotic machines, which force us to look at animals as ourselves and ourselves as animals."[35] In this particular case, the animal attributes contribute to the design (and the depth) of the character and determine the relationship/interaction they will develop with human characters. At the same time, these attributes help give shape to particular symptoms or manifestations of mental health conditions in a clear and accessible manner. In this way, they guide the audience into really seeing and recognizing the signs, thus de-tabooing the topic and making bold steps toward removing the stigma. Depression Kitty, the anthropomorphized animal that portrays depression, has the form of an oversize bipedal purple cat. She first appears in episode 10 of season 2, as an external consultant from the Depression Division, called in to advise on the case of Jessi who is having trouble coping with everything. Eventually, Depression Kitty takes over as Jessi's helper. Embodying all the stereotypical attributes of a cat, Kitty is depicted as moving slowly but consciously, as if her every move is planned carefully. A key cat attribute that is successfully utilized in the series is lying on top of humans; Kitty does it with Jessi in her attempt to immobilize her and lure her into a condition of idleness and melancholy. In terms of personality, she is smooth, seductive, and cunning; she has the ability to convince others to give into their sadness, to surrender to their misery, and to withdraw from everyday life. The same logic shapes the character of Tito, the Anxiety Mosquito, the main antagonist of season 4. Tito first appears in episode 1of season 4 while the kids are at sleepaway camp, voicing anxious thoughts to Natalie (Josie Totah), the first transgender character that appears on *Big Mouth* and starts circling Nick after he has a panic attack. Being a mosquito, Tito is depicted as flying around and buzzing in an annoying manner, while at the same time uncontrollably uttering intrusive thoughts that cause great distress.

Similarly to the Hormone Monsters, Depression Kitty and Tito the Anxiety Mosquito are depicted as externalized, independent creatures who visit the characters and engage in a relationship with them. By narratively positioning them as antagonists, Kitty and Tito—and by extension the conditions that they embody—become concrete obstacles in the human characters' road to development and well-being. The important thing to observe here is that *Big Mouth* openly deals with topics that previous generations of entertainment and TV series would not dare to tackle head-on, that is "series that avoid naming diagnoses for their characters, instead relying on certain unusual behavior or personal quirks as code for particular disorders."[36] Instead, *Big Mouth* openly names and confronts mental health conditions both verbally and visually. In fact, *Big Mouth* does not only give shape to such conditions, their symptoms, and their consequences, but also proposes concrete solutions, or rather concrete ways to fight the antagonists. In episode 9 of season 4, entitled "Horrority House," Jessi—who is at this point distressed because of both anxiety and depression—is depicted in a session with psychologist Nancy (Maria Bamford). In her attempt to help Jessi cope with her problems and establish a positive attitude to life, Nancy mentions the value of practicing gratitude:

Jessi: And now I'm home, but I have this nagging feeling that something is wrong and I'm just a nagging loser.
Nancy: Jessi, what you're describing, that's anxiety.
Tito: [gasping] She's talking about me!
Nancy: Anxiety is that feeling we get inside that there's danger all around us.
Tito: I feel so seen.
Kitty: You're also depressed. You had yellow mustard on a tortilla for dinner last night.
Jessi: Oof.
Nancy: And when I feel anxious, you know what I do? I practice my gratitude.
Jessi: Well, I'm not feeling that grateful right now.

Nancy: Well, gratitude, like your pelvic floor, is a muscle that needs to be strengthened. In my case, a lot.
Jessi: Okay.

While Jessi is not automatically convinced about the value of gratitude (the fact that her psychologist is obsessively collecting toads does not help much), she starts warming up to the feeling after drinking some spiked punch at a Halloween party. The drink knocks her out and she starts having weird dreams about first being in a mental institution in a straitjacket and then landing in a swamp. That's where she first meets the Gratitoad (Zach Galifianakis), a friendly toad with a tiny beard who represents the emotion of gratitude and plays a critical role in introducing a clearly defined way to deal with negative emotions and intrusive thoughts:

Gratitoad: I am the Gratitoad and I'm just so grateful to meet you.
Jessi: Yeah, I can't shake your hand. I'm stuck in a straitjacket, okay? Everything's fucked.
Gratitoad: You know, when I feel my lily pad sinking down into the muck, you know what I do?
Jessi: I think you're gonna tell me.
Gratitoad: I try to think about all the things I'm grateful for. Makes me think a little better [chuckles].
Jessi: Um, what are toads grateful for?
Gratitoad: Well, let's see. I'm grateful that my skin looks like a rock so my predators can't see me. Grateful for my predators. They make me wanna jump higher. And all that jumping makes my tush look high and proud.
Jessi: Yeah, that's a nice butt.
Gratitoad: Oh, well, shoot. I'm grateful for the compliment. Now, come on, now. Your turn. What are you grateful for?
Jessi: No, I can't. It makes me feel weird and embarrassed.
Gratitoad: Well, gratitude does take practice. Like the maracas! Come on, Jessi. Gratitude, Gratitoad. What about you? Give it a go.

In other words, Gratitoad teaches about the value of gratitude, enabling the kids to re-wire their emotional state and actively turn to gratitude whenever they want, although some practice might be required. In the aforementioned examples, the pedagogical aspects of *Big Mouth* become even more evident as the Gratitoad shows the way, educates, and relieves. In another episode, and after an anxiety-ridden Nick takes the time to appreciate all the things in his life that he is grateful for, the Gratitoad eliminates Tito by eating him, thus drawing the parallel between the toad as natural predator of the mosquito and gratitude as the antidote to anxiety. From a psychological point of view, *Big Mouth* picks up on an example of practicing positive psychology, which has to do with psychological perspectives that focus on development, flourishing, well-being, and ultimately, eudaimonia. According to relevant literature, *gratitude* is an important concept in positive psychology, albeit an emotion neglected by psychologists (however not by religion and philosophy), despite it being an important part of positive psychology and the path to well-being: "Gratitude is a virtue, the possession of which enables a person to live well, and therefore must receive a hearing in any comprehensive treatment of the topic."[37] By inserting the notion of gratitude into the equation, *Big Mouth* offers yet another path toward eudaimonia, one that introduces the practice and beneficial outcomes of positive thinking.

CONCLUSION

Building on the notion of eudaimonic entertainment, this chapter has explored the ways in which Netflix series *Big Mouth* functions as televisual pedagogy, successfully merging entertainment and education, especially when it comes to issues of adolescent mental health and well-being. Additionally, this chapter contributes to a broader discussion around the thematic specificities of contemporary (teen) television, especially with respect to issues of growing up and dealing with identity-defining emotions and situations. Through the use of cute monstrous creatures, visualizing hormonal changes and urges, who coach the kids as they jump through the hoops of puberty, *Big Mouth* provides the space for the negotiation of the latter as a morally neutral sphere where teenagers are encouraged to experiment and embrace change. By animating mental health conditions as animals, *Big Mouth* visualizes how they manifest themselves and how they operate in an accessible, non-scary manner. This "in-narrative diagnostic representation"[38] has been hailed as a positive development when it comes to the representation of mental health disorders on television and has been partly attributed to the so-called "Netflix effect," and more specifically the shift away from mainstream content toward the needs and pleasures of "underserved audiences," and the involvement of storylines that have previously been deemed too risky by channel executives.[39] We know from previous research that representations of mental illness within popular media are critical because they constitute a key source of information for both the general population and those with diagnoses. As such, *Big Mouth* contributes to the on-screen representation of mental health in open, non-judgmental, and pedagogical ways, confirming the view of animal representations as "embroiled within human matters, norms and ideologies."[40] At the same time, the series potentially contributes to the public's exploration of their own identities, experiences, and attitudes to mental illness.

Especially within the context of the digital streaming era and the appearance of television shows such as *Euphoria* (HBO, 2019-), *Sex Education* (Netflix, 2019-), *East Los High* (Hulu, 2013-2017), *Genera+ion* (HBO, 2021), and *Betty* (HBO, 2020-2021), research has emphasized the role of teen and youth TV in making various models of being available to young people, often with a focus on mental health, sexuality and gender identity, in educational, progressive, queer, and "woke" ways. *Big Mouth*'s use of the codes of animation, including the utilization of monstrous creatures (encompassing a variety of animal characters) as a means to express the intricacies of growing up and getting to know yourself and others, contributes to an understanding of early puberty as a chaotic, intense, and at times dangerous, experience, often associated with the emergence of various emotional and behavioral problems. However, the same codes also offer the opportunity for a decisive separation of the person from puberty itself and from potential mental health conditions that might surface. Behind the raunchy façade, *Big Mouth* sends out the message that puberty is not about learning through making the right choices but learning through understanding yourself. The pedagogical potential of contemporary teen and youth TV is therefore less bounded by "the after-school special" morality defined by clear-cut moral values as the (conservative) path to eudaimonia[41] and determined more by the acceptance of the moral complexity and ambiguity of puberty.

NOTES

1. Stefania Marghitu, *Teen TV* (New York: Routledge, 2021), 3–4.
2. Jonathan Gray, *Television Entertainment* (New York and London: Routledge, 2008), 5.
3. Gray, *Television Entertainment*, 6.
4. Alan McKee, Christy Collis, Tanya Nitins, Mark Ryan, Stephen Harrington, Barry Duncan, Joe Carter, Edwina Luck, Larry Neale, Des Butler and Michelle Backstrom, "Defining entertainment: An approach," *Creative Industries Journal* 7, no. 2 (2014): 117. doi: 10.1080/17510694.2014.962932.
5. Jonathan Gray, "Entertainment and Media/Cultural/Communication/etc. Studies," in *Entertainment Industries: Entertainment as a Cultural System*, ed. Alan McKee, Christy Collis and Ben Hamley (New York and London: Routledge, 2012).
6. Ava Laure Parsemain, *The Pedagogy of Queer TV* (Cham: Palgrave Macmillan, 2019), 4.
7. Mary Beth Oliver and Anne Bartsch, "Appreciation as Audience Response: Exploring Entertainment Gratifications beyond Hedonism," *Human Communication Research* 36, no. 1 (2010): 53–81. doi: 10.1111/j.1468-2958.2009.01368.x; Mary Beth Oliver and Anne Bartsch, "Appreciation of Entertainment: The Importance of Meaningfulness via Virtue and Wisdom," *Journal of Media Psychology: Theories, Methods, and Applications* 23, no. 1 (2011): 29–33. doi: 10.1027/1864-1105/a000029;

Mary Beth Oliver and Tilo Hartmann, "Exploring the Role of Meaningful Experiences in Users' Appreciation of 'Good Movies'," *Projections* 4 (2010): 128–150.

8. Mary Beth Oliver and Arthur A. Raney, "Entertainment as Pleasurable and Meaningful: Identifying Hedonic and Eudaimonic Motivations for Entertainment Consumption," *Journal of Communication* 61, no. 5 (2011): 984–1004.

9. Parsemain, *The Pedagogy of Queer TV*.

10. Werner Wirth, Matthias Hofer and Holger Schramm, "Beyond Pleasure: Exploring the Eudaimonic Entertainment Experience," *Human Communication Research* 38, no. 4 (2012): 408–9.

11. Wirth et al, "Beyond Pleasure," 408–9.

12. See for instance: Arvind Singhal, Michael J. Cody, Everett M. Rogers and Miguel Sabido, eds., *Entertainment-Education and Social Change. History, Research and Practice* (Mahwah, NJ: Erlbaum, 2004); Arvind Singhal and Everett M. Rogers, "A Theoretical Agenda for Entertainment-Education," *Communication Theory* 12 (2002): 117–35; Parsemain, *The Pedagogy of Queer TV*.

13. Beverley Skeggs and Helen Wood, *Reacting to Reality Television: Performance, Audience and Value* (London: Routledge, 2012), 136.

14. Mauro P. Porto, "Political Controversies in Brazilian TV Fiction: Viewers' Interpretations of the Telenovela *Terra Nostra*," *Television & New Media* 6, no. 4 (2005): 345.

15. Lesley Henderson, *Social Issues in Television Fiction* (Edinburgh: Edinburgh University Press, 2007).

16. Colin Jon Mark Crawford, *Netflix's Speculative Fictions* (Lanham: Lexington Books, 2021), 88.

17. Christopher Campbell and Loren Saxton Coleman (eds.), *Media, Myth, and Millennials: Critical Perspectives on Race and Culture* (Lanham: Lexington Books, 2019).

18. Brett Mills, *Animals on Television: The Cultural Making of the Non-Human* (London: Palgrave MacMillan, 2017), 5.

19. Miquel Porta and John M. Last, *A Dictionary of Public Health* (Oxford: Oxford University Press, 2018).

20. Sarah Gosling, "*Big Mouth* – the Cartoon That Makes a Joke Out of Puberty," *The Guardian*, October 23, 2017, https://www.theguardian.com/tv-and-radio/2017/oct/23/big-mouth-the-cartoon-that-makes-a-joke-out-of-puberty

21. Jen Chaney, "Netflix's *Big Mouth* Is Your Childhood in Disgusting, Humiliating Detail," *Vulture*, September 28, 2017, https://www.vulture.com/2017/09/big-mouth-review.html

22. See for instance: James McMahon, "'*Big Mouth*' Season 3 review: Proof That 'Woke Culture' Hasn't Ruined Comedy," *NME*, October 7, 2019, https://www.nme.com/reviews/big-mouth-season-3-review-2554566; and Randall Colburn, "Nick Kroll On Making Comedy in a "Woke Culture": "You Can Still Do and Say Some Pretty Crazy, Wild Shit"," *AV Club*, October 22, 2019, https://www.avclub.com/nick-kroll-on-making-comedy-in-a-woke-culture-you-c-1839265725

23. "Nick Kroll on Why His Crude Cartoon "Big Mouth" is a Teachable Moment for Kids and Parents," *Salon*, u.d., https://www.salon.com/tv/video/2gwbw7

24. Particularly on the topic of shame, the character of the Shame Wizard (David Thewlis) is introduced as the main antagonist for season 2; he manifests himself to a number of kids and his aim is to make them feel isolated and wretched with feelings of pity and shame.

25. Derritt Mason, *Queer Anxieties of Young Adult Literature and Culture* (Jackson: University Press of Mississippi, 2021).

26. Catherine Lester, *Horror Films for Children: Fear and Pleasure in American Cinema* (London: Bloomsbury, 2022).

27. Eddie Falvey, "Situating Netflix's Original Adult Animation: Observing Taste Cultures and the Legacies of 'Quality' Television through *BoJack Horseman* and *Big Mouth*," *Animation: An Interdisciplinary Journal* 15, no. 2 (2020): 116–29.

28. Lester, *Horror Films for Children*.

29. Niall Scott, "Introduction," in *Monsters and the Monstrous: Myths and Metaphors of Enduring Evil*, ed. Niall Scott (Amsterdam and New York: Rodopi, 2007), 1.

30. Mason, *Queer Anxieties of Young Adult Literature and Culture*, 114.

31. Maja Brzozowska-Brywczyńska, "Monstrous/Cute. Notes on the Ambivalent Nature of Cuteness," in *Monsters and the Monstrous: Myths and Metaphors of Enduring Evil*, ed. Niall Scott (Amsterdam and New York: Rodopi, 2007), 213–28.

32. Liza Tsaliki and Despina Chronaki, "Introduction: Anxiety over Childhood and Youth Across Cultures," in *Discourses of Anxiety over Childhood and Youth across Cultures*, ed. Liza Tsaliki and Despina Chronaki (Cham: Palgrave Macmillan, 2020), 8.

33. Mason, *Queer Anxieties of Young Adult Literature and Culture*, 120.

34. Jule Selbo, Film Genre for the Screenwriter (New York and London: Routledge), 216.

35. Laurel Schmuck, "Wild Animation: From the *Looney Tunes* to *Bojack Horseman* in Cartoon Los Angeles," *European Journal of American Studies* 13, no. 1 (2018): 2.

36. Kimberley McMahon-Coleman and Roslyn Weaver, *Mental Health Disorders on Television: Representation Versus Reality* (Jefferson: McFarland, 2020), 4.

37. Robert A. Emmons and Michael E. McCullough, eds., *The Psychology of Gratitude* (Oxford: Oxford University Press, 2004), 6.

38. McMahon-Coleman and Weaver, *Mental Health Disorders on Television*, 4.

39. McMahon-Coleman and Weaver, *Mental Health Disorders on Television*, 4.

40. Mills, *Animals on Television*, 6.

41. Richard Green and Wayne Yuen, "Why We Can't Spike Spike?: Moral Themes in *Buffy the Vampire Slayer*," *Slayage* 2, no. 1.2 (March 2001).

BIBLIOGRAPHY

Brzozowska-Brywczyńska, Maja. "Monstrous/Cute. Notes on the Ambivalent Nature of Cuteness." In *Monsters and the Monstrous: Myths and Metaphors of Enduring Evil*, edited by Niall Scott. Amsterdam and New York: Rodopi, 2007, 213–228.

Campbell, Christopher, and Loren Saxton Coleman, eds. *Media, Myth, and Millennials: Critical Perspectives on Race and Culture*. Lanham, MD: Lexington Books, 2019.

Chaney, Jen. "Netflix's Big Mouth is Your Childhood in Disgusting, Humiliating Detail." *Vulture*, September 28, 2017. https://www.vulture.com/2017/09/big-mouth-review.html.

Colburn, Randall. "Nick Kroll on Making Comedy in a "Woke Culture": "You Can Still Do and Say Some Pretty Crazy, Wild Shit."" *AV Club*, October 22, 2019. https://www.avclub.com/nick-kroll-on-making-comedy-in-a-woke-culture-you-c-1839265725.

Crawford, Colin Jon Mark. *Netflix's Speculative Fictions*. Lanham, MD: Lexington Books, 2021.

Emmons, Robert A., and Michael E. McCullough, eds. *The Psychology of Gratitude*. Oxford: Oxford University Press, 2004.

Falvey, Eddie. "Situating Netflix's Original Adult Animation: Observing Taste Cultures and the Legacies of 'Quality' Television Through *BoJack Horseman* and *Big Mouth*." *Animation: An Interdisciplinary Journal* 15, no. 2 (2020): 116–129.

Gosling, Sarah. "Big Mouth – The Cartoon That Makes a Joke Out of Puberty." *The Guardian*, October 23, 2017. https://www.theguardian.com/tv-and-radio/2017/oct/23/big-mouth-the-cartoon-that-makes-a-joke-out-of-puberty.

Gray, Jonathan. "Entertainment and Media/Cultural/Communication/etc. Studies." In *Entertainment Industries: Entertainment as a Cultural System*, edited by Alan McKee, Christy Collis, and Ben Hamley. New York & London: Routledge, 2012, 1–19.

Gray, Jonathan. *Television Entertainment*. New York & London: Routledge, 2008.

Green, Richard, and Wayne Yuen. "Why We Can't Spike Spike?: Moral Themes in Buffy the Vampire Slayer." *Slayage* 2, no. 1.2 (March 2001).

Henderson, Lesley. *Social Issues in Television Fiction*. Edinburgh: Edinburgh University Press, 2007.

Lester, Catherine. *Horror Films for Children: Fear and Pleasure in American Cinema*. London: Bloomsbury, 2022.

Marghitu, Stefania. *Teen TV*. New York: Routledge, 2021.

Mason, Derritt. *Queer Anxieties of Young Adult Literature and Culture*. Jackson: University Press of Mississippi, 2021.

McKee, Alan, Christy Collis, Tanya Nitins, Mark Ryan, Stephen Harrington, Barry Duncan, Joe Carter, Edwina Luck, Larry Neale, Des Butler, and Michelle Backstrom. "Defining Entertainment: An Approach." *Creative Industries Journal* 7, no. 2 (2014): 108–120. https://doi.org/10.1080/17510694.2014.962932.

McMahon, James. "'Big Mouth' Season 3 review: Proof that 'Woke Culture' Hasn't Ruined Comedy." *NME*, October 7, 2019. https://www.nme.com/reviews/big-mouth-season-3-review-2554566.

McMahon-Coleman, Kimberley, and Roslyn Weaver. *Mental Health Disorders on Television: Representation Versus Reality*. Jefferson: McFarland, 2020.

Mills, Brett. *Animals on Television: The Cultural Making of the Non-Human*. London: Palgrave MacMillan, 2017.

Oliver, Mary Beth, and Anne Bartsch. "Appreciation as Audience Response: Exploring Entertainment Gratifications Beyond Hedonism." *Human Communication Research* 36, no. 1 (2010): 53–81. https://doi.org/10.1111/j.1468-2958.2009.01368.x.

Oliver, Mary Beth, and Anne Bartsch. "Appreciation of Entertainment: The Importance of Meaningfulness Via Virtue and Wisdom." *Journal of Media Psychology: Theories, Methods, and Applications* 23, no. 1 (2011): 29–33. https://doi.org/10.1027/1864-1105/a000029.

Oliver, Mary Beth, and Arthur A. Raney. "Entertainment as Pleasurable and Meaningful: Identifying Hedonic and Eudaimonic Motivations for Entertainment Consumption." *Journal of Communication* 61, no. 5 (2011): 984–1004.

Oliver, Mary Beth, and Tilo Hartmann. "Exploring the Role of Meaningful Experiences in Users' Appreciation of 'Good Movies'." *Projections* 4 (2010): 128–150.

Parsemain, Ava Laure. *The Pedagogy of Queer TV*. Cham: Palgrave Macmillan, 2019.

Porta, Miquel, and John M. Last. *A Dictionary of Public Health*. Oxford: Oxford University Press, 2018.

Porto, Mauro P. "Political Controversies in Brazilian TV Fiction: Viewers' Interpretations of the Telenovela Terra Nostra." *Television & New Media* 6, no. 4 (2005): 342–359.

Salon. "Nick Kroll on Why His Crude Cartoon "Big Mouth" is a Teachable Moment for Kids and Parents." *Salon*, u.d. https://www.salon.com/tv/video/2gwbw7.

Schmuck, Laurel. "Wild Animation: From the *Looney Tunes* to *Bojack Horseman* in Cartoon Los Angeles." *European Journal of American Studies* 13, no. 1 (2018): 1–16.

Scott, Niall. "Introduction." In *Monsters and the Monstrous: Myths and Metaphors of Enduring Evil*, edited by Niall Scott. Amsterdam and New York: Rodopi, 2007, 1–6.

Selbo, Jule. *Film Genre for the Screenwriter*. New York and London: Routledge.

Singhal, Arvind, and Everett M. Rogers. "A Theoretical Agenda for Entertainment-Education." *Communication Theory* 12 (2002): 117–135.

Singhal, Arvind, Michael J. Cody, Everett M. Rogers, and Miguel Sabido, eds. *Entertainment-Education and Social Change: History, Research and Practice*. Mahwah, NJ: Erlbaum, 2004.

Skeggs, Beverley, and Helen Wood. *Reacting to Reality Television: Performance, Audience and Value*. London: Routledge, 2012.

Tsaliki, Liza, and Despina Chronaki. "Introduction: Anxiety over Childhood and Youth Across Cultures." In *Discourses of Anxiety Over Childhood and Youth Across Cultures*, edited by Liza Tsaliki and Despina Chronaki. Cham: Palgrave Macmillan, 2020, 1–26.

Wirth, Werner, Matthias Hofer, and Holger Schramm. "Beyond Pleasure: Exploring the Eudaimonic Entertainment Experience." *Human Communication Research* 38, no. 4 (2012): 408–409.

Chapter 9

The Transcendence of the Borders

The Animal Hero in Hosoda Mamoru's The Boy and the Beast

Katsuya Izumi

The Boy and the Beast (*Bakemono no ko*, 2015) is an animation film that Hosoda Mamoru (1967–), one of the most well-known Japanese animators, directed after *Wolf Children* (*Ōkami kodomo no ame to yuki*, 2012) which depicts a human mother's challenges involved in raising her hybrid children of human and wolf.[1] While both films are about the problems of educating children, *The Boy and the Beast* depicts an animal (bear) hero, Kumatetsu, who tries to raise and educate a human child, Ren (later nicknamed Kyūta).[2] Similar to the bathhouse world that Miyazaki Hayao (1941–) creates for the setting of his film *Spirited Away* (*Sen to Chihiro no kami kakushi*, 2001), the Beast Kingdom called Jyūtengai, where various animalistic creatures including Kumatetsu live, is an alternate world (or *ikai*) to which Ren accidentally gains access. Hosoda deliberately creates the Beast Kingdom as a space that cannot be identified as any specific country; he uses various cultural traits for the buildings, roads, and creatures. Hosoda presents the various traits not only for his setting but also for his literary references to create this film: the most obvious example of intertextuality includes a reference to Herman Melville's *Moby-Dick or, the Whale* (1851) to describe Ren's insinuation into higher education to ponder on his life and to depict the power of darkness that Ichirōhiko, the other human child living in the Beast Kingdom, carries in his mind. Hosoda also uses a novella "Gojyō shusse" (1942) which Nakajima Atsushi (1909–1942), a twentieth-century Japanese author, wrote by focusing on one of the main monster characters of the Chinese classical novel *Journey to the West* (1592) written by Wu Cheng'en (1500 or 1505–1582 or 1580). In other words, Hosoda's *The Boy and the Beast* draws on the tales of animals from three different countries. In this chapter, I will look at the various characteristics and hybrid traits that the film uses to depict the Beast Kingdom and the animal characters as preparatory devices for Hosoda to convey the importance of transcending the borders that exist between different species. Through Hosoda's literary borrowings and revisions, I will argue that the protagonist Kumatetsu's heroicness stems from his ability to transcend the border between the human and the animal, and by extension, his ability to practice the transcendence between the self and the other near the end of the film. To highlight the importance of the border transcendence, I compare this film with Hosoda's *Wolf Children*, a film that ends up emphasizing the difficulty of transcending the border between the human and the animal worlds even with Hosoda's attempts to show animality and its ferociousness as cultural constructs.

In his study, *Narratology Beyond the Human* (2018), David Herman analyzes the use of nonhuman animals in graphic narratives. While summarizing previous studies about animal comics, he attempts to understand how the narrative strategies of comics and graphic novels "index ways of understanding the boundary [between human and nonhuman worlds]." To consider the same boundary in animation films, Susan J. Napier's remark about identity and anime's narrative speed is useful:[3]

> Indeed, anime may be the perfect medium to capture what is perhaps the overriding issue of our day, the shifting nature of identity in a constantly changing society. With its rapid shifts of narrative pace and its constantly transforming imagery, the animated medium is superbly positioned to illustrate the atmosphere of change permeating not only Japanese society but also all industrialized or industrializing societies. Moving at rapid—sometimes breakneck—pace and predicated upon the instability of form, animation is both a symptom and a metaphor for a society obsessed with change and spectacle. In particular, animation's emphasis on metamorphosis can be seen as the ideal artistic vehicle for expressing the postmodern obsession with fluctuating identity.[4]

In *The Boy and the Beast*, Hosoda does not use metamorphosis very much, but he benefits from the traits of anime by depicting the hybridity of the human and the animal. Whereas he depicts the characters in Jyūtengai by attaching traits of different animals to the characters during the first half of the film, the second half of the narrative introduces the famous sperm whale from Herman Melville's *Moby-Dick* even though Hosoda stages it in one of the busiest towns in Tokyo, Shibuya. It is this disruptiveness of the narrative and the freedom from the rules of the rational and the orderly that I wish to address first.

Melville's *Moby-Dick* has attracted many artists for many years. Hosoda's 2021 film, *Belle* (*Ryū to sobakasu no hime*), starts with the main character singing on the back of a whale in the virtual world called "U." The whale used in the film resembles a blue whale because of its shape, and is different from the white whale that is depicted as a sperm whale in Melville's novel. Nonetheless, Hosoda's references to *Moby-Dick* in *The Boy and the Beast* are visible throughout the film. The appearance of material from the novel in the middle of the film is so sudden that they seem to disrupt the film's plot. The story involves a high school girl named Kaede who shows up to teach Ren how to read the book along with some other subjects. As she explains, *Moby-Dick* is a story about the protagonist, Captain Ahab, who wants to kill the white whale as a form of revenge because it has bitten off one of his legs. The reason that Hosoda uses the novel in this film is at least partly explained by what Kaede says when she continues to argue about the novel: she indicates that the protagonist fights against himself because the whale is a mirror that reflects him.

While the appearance of *Moby-Dick* and the use of the whale seem disruptive and random, the theme of finding oneself in the other, which results in the obfuscation of the border between the self and the other, is consistent throughout *The Boy and the Beast*. According to the animalistic creatures in Jyūtengai, human beings are supposed to carry "darkness" in their hearts, and are thus considered dangerous. Ichirōhiko, who is introduced as the first son of Kumatetsu's rival Iōzen, a lion-shaped creature, is in fact an abandoned human child. When Kumatetsu wins the fight against Iōzen to be named Sōshi, or the master leader, of their world, Ichirōhiko is swallowed by the darkness that has resided in his heart and throws a sword into Kumatetsu's back by using his psychic force. After that, Ichirōhiko goes to the human world, and the power of darkness changes him into a sperm whale. The vengeful hatred that takes over Ichirōhiko is similar to that of Captain Ahab toward Moby Dick, which reflects Ahab's self in Melville's novel. However, Hosoda does not depict the problem of dealing with the power of darkness as Ichirōhiko's individual problem. Ren also carries the same darkness that almost takes him over when Ichirōhiko stabs the sword into Kumatetsu. He admits that he needs to fight against Ichirōhiko because the problem of the internal darkness is also his own problem. When Kaede faces the sperm whale, she confesses that she, just like Ren, has the same darkness against which she keeps struggling. In other words, *The Boy and the Beast* has a consistent theme: the human characters invariably fight with their internal selves in the same way that Captain Ahab fights with Moby Dick.

Before the appearance of Melville's *Moby-Dick*, the first half of *The Boy and the Beast* depicts Kumatetsu as Kyūta's educator in the animal world. In other words, Kumatetsu works as a surrogate for the boy's parents. Ren's parents are minor characters, but Hosoda attaches family issues to his parents' background. Ren's mother has just passed away when we are first introduced to the character. Without showing any sympathy to Ren, his family members and relatives only emphasize the importance of inheriting the family lineage because Ren is the only son, and, therefore, an only heir. His deceased mother shows up in his imagination a couple of times in the film to encourage him to be mature. His father appears in the second half of the film as a sincere father who has been worried about his son and who kept looking for him even after the police gave up. (There is no way that he could find Ren who, right after leaving his family, has been lost in Jyūtengai to which humans have no access. They do not even know the existence of the animal community.) According to Ren's relatives, his parents divorced before his mother passed away, but their sincerity and kindness imply that his father might have had a hard time in their marriage because of the relatives who are so immersed in the conservative and patriarchal system that they can only care about their family lineage and traditions. One could posit that Hosoda uses the form of education which Kumatetsu and other animalistic creatures provide Kyūta in the film because the form of human education depicted here is conservative and patriarchal and therefore inadequate.

After Ren accidentally steps into Jyūtengai, the film's viewer soon learns that Kumatetsu entices Ren into the animal kingdom because he was looking for someone who could potentially be his disciple. With Kumatetsu playing the role of Kyūta's father, Hosoda deals with the problem of the fathers' education of children in Japan in *The Boy and the Beast* after *Wolf Children*, which is about a mother's struggle to raise two children. Referring to his choice of a boy as the film's protagonist, Hosoda explains that he chose a boy as his central character because coming-of-age stories about boys are not so readily available these days.[5] Nonetheless, it is not difficult to place this film in the historical contexts of Japanese films and Japanese society in terms of the importance of paternity, as Fukushima Ryōta has done in his analysis of this film. He points out that Japanese film directors such as Ozu Yasujirō and Mizoguchi Kenji have depicted unstable parent-child relationships by bringing in something "unnatural," "erotic," and even "violent." Fukushima continues to observe that the hollowness of paternity is prevalent in the 1980s Japanese action films. Needless to say, the authority of the Japanese father has collapsed both in the household and in society since Japan experienced the economic stagnation after the burst of the bubble economy during the 1990s. Placing Kumatetsu in this context of the father's eviscerated position, Fukushima argues that "*The Boy and the Beast*, from the beginning, brings the father and the son close to each other without making forced effort [to regenerate paternity]."[6] As Hosoda makes Sōshi state in the film, through training Kyūta, Kumatetsu trains himself. Fukushima places this parent-child relationship in the context of postmodern society in which people desire to remove the absolute authority of the father. Whereas Hosoda effectively breaks the hierarchical order of the human and the animals by having the animalistic creatures educate the human boy, he carefully avoids reestablishing the reversed hierarchy with the animals placed higher than the human. This form of education is what Ren's relatives who embody the Japanese conservative patriarchy cannot provide to Ren because they still live with the social values that had noticeably started to collapse since Japan's bubble economy burst.

Kumatetsu's education of Kyūta is only possible because of the reciprocal relationship between these animal and human characters. When he comes across Kyūta, who has lost his family ties and is all alone in Shibuya, Kumatetsu may be seeing himself in Kyūta because he grew up without his parents and mentors. This reciprocal relationship between the self and the other is the linkage between the first and the second half of the film in relation to the process of how Kyūta/Ren is educated. The film's consistent theme comes from Hosoda's use of the human Kyūta as a mirror that reflects the animal Kumatetsu and his reference to Moby Dick, or a whale that reflects the human Captain Ahab. I thus contend that Kumatetsu's heroic trait resides in his ability to transcend the border between himself and Kyūta, or between the animals and the human.

In order to set up the significance of the transcending borders in the film, I would like to discuss the literary contexts that Hosoda constructs in the film's first half. When Ren reads or tries to read Melville's *Moby-Dick* in the high school library at the beginning of the film's second half, he takes the volume from the shelf of the world literature's anthologies. Although the location tells us that the novel has achieved its high literary status in the world, it is not natural for Ren's initiation into higher education to start with an esoteric novel because he has not even finished his elementary school. Because of the difficulty of reading the novel and the unfamiliar theme of cetology, however, Ren starts studying the Bible, whales, histories of Americans hunting whales, and so on. This derivative power of the novel plants *The Boy and the Beast* in the context of world literature and multiple cultural contexts because Hosoda uses other works to create this animation film and, I argue, to prepare borderlessness which enables Kumatetsu to become a hero.

In addition to Melville's *Moby Dick*, Hosoda lists Nakajima Atsushi's novella "Gojyō shusse," which uses a *yōkai*, or an animalistic character as the protagonist in the film's end credits. Nakajima bases his main *yōkai* on a character from Wu Cheng'en's *Journey to the West* whose main characters are based on animals. Nakajima was prolific from the early 1930s until his death in 1942. His works are well-known for two traits: he was greatly influenced by Chinese classical works; he observed and wrote stories about people in the South Sea Islands when he received his post in the Ministry of the South Sea during the Pacific War. The model of the protagonist in his "Gojyō shusse" is Sha Wujing, one of the main *yōkai* who travel to India with a Buddhist monk, Tang Sanzang who wants to bring Buddhist scriptures from Leiyin Temple in India back home during the Tang dynasty (618–907). Sha Wujing's Japanese rendering of the name is Sa Gojō, and he is the river ogre, usually called *kappa* in Japanese. Nakajima's novella depicts the process through which Sa Gojō tries to find who he is or what one's self is by meeting with various *yōkai* masters until he encounters Tang Sanzang's group. It is interesting that Nakajima decides to bring him into the spotlight in his novella because some consider him as a minor character among the three disciples of Tang Sanzang. Compared to the other two disciples, a monkey beast figure Sun Wukong and a pig beast figure Zhu Bajie, who engage in quarrels and fights, Sha Wujing is polite and logical. At the same time, it is therefore understandable that Nakajima chooses this character as the one who ponders philosophical questions concerning the self.

Hosoda's conspicuous borrowings from Nakajima's "Gojō shusse" in *The Boy and the Beast* are located in the first half of the film when Kumatetsu and Kyūta visit various sages with a monkey-like creature Tatara and a pig-like creature Hyakushūbō, who seem to be Kumatetsu's guardians and friends, in order to ask them about the meaning of true strength (*shin no tsuyosa*). Despite the shift from asking what the self is to what strength is and the change from Sa Gojō's traveling all alone to four characters traveling together, Hosoda still draws a clear parallelism between Nakajima's novella and his film by expressing the difficulty of finding one specific answer to the question about true strength. In Nakajima's "Gojō shusse," Sa Gojō meets four *yōkai* sages, the same number of the sages that Hosoda uses during his characters' journey, but the novella ends before he finds any answer to his question about what the self is. Refusing to use Sa Gojō in his film, Hosoda goes further by using *Journey to the West* as the source of the journey that Kumatetsu and Kyūta undertakes with the other animal characters Tatara and Hyakushūbō.

Michael Dylan Foster indicates that "the word yōkai 妖怪 [is] variously translated as monster, spirit, goblin, ghost, demon, phantom, specter, fantastic being, lower-order deity, or, more amorphously, as any unexplainable experience or numinous occurrence."[7] Considering that Sun Wukong and Zhu Bajie are modeled after animals, a monkey and a pig, respectively, one can contend that Sa Gojō is the most imaginative character among the three disciples of Tang Sanzang because he is modeled after the amorphous *yōkai*.[8] Although Hosoda does not use any character that noticeably inherits Sa Gojō's traits as the river *yōkai* in *The Boy and the Beast*, this absence is informative especially when he lists Nakajima's "Gojō shusse" as one of the references in the end credits for the film. While the river *yōkai* creature is absent in *The Boy and the Beast*, the film does present unusual creatures in the form of animal-like characters or beasts. It is therefore important to look at the physical appearances of Tatara and Hyakushūbō in greater detail. Tatara has the face of a monkey; Hyakushūbō's face is that of a pig while his accoutrements are those of a monk's. The film's Japanese viewers who are familiar with the Japanese version of *Journey to the West* notice that Tatara would be equivalent to Sun Wukong and Hyakushūbō to Zhu Bajie. However, the relationships between Hosoda's characters and the characters from the Chinese classical novel are not straightforward. While Sun Wukong is considered a major protagonist of *The Journey to the West*, Tatara, just like Hyakushūbō, serves as the supporter of Kumatetsu. Hyakushūbō, a calm and prudent monk in the film, cannot be an equivalent to Zhu Bajie who is a pig *yōkai*, but cannot be linked to Tang Sanzang (a Buddhist monk) either because his facial traits are like those of a pig. Both Kumatetsu, a bear-like beast, and Kyūta, a human child, seem to fill in the role that would be equivalent to Sun Wukong's in *Journey to the West* with their untamable characteristics although they are both far from the monkey *yōkai* in terms of their physical appearances.

In other words, Hosoda has borrowed the structures and characters both from *Journey to the West* and from Nakajima's "Gojyō shusse" to create the first half of *The Boy and the Beast* with many of his revisions. Comparatively speaking, Nakajima's "Gojyō shusse" is not widely known to Japanese general readers, but *Journey to the West* has been used and adapted to various genres and media such as picture books, children's literature, TV series, and action films in Japan. Japanese viewers of Hosoda's film are familiar with the adapted versions of the novel to the extent that they might be surprised to see the monk that has the porcine facial traits, for instance, because of the discrepancies between Hosoda's characters and those in all these adapted versions of the Chinese novel. These borrowings from the Chinese classical novel and Nakajima's novella create the film's space and the characters that have similarities and dissimilarities to those of their sources, and as a result, create a kind of borderlessness. For example, as Kyūta matures in the first half of the film, he tries to imitate Kumatetsu completely thus indicating an animal's imitation of a human being. Imitations suggest a crossing of the border between the self and the other, and they also gesture toward the demonstration of affections toward another entity. In this film, the ability of transcending borders is used as a gateway to success, and Hosoda depicts Kumatetsu as a hero who can convey the ability to Kyūta.

If Hosoda's project is to transcend the border between the animalistic and human communities in this film, he tries to achieve this through bringing two different types of education: animalistic and human education. *The Boy and the Beast* does use the division between animals and humans. The animalistic creatures in Jyūtengai are critical of humans who carry darkness in their hearts. Through the perspective of Ren/Kyūta who accidentally discovered the animalistic kingdom, viewers know that the creatures are aware of the human and the human world. As Kumatetsu and Tatara roam around in Shibuya at the film's beginning, they can move between the two worlds implying that this ability of transcendence is because of their animal identities. Growing up in Jyūtengai since he was nine, Kyūta again accidentally gains access back to the human world when he turns seventeen years old. Although the humans do not know the existence of Jyūtengai, Kyūta, just like the animalistic creatures, is now able to move between the two worlds freely. Hosoda thus shows that Kumatetsu's animalistic education enables Kyūta to transcend the border.

Kyūta's movement between the two worlds reflects Hosoda's originality as a director and animator. Some have noticed that Jyūtengai shares many traits with the bathhouse town that Miyazaki Hayao uses in *Spirited Away*. The latter is also a space that seems borderless in that it consists of various cultural traits. The ten-year-old girl protagonist, Chihiro, however, cannot move between the two worlds. After going out of the eerie space of the bathhouse, she does not even remember what she has experienced. It is thus unclear if Miyazaki wants to depict the communication between the two worlds. In contrast to the ambiguity of Miyazaki's use of the two worlds, Hosoda's decision to allow Ren/Kyūta to move between the animal and human realms leads to the loss of the border, and he also adds reality to that. Unlike the bathhouse town, Jyūtengai gains its realistic tinge partly because of the fact that Kyūta comes in and out of the animalistic world. It has its own flow of time without Kyūta's perspective when he is in the human world; Iōzen's sons, Ichirōhiko and Jirōmaru, grow into their adolescence; the match between Kumatetsu and Iōzen to be the next Sōshi has been scheduled when Kyūta comes back from the human world. Hosoda succeeds in attaching the same level of reality to the two worlds, but it is still not without the sense of disruption when Kyūta is suddenly placed in the human world in the middle of the film.

Although this transition from Kyūta in Jyūtengai to Ren in the human world is rather too sudden, this is not without purpose. Hosoda describes Kyūta's/Ren's access to the human world as his ability to access human education. When he encounters Melville's *Moby Dick* in the library at the start of the sudden turn of the plot, he encounters Kaede who becomes a gateway for Ren to aspire to enter university. Significantly, the film ends with Kaede's reconfirmation and Ren's agreement that he will take the exam to earn the certificate equivalent to a high school diploma so that he can take a college entrance exam. Although Hosoda juxtaposes his human and animal characters because the former, unlike the latter, is depicted as a bearer of darkness, he does not abandon the human education component, thus allowing Ren to mature. In other words, as I have argued above, Kumatetsu's education of Kyūta is not the one that Ren's relatives with their conservative and patriarchal values can provide, but this does not mean that

Hosoda distinguishes the animal education from the human education clearly; it is precisely this binary which he opposes.

Like *The Boy and the Beast*, Hosoda's *Wolf Children* places an importance on education because it starts with a university setting. The wolf man who later marries the protagonist Hana and has two children with her sneaks into a national university in the outskirts of Tokyo. The wolf man, whose name is unknown, is a descendant of the Japanese wolf (*Nihon ōkami*) that became extinct at the beginning of the twentieth century. Being half human and half wolf, the wolf man is not, and probably cannot be, a college student. The fact that he sneaks in to learn there suggests that Hosoda highly values the human educational institution. Yet he never views education in human society as superior to the kind of education or learning experience available in the forest environment as depicted in *The Boy and the Beast* and *Wolf Children*. While the first child of Hana and the wolf man, Yuki, decides to stay in the human world, the second child Ame leaves his mother to grow up in the forest with other animals. Although the film's end remarks that an individual cannot belong to the two worlds, Hosoda conveys that both kinds of education are valuable by having two characters who choose different paths.

While Hosoda uses two different forms of education without placing them in a hierarchical relationship in both films, *The Boy and the Beast* seems more radical than *Wolf Children* because the director uses two different kinds of education to raise an individual, or Ren/Kyūta, in the former rather than dividing them into two children Yuki and Ame in the latter. By giving Ren/Kyūta the ability to move between the two worlds, Hosoda tries to make a flexible mixture of the human and animal education systems for the boy protagonist while creating a space in which one does not have to choose a particular form of education over the other in *The Boy and the Beast*.

In *Wolf Children*, whenever Yuki and Ame cross the boundaries of species between human and wolf, they notice the territorial border because the metamorphoses between the human and wolf forms in each of the human and the animal communities are not acceptable. If the originality of *The Boy and the Beast* resides in the transcendence of the borders between the two worlds in terms of two different types of education, Kumatetsu then is already a heroic figure when he chooses Ren as his disciple because, in Jyūtengai, humans are considered dangerous. Whereas the other creatures admonish Kumatetsu for taking human Ren into their animal world, Kumatetsu does not have the strong sense of the boundary between the species. Ren, who now becomes Kyūta, matures by imitating what Kumatetsu does. Kyūta's eating of a bowl of rice with raw eggs is one of the significant actions that demonstrates the transcendence of the boundary between humans and animals. It is normal to eat raw eggs with rice in Japan, but Kyūta obviously has not had raw eggs before. Emphasizing the contrast between animals and humans, Hosoda includes an omelet with ham in the film since this was Ren's favorite food when Ren lived with his parents. When his deceased mother appears in his imagination and when his real father shows up in the film's second half, they both offer to make omelets. Refusing to eat the bowl of rice with raw eggs that Kumatetsu prepares in the morning because "it smells raw," Kyūta in the evening of the very same day starts eating it after deciding to become his disciple. This quick initiation into the animalistic world through eating shows that Kyūta does not have a strong sense of the border either. Both Kumatetsu and Kyūta, the heroic figures in the film, are able to cancel out the species specific boundaries.

To return to Hosoda's literary borrowings, *Journey to the West* makes the same kind of attempt to transcend the species' boundaries which accompany the hierarchical relationship between the human and animal. The Buddhist monk Xuangzang is sometimes childish enough to have arguments with Sun Wukong and Zhu Bajie. Sha Wujing [Sa Gojyō], who is rarely involved with their arguments and makes composed interventions, often appears more mature than the human monk. With the absence of an animalistic creature who would carry some physical traits of the river *yōkai kappa*, Kumatetsu seems to occupy this position when he makes the journey with Hyakushūbō, Tatara, and Kyūta. In fact, Kumatetsu provides a solution to another philosophical problem about the true strength in the film: after visiting all the sages, Kumatetsu says that they must find answers in themselves. His remark turns Kyuta's outward journey into his inward journey before he starts to become more mature by imitating every one of Kumatetsu's movements. The close relationship or the reciprocity between the outward and inward or the exterior and the interior is reflected in Kumatetsu's teaching method when he earlier instructs Kyūta about how to use a sword: unable to explain to Kyūta logically how to use a sword, Kumatetsu ends up saying that "what is important is a sword in one's heart." His teaching also demonstrates that he does not have a strong sense of border between the exterior and the interior.

Hosoda's drastic change from the question about the self with which Sa Gojyō struggles in Nakajima's "Gojyō shusse" to the question about the notion of true strength in the film demonstrates that the animalistic creatures in Jyūtengai do not have any skepticism about their selves. Ichirōhiko is the only one who experiences the agony of not knowing himself. Found and raised by Iōzen when he was only an infant, Ichirōhiko believes that he is also one of the animalistic creatures and thus questions Iōzen why his nose does not become like his father's and why he does not have any tusks. As a human who has lived in Jyūtengai, he suffers from being on the border between the human and animal worlds. In her article about Hosoda's films, Saiga Keiko defines "monsters" (*bakemono*) as the ones who "are creepy and fearful because they are ambivalent, unsettling anywhere, and ambiguous."

She continues to explain, however, that "while the monsters are stable as monsters [in Hosoda's *The Boy and the Beast*], the humans, who are foreign entities, are the darkness in the monster world. The unsettling identity is considered the darkness."[9]

Kumatetsu's heroicness appears to come from the solid sense of his self, but this strength is possible because he is not an authoritarian. Although Kyūta is flexible because he is open to various definitions and non-definitions of the true strength, Kumatetsu retains his greatness by insisting that one has to find "meanings" on one's own. This, by the way, means that he is also open to different kinds of definitions of the true strength, and Hyakushūbō ties this into how Kumatetsu grew up and became strong without having any parents and mentors. In other words, the meaning of his self is not given by others but created and found by him. Able to move between the two worlds, he does not have an unsettling identity because the border does not matter to this hero who does not harbor binary thinking. One might want to argue that all other creatures in Jyūtengai are also able to move between the two worlds without having their identity crises. Yet unlike others who look down upon the humans because they have darkness in their minds, Kumatetsu does not categorize the humans and the animalistic species so clearly. That is the reason that he entices Kyūta into Jyūtengai and decides to train him as his disciple despite the initial oppositions from Hyakushūbō, Tatara, and others. Rather, he sees similarities between himself and Kyūta who also does not seem to have anyone on his side. Not only does the spatial border matter little to Kumatetsu, but the border between species is also insignificant to him.

As Hosoda depicts humans with darkness in their minds, his human world is also a suffocating place in the film. If Ren had stayed with his mother's family at the film's beginning, his life would have been controlled by a traditional and conservative family's mindset; Kaede's parents seem controlling because she confesses to Ren that she has lived her life according to her parents' desires and not her own, and sometimes her relationship with them is non-existent because they are busy with their jobs; most importantly, when Ren leaves his mother's family and roams around in Shibuya, Hosoda uses the view of security cameras to show that people are under constant surveillance. In that suffocating, controlling, and dangerous space of the human world, the human form of education is an exception. When comparing the ways in which Hosoda uses the human and animalistic (Kumatetsu's) educational elements in *The Boy and the Beast*, I have suggested that Hosoda regards the two kinds of education as mutually cooperative.

In *Wolf Children*, however, the border between the human and animal worlds is much more difficult to transcend than the one in *The Boy and the Beast*. The world in the former is cruel in that the animal forest and the human village do not allow hybridity. The hybrid children of Hanna and the wolf man can choose to belong to the animal world or the human world as Ame goes to the forest to live with other animals and Hanna stays with her mother and other humans. However, Ame and Hanna still have to choose one world or the other even though they have lived close to the border. They cannot stay on the border nor continue to move between the two worlds. When Hanna changes into her wolf figure in the yard when their neighbors visit their house, one of the visitors think of her as a cute dog even though Hanna in wolf form wears her clothes. Ame and Hanna are constantly categorized into either humans or animals.

In that context, it is important to note that Hosoda makes an effort to show that animality is also a "cultural" or social construct. Hosoda deliberately chooses Ame as the one who decided to leave his family for the animal world. In contrast to Yuki who chases after and catches all kinds of animals in her childhood, Ame is scared of small animals and insects and asks his mother to caress him. As an initiation ritual into animality, he succeeds in catching a bird in the forest (although he will be saved by Yuki because he slips on a rock and almost drowns himself in the river), and since that initiation, Hosoda depicts the process through which Ame is trained to gain his animality. Encountering a wolf in the forest and calling it his teacher, Ame learns from him how to hunt animals. Hosoda vividly depicts the scene in which Ame bites off the body of a running rabbit with his teacher wolf to show that the whimpering child can grow ferociousness in himself and to show that that ferociousness is only one of Ame's aspects because he continues to function in the human community in his human form and continues to respect his teacher wolf in his animal form.

Exhibiting the ferocious animality as a cultural construct, Hosoda makes another attempt to revise the image of wolf as a scary animal that humans try to get rid of from their settlement as depicted in picture books and children's literature. Ame, still a young boy, laments to Hanna in his feeble voice that the books he has read invariably depict wolves as blood-thirsty animals. Earlier in the film, a grown-up Yuki, who now has become the film's narrator, indicates that her mother has learned from the wolf man that stories about animals who metamorphose into different shapes at night during a full moon and who attack people are merely legends that are not based on facts. Still, the film's narrative ends up dividing the people and the animals into the logical and the emotional, respectively. For example, when Yuki and Ame fight because of the difference of their opinions about how they live their lives, they turn into wolves. When Yuki is cornered by Sōhei, the boy who transfers to Yuki's school and who notices that Yuki smells like a beast, she scratches his right ear with her hand which has turned into a wolf's paw.

In *The Boy and the Beast*, Hosoda is not as much interested in showing animals' ferociousness as a cultural construct as he is in *Wolf Children*.

He depicts the transcendence of the border between the human and animal worlds especially in terms of education. His literary borrowings and revisions that obfuscate the different species and nullify the hierarchy of animals work as preparatory devices for the transcendence of borders. In order to fight against the sperm whale, or the embodiment of the power of darkness that swallowed Ichirōhiko, Kumatetsu, who has transmigrated into a god called *tsukumo-gami* that attaches its spirit to a thing, becomes a sword and enters into Kyūta's heart. This signifies the climax of the border transcendence between the self and the other as well as between different species in *The Boy and the Beast* because Kumatetsu, an animal creature who has become a god, transforms into an object, by which he also continues to live in Kyūta thus becoming a human. These layered/multiple images of transcendence show that Hosoda has deepened his understanding about the relationship between the animal and the human since his earlier film *Wolf Children*.

NOTES

1. In Japan, the surname comes before the given name. I use this order when I refer to Japanese names in this chapter.

2. Kumatetsu gives Ren the nickname Kyūta because he is nine (kyū in Japanese) years old when they meet for the first time. Hereafter, I use Kyūta when I discuss him in relation to Kumatetsu, and I use Ren when I discuss him in relation to the other human characters. On other occasions, I use Kyūta/Ren to avoid creating an impression that the human or animal world is more significant than the other.

3. David Herman, *Narratology Beyond the Human: Storytelling and Animal Life* (New York: Oxford University Press, 2018), 121.

4. Susan J. Napier, *Anime from Akira to Princess Mononoke: Experiencing Contemporary Japanese Animation* (New York: Palgrave, 2001), 12.

5. Hosoda Mamoru, "Hito natsu no eiga ni mukatte" ひと夏の"映画"に向かって [Toward a "Movie" for a Summer], *Eureka* ユリイカ 47, no. 12 (September 2015): Kindle e-book.

6. Fukushima Ryōta, "Fusei no sakuran to shūsoku: *Bakemono no ko* to sono bunmyaku" 父性の錯乱と収束：『バケモノの子』とその文脈 [Paternity's Confusion and Convergence: *The Boy and the Beast* and its Context], *Eureka* ユリイカ 47, no. 12 (September 2015): Kindle e-book. All quotes from Japanese texts in this chapter are my translation.

7. Michael Dylan Foster, *Pandemonium and Parade: Japanese Monsters and the Culture of Yōkai* (Berkeley: University of California Press, 2009), 2.

8. This is not to undermine the complexity of the other two characters. For example, Hongmei Sun focuses on Sun Wukong's multivalent character to study the character's adaptation and representation in *Transforming Monkey: Adaptation and Representation of a Chinese Epic* (Seattle, WA: University of Washington Press, 2018).

9. Saiga Keiko, "Monstā to wa nani mono ka" モンスターとはなにものなのか [What are the Monsters?], *Eureka* ユリイカ 47, no. 12 (September 2015): Kindle e-book.

BIBLIOGRAPHY

Foster, Michael Dylan. *Pandemonium and Parade: Japanese Monsters and the Culture of Yōkai.* Berkeley: University of California Press, 2009.

Fukushima, Ryōta. "Fusei no sakuran to shūsoku: *Bakemono no ko* to sono bunmyaku" 父性の錯乱と収束：『バケモノの子』とその文脈 [Paternity's Confusion and Convergence: *The Boy and the Beast* and its Context]. *Eureka* ユリイカ 47, no. 12 (September 2015). Kindle e-book.

Herman, David. *Narratology Beyond the Human: Storytelling and Animal Life.* New York: Oxford University Press, 2018.

Hosoda Mamoru. "Hito natsu no eiga ni mukatte" ひと夏の"映画"に向かって [Toward a "Movie" for a Summer]. *Eureka* ユリイカ 47, no. 12 (September 2015). Kindle e-book.

Melville, Herman. *Moby-Dick; or, the Whale.* Edited by Harrison Hayford, Hershel Parker, and G. Thomas Tanselle. Evanston: Northwestern University Press, 1988.

Nakajima, Atsushi. "Gojyō shusse" 悟浄出世 [Gojyō's Personal Advancement]." In *Nakajima Atsushi Zenshū Vol.1* 中島敦全集第一巻 [*Nakajima Atsushi Anthologies Vol.1*], 309–335. Tokyo: Chikuma bunko, 2009.

Napier, Susan J. *Anime From Akira to Princess Mononoke: Experiencing Contemporary Japanese Animation.* New York: Palgrave, 2001.

Saiga, Keiko. "Monstā to wa nani mono ka" モンスターとはなにものなのか [What Are the Monsters?]." *Eureka* ユリイカ 47, no. 12 (September 2015). Kindle e-book.

Spirited Away. 2001. DVD. Directed by Miyazaki Hayao. Studio Ghibli.

Sun, Hongmei. *Transforming Monkey: Adaptation and Representation of a Chinese Epic.* Seattle, WA: University of Washington Press, 2018.

The Boy and the Beast. 2015. DVD. Directed by Hosoda Mamoru. Studio Chizu.

Wolf Children. 2012. DVD. Directed by Hosoda Mamoru. Studio Chizu.

Wu, Cheng'en. *Journey to the West.* Beijing: Foreign Language Press, 1990.

Chapter 10

The Esperpento of *Kipo and the Age of Wonderbeasts*

Sumor Ziva Sheppard

Answering the question of how best to live in the world and what constitutes a good person has been a reoccurring concern in popular, Western culture previous to and during the pandemic. *Avatar: The Last Airbender*, set in an undefined amalgamated universe of Asian cultures, investigated prejudice and hate, colonialism, self-development, capacity for change, and choosing the "good" beyond familial ties or personal fears. Series like *The Good Place* (2016–2020) posited not only what a heavenly (or hellish) afterlife would consist of and why, but also imagined who would or should make it there. In this vein, the animated television series *Kipo and the Age of Wonderbeasts* (KAWB) approaches the Aristotelian themes of how to live best and the concept of goodness in society through the structure of an *esperpento*[1] (an early, twentieth-century Spanish theatrical genre used to make social critiques that often included racist or antisemitic ideas). The deft use here of the *esperpento* form allows KAWB to function unlike any of its predecessors. KAWB creates a double narrative of its possible world: one in which a hybrid human is a hero and bridge to a new paradigm; and another in which racist and misogynistic dog whistles warn of societal decay due to the very same hybrid visibility, acceptance, leadership, and power. Contrary to its popular reception, the function of animals in *Kipo and the Age of Wonderbeasts*—whether anthropomorphized, hybridized, mutated, or in their natural state—warns of, rather than promotes, a reality in which human civilization has fully embraced social inclusivity and diversity.

In brief, *Kipo and the Age of Wonderbeasts* (KAWB) relates the creation myth of a new society after an apocalyptic event. It tells the story of an adolescent girl who is thrust into navigating a mysterious and dangerous world alone as she tries to reconnect with her father and their human village. The young teen, the titular Kipo, lives in a distant Earth future in which a catastrophe (hinted to have origins in modern-day science) has caused widespread mutations in animal species which make living above ground impossible for humanity. Some animals have become enormous, mutated versions of themselves (called "mega-mutes") while others have become anthropomorphized and now reside in the remnants of human civilization. Throughout her quest to reconnect with her village (called a "burrow" in the series), Kipo functions as a bridge for the anthropomorphized animals and humanity. Her calls for unity ultimately birth a world in which all species live together. This is directly due to Kipo's innate nature and singular state of being a prophesied, human-animal hybrid "mega-mute" leopard. Thus, Kipo's story is not just a coming-of-age story, but rather a narrative of the origins of a messiah figure and a creation myth in this fictional universe. Ironically, it is within the history of religious, medieval texts that the relevance and meaning of animal hybridity in KAWB is found. Kipo and the Oak family are contrasted against the antagonist Dr. Emilia in esperpentic form[2] visually using animal hybridity and racist tropes to make a critique of the direction of modern, American society and its rising value of diversity and inclusion.

The historical use of the hybrid creature in European medieval marginalia was a depiction of the villain of society and those who supposedly posed a threat to a positive evolution of their civilization. During this period, the definition of *humanity*, as shown by Caviness,[3] was being formed as White, European and Christian. Many populations that did not conform to that category were subject to a type of literary Othering which was manifested in a hybrid creature created to represent them in the marginalia. This is best exemplified in the case of the Jewish populations.[4]

The animal-hybridized Jewish character had many manifestations. One of the most popular was the horned or hooved Jewish figure. This depiction's history lies in a mistranslation in which Moses is "horned" instead of "radiant" after having divine contact. This error and the dissemination of this mistranslation gave rise to the popular, antisemitic belief that beneath the kippah or any covering, Jewish people were horned—and maybe even hooved—hybrid creatures. Following the spread of this belief, we see these visualizations of horned and hooved Jewish people. Coupled with the simultaneous developing imagery in Europe of devils and demons being horned and hooved creatures, this image of horned Jewish populations in the medieval imaginary relegated them to being a demonic force in society.[5] Head coverings, hats, and kippahs became symbols of the methods used to conceal their horns, but all was apparently "revealed" in the visuals of the marginalia.

It is in the fringes, then, of these Christian, religious texts that the reader is shown the supposedly true, vile nature of the Othered, hybridized population. The animal mixture chosen was symbolic of the hidden characteristics of the Other. It was inferred in these visuals that they were wolves in sheep's clothing through the partial hiding of the animal hybridity in the drawings. Thus, the use of hybridity in the medieval, European text is meant to expose weakness and vice, not virtue and strength. The power of this antisemitic image is apparent and persists today, along with the connection of animal-hybridity as a marker of an inherently evil or inhuman aspect of the Other. Kipo's story in KAWB does not escape this historical use. The use of animal hybridity in KAWB is clearly intended to convey a negative message about Othered groups through the visually racist narrative created by the patterns of hybridization in the series.

As a messiah figure prophesied to save the emerging world, Kipo's provenance is important to her narrative. Kipo's father is a Black man named Lio (Leo/lion) who is never visually hybridized in the series. Instead, manifestations of hybridity are associated with him, and they are most often those of various simians. In KAWB, Lio serves as a type of asymptomatic carrier of simianization through familial connection or sex. All members of his family are visually hybridized usually as either monkeys or felines through him. Much like the medieval marginalia, these "silent" visuals have a great impact on the meaning of the work for the audience.

To fully appreciate the significance of the simianization of the Oak family in KAWB, a fuller understanding of the place of the image of the monkey or ape and its specific racist uses in the Western literary tradition is necessary. The simianization of Africa and peoples of African descent is a relatively modern phenomenon that is explicitly linked to Anti-Black racism. The ape or monkey images in the Western canon—most notably in Christian texts—were first used to symbolize a wide range of spiritual deficiencies and undesirable traits: laziness, dirtiness, over-sexualization, a general symbol of sin as well as the devil himself.[6] As such, the ape/monkey also lived in the marginalia of medieval religious and illuminated texts.[7] The ape was a universal figure associated with general vice and to a lesser degree Egypt/Africa ("the land of darkness") as well.[8] This image, as a signifier, spread beyond texts to adorn buildings, church façades, and even textiles of the era.

In the early modern period, and with the advent of colonialization, the racist simianization of Afrodescendants was solidified through a literature of travel. This specific, travel lore told, with little variation, the story of an Iberian woman shipwrecked in Africa who is forced to mate with an ape to survive.[9] She bears the ape's children and later abandons her unnatural family when she is able to hail a ship. It ends with the distraught ape murdering the children after the woman escapes and the woman being pardoned in Europe and sent to a cloister to repent. The first record of these stories is usually attributed to Spain's Torquemada who relates it as a tale of a Portuguese woman who suffers the fate. Although the woman figure in this story functions as a warning of the spiritual weakness of women in general, the story's primary function was to point to the dangerous, sexual nature of the entire African continent—and specifically its male populations.

Furthering the development of visualized Afrodescendant simianization was the development of a biologic/scientific racism which placed the African as a race of human being more closely resembling the simian than other modern humans—and especially far from the European who occupied the highest evolutionary point in that hierarchy. Africans and Afrodescendants were rewritten as missing links between the simian and the modern man.[10] Using pseudo-scientific knowledge to support these claims of White supremacy, the Afrodescendant ceased being imagined as a harmless, child servant as in the painting *Young Black Holding a basket of Fruit and a Young Woman Stroking a Dog*.[11] They began, in the Western imaginary, to take on the previous medieval qualities associated with monkeys and apes developed in the aforementioned religious texts as beings of vice, the demonic, or mere mimickers who aimed to subvert the spiritual and social development of true humanity.[12]

Afrodescendants were continuously simianized as a special form of dehumanization starting in the eighteenth century. Throughout the colonial periods in Africa, European colonists often referenced the indigenous as monkeys (the use of "macaque" in Portuguese-held areas, for example). These racist slurs functioned no differently than the previously developed antisemitic images of horned and hooved Jewish characters. For the Afrodescendant, the image of the simian became further superimposed on their international image as the West's cultural racism spread through the advent of globalism, exported as if it were one of the many goods of the West.

The veracity of this racist trope continues to the present day. We are all well aware of the dehumanization of Afrodescendants that it easily conveys to its international audience. Examples in just this past couple of decades alone are astounding in number. In athletics, European football clubs have been sanctioned, players fined or sanctioned, and fans ejected or banned from attending future games for using monkey slurs, images, sounds, and related objects to racially harass players of African descent. These forms of racial abuse have additionally caused some European nations and clubs to be labeled as places hostile to Afrodescendant presence. In politics across the globe, the monkey trope has been employed to denigrate and question the credentials of Afrodescendant politicians and world leaders. The most famous of these would be the relentless simianization of former U.S. president Barack Obama and his wife Michelle Obama. Widespread images and the verbal use of racial slurs by other world leaders constantly assailed them in formal and informal media.[13] In Italy, the virulent, racist attacks against Cecile Kyenge, based on her Afrodescendant heritage, also employed the image of the African as monkey to question her ability to govern and participate in politics at all. In that case, it was suggested that her true aim in Italian politics was, in fact, to destroy Italian political structures by infusing them with a supposedly inferior and ape-like, African system.[14] We see again, sadly, the visual being used to spread racist beliefs which represent Afrodescendants as devilish contagions with intentions to attack and destroy true, "human" civilization. Even schools and workplaces are not immune to the racist beliefs concerning the simianized African. In the United States, this same category of slur has been used to abuse, humiliate, and intimidate people of African descent through the creation of hostile student and work environments. Tactics such as placing bananas on desks or locker rooms as well as assailing colleagues with monkey sounds, though not common, are not unknown. It is, thus, undeniable that the trope continues to thrive in the modern world. Its placement and use in KAWB cannot then be said to be happenstance as any use of monkeys with Afrodescendants in any context—even in the modern day—calls to the minds of the audiences its international signifying, racist meanings.

Returning to the central family of KAWB, then, we find that it is led by a Black, male character named Lio Oak. His appearance throughout the series is as a non-hybrid and positive figure. He is a highly educated scientist and doting, single, supposedly widowed father that is loyal to his burrow village and, on the surface, to their mission to save humanity. Secretly, he is shown to have decided a path which runs counter to realigning his world to its natural state. He is consistently presented as a harmless, asexualized, and even pitied character, incapable of harming others or doing wrong intentionally; yet the trajectory of his character reveals that he is indeed a type of king of beasts hidden in a mostly White or White-presenting human enclave of human survivors and scientists. Lio (accompanied by wife Song, an extremely intelligent, Asian woman) violates the basic tenets of human and animal experimentation. Their experiments result in the creation of two designer babies: one, a male mandrill, Lio's first son, who is anthropomorphized using possibly Lio's genetic material; the other, Kipo, his genetically engineered, mega-mute daughter conceived with his wife. Though not apparent in the beginning of the series, Lio is the catalyst of animal-hybridity in KAWB. It is through his implied/hidden simianization and the extensive use of the racist monkey trope in the series that this becomes apparent. Much like the Torquemada tale mentioned previously, his hybridity is apparent in his progeny and in those with whom he has sexual contact.

Lio Oak's first child is the human-mandrill hybrid Hugo (alluding to Victor Hugo). He is the first missing link in the data the Oaks and their human village-burrow need to reverse the mutations that have destroyed human civilization. His creation violates the human civilization's ethical rules against animal-human genetic blending and experimentation. As such, his parents, the Oaks, hide and raise him as their son. The implied origin of his DNA is Lio as later in the couple's history they (again) use their own DNA in the creation of the titular, main protagonist Kipo. Thus, the first representation of the offspring of the hidden, hybrid character Lio is a monkey. By way of Hugo's existence, he affirms the simian hybridity of his father while alluding to the other characteristics of vice historically attributed to monkeys in the Western canon.

It is important to note that the simian in East Asian cultures does not have such a uniform meaning. Sometimes it is clever while other times it is mischievous and slow-witted—although it is often used as a metaphor for humanity and the human condition. One particularly negative use of the monkey is in Buddhism where the unenlightened mind is literally "monkey mind" or *shin-en*. In KAWB, the hybridized monkeys capture some of the negative, East Asian depictions of the anthropomorphized simian but since the work is not centered in Eastern culture these connections are peripheral. KAWB is merely drawn in an anime style, but is a decidedly Western piece in theme, character, societal representation, and narrative arc.

As a visible monkey, Hugo openly displays many historical, medieval vices attributed to simians. His character development is hinged upon his early imitation of humanity, obsession with high Western culture, and the sinister use of a supernaturally, sexual biology. Much like a Western hot-housed child,[15] he is infused with cultural knowledge of the heights of European civilization, but is only a façade of human giftedness. He remains a mere monkey, nonetheless, set apart and rejected in a human enclave. The visual of the Black boy/monkey and his mimicry is a highly charged aspect of the racist, monkey trope being employed here. As discussed earlier, the monkey's mimicry of humanity was only to subvert it in the European imagination. They were symbols of beings naturally incapable of true humanity.

When later in the series, the character of Hugo becomes Scarlemagne (his version of Charlemagne complete with a desire to unify the mute population under his reign), the visualization of dangerous monkey mimicry is complete, but added to this is the sexualized aspect of the racist trope. Hugo's manner of control and rise to power is discovered later in the series as his use of his sexual pheromones to mind-rape his victims (mostly White or White- presenting humans as well as mutated animals) into submission. His obsession with eighteenth-century France and European high culture is presented as a farce—yet another example of pitiful, simian imitation. His power is found to be his brute, unnatural, and irresistible sexuality. Hugo is ridiculous and terrifying as a mandrill dressed in the fashion of nineteenth-century French nobility. As a self-crowned emperor of beasts, he boasts of his culture, but is devoid of humanity in his vicious savagery.

Hugo/Scarlemagne is an encapsulated synopsis of the racist, monkey trope whose traits span the entire historical development of the slur. As a child, he is harmless and obedient like the Afrodescendant servant children painted in the late Middle Ages surrounded by monkeys.[16] As an adolescent, he further gains the "knowledge of the White" while his "savage of the Black" increases in force.[17] In adulthood, he is a terrifying parody of European civilization bent on the destruction of the remaining White, Western world that the human burrow from which he came represents.

The fate of Song Oak, Lio's wife, expands anti-Black simianization as linked to misogyny. As discussed earlier, women were subject to misogynistic attacks related to the monkey trope from the medieval period to the modern era. Key to furthering the characterization of the Afrodescendant man as a dangerous simian-hybrid or dehumanized creature who needed to be controlled or eradicated was establishing the sexual danger he posed to the non-Black woman. Most often, the same story conjured by Torquemada was repeated and embellished by later authors to focus more heavily on misogynistic aspects of the tale. In the sixteenth century, Cardinal Jean Bodin and Church Doctor Peter Damian disseminated a tale of the Count of Liguria who was cuckolded by his wife with a monkey who later murdered him.[18] In this story, the wife also produces heirs and chooses her monkey beau over her faithful husband. Hers is the beginning of the treacherous woman who chooses the monkey over the man. Bodin was known to describe sub-Saharan Africa as a land of monsters, asserting that there are unions between men and animals.[19] Song becomes part of the misogynistic and racist treacherous woman character of the ape trope. She is despicable as she openly chooses to be with the simianized, Black man over the "real" human men. Her punishment comes in three forms. She first produces a mandrill son.[20] Later, she produces a second, animal-hybrid child that, as third punishment, in turn affects her physically and mentally. The difference between her two maternal experiences lies in the fact that her first child, Hugo, is conceived in the lab and does not seem to contain her genetic material. His existence does not confirm her sexual relations with her husband nor "taint" her body. Although she is associated and implicated as his mother, she still has not fully taken on the treacherous woman role. With the implied natural (sans genetically engineered egg) pregnancy of Kipo, Song's sexual relation with her visually simianized husband is made concrete. Her third punishment in the series is the shocking, physical transformation of her into a mega-mute macaque[21] monkey herself—losing all her humanity and intelligence through the simianization brought upon her by sexual association with her husband. It is the sexual contact with Lio that is the catalyst for this transformation. Her mutation is a visual reminder of the racist simianization of her husband Lio and the silent, authorial condemnation of those who choose willingly to reproduce or mate with the Black man in this universe. They are castigated by becoming wildly simianized themselves.

Song's inner torture and descent is further elaborated in the story in ways similar only to the psychological and emotional cracking of Hugo. In becoming the mega-mute macaque monkey, she loses her human abilities of communication and self-awareness. She is literally and visually swallowed—losing her sense of self—by the implied infection her simianized husband holds. Following her degradation by the racist trope, she is then mind-raped by the power of the sexual hormones of her own son Hugo/Scarlemagne. This final occurrence implies an uncontrolled and heightened, unnatural sexuality that includes incest or the ability/desire for incestuous relationships post-contact with her husband Lio. Song's semi-liberation from this descent into hell can only be gained through a connection with her daughter Kipo, a purpled copy of herself. Kipo, through the use of music and her inherited hybridity, helps her mother cope and partially restores her inner humanity lost due to the visualized prohibition of miscegenation in the series. In the concave mirror of the *esperpento*, the supposed "good family" of Lio and Song are methodically stripped of their humanity, tortured, and made grotesque with striking moral deficiencies. Visually, they are not heroes but rather infiltrators and villains of the human community. This conceit is continued in the development of the main protagonist, Kipo.

Unlike her mother Song and brother Hugo/Scarlemagne, Kipo is not associated with simianization as a visualized monkey. Instead, it is through a transformation into a gigantic leopard at the start of her menstruation. Her animal hybridity focuses on her as a hypersexualized feminine progeny of Lio just as Hugo/Scarlemagne's ultimate superpower is based in his inherited sexual nature. Kipo is transformed into an amplified object of sex instead of the victim/subject of sexual intercourse. This simian-linked, sexual perversity makes it impossible for the Oak family to be a benign protagonist group. The family is an evolved, modern, sophisticated version of the medieval monkey—controlling, dangerous, and infectious. They are less able to be identified and thus have found acceptance—are even uplifted as role models—but their role as defined by the racist, visual history remains. Through Kipo, the audience encounters the imaged and imagined crossroads of racism, patriarchal status quo, and misogyny.

Chronologically, Kipo's character development begins with three sister goat witches of the forest who received visions of her birth. Later, they guide Lio in the raising of Kipo, help her to control her mutation until she reaches puberty (unbeknownst to Kipo), and guide her to a full realization and control of herself. Women, cats, and witches: women as witches with cats, and witches who turn into cats are all familiar occult and misogynistic themes to audiences. Historically a way of demonizing women, the woman-witch-cat connection has also been a symbol of female divinity and innate connection with the supernatural. As a prophesied, mythical, feminine cat, Kipo is elevated to the status of a savior deity for the "mute" world. The revelation frames her entire story although it is not initially divulged to audiences.

Kipo's occult connection is normalized as a natural part of her origin story. The ridiculous occult rites of the witches at once poke fun at non-organized mystical traditions often associated with "barbaric" peoples and underdeveloped regions while supporting the veracity of the goat witches' claims through the rise to power of Kipo in this apocalyptic world. When Kipo reaches the goats, she is already a proven leader and uniter of the different species in the predominantly male-dominated spaces of conflicts she encounters. It is here in the den of the witch goats that her place as founder of the new world and leader of a united, cognizant, "mute" Other is officially ratified as the mission of her existence. Her rise is positioned as a triumphant, misogynistically, enveloped moment.

The idea of a powerful, independent woman being associated with witchcraft is a popular, well-trod one that has been consistently used against the non-conformist woman in male-dominated society. The belief that such behavior was innately unnatural supported calls for murder, exile, social stigma, and repression of such women as they shifted away from their ascribed roles in traditional patriarchal societies. It could be argued that in KAWB this trope is challenged as Kipo's leadership role is mostly supported by her compatriots and other males, but I contest that it is not challenged, precisely because of the embedded, visual, racist message produced by the *esperpentic* lens with which the viewer experiences this series. The normal protests against the independent, female leader arise from representatives of the male patriarchy and women who support it, but in both cases, such characters have been made ineligible as valid representatives. Her male family members have been simianized; the only other male friend in the series is a young, Black male who is analogously simianized as a hidden hybrid; and the only other female is a contradiction of all other female characters. She is Wolf, the "angry Black girl."

In Wolf, the audience meets a primary school-aged, Black girl. Although her history is never told, it seems that she was the victim of a catastrophe on the surface. Orphaned suddenly, she ran for her life and ended up being adopted by a pack of wolves. She is a literal *enfant savage*. As the sole representation of the unambiguous, Black feminine, Wolf has no human background or family, is unnaturally strong, agile, and aggressive, lacks trust, and has no traditionally feminine personality qualities. Adopted by a family of sophisticated wolves, she, in fact, shows herself even more beastly and wolfish than the actual wolves themselves—eventually besting them, skinning one of her adopted siblings and wearing their skin and head over her like a costume throughout the entire series. In Wolf, there is a consistent presence of the "angry, Black woman" who is not afforded sincere narrative compassion. The child's general ignorance and coping mechanisms are interpreted as biological faults innate to her as the sole representative of unambiguous,

Black femininity. Compounded in this character is also the image of the savage; she possesses an extraordinary athleticism that cannot be attributed to her wolf-in-training time with her adopted family. The audience sees that Wolf is later a serious match for the adult, martial arts-trained antagonist Dr. Emilia as well as the mutated animals of the series. Kipo, on the other hand, must mutate into a mega-mute leopard to achieve the same feats. Wolf's animalized hybridity is truly hidden within her as it is for all the other designated Black characters. It is biological and connected with her Blackness through the tropes used to flesh her out. It negates her ability to join the humans of the series, muting her as a possible, legitimate voice to challenge Kipo or the Oak family.

In contrast, Kipo is the soft and yielding mediator. She is the opposite of Wolf. Instead of an aggressive canine, she is the giant pussy cat, slow to anger and eager to find a way to appease all sides in her quest for unity. Hers is an outsized femininity and sexuality, while Wolf embodies a costume of masculinity in her response to the violent, apocalyptic world they inhabit. The superhuman, superbestial, sexual power inherent in Kipo's visualization as the mega-mute leopard and her access to an enhanced and understated feminine persuasion see both of Lio's children exhibiting characteristics of the sexual aspect of the monkey trope but in markedly different ways. Where Hugo/Scarlemagne mind-rapes, Kipo succeeds ultimately not through her reasoned persuasion but rather through her visage as the powerful, enormous cat who chooses to be soft and petable when it suits her goal to defeat her enemy.

The main protagonists and stylized heroes of KAWB seem to be neatly packaged answers to the calls from the mainstream West for more inclusion and representation of heroes of diverse backgrounds. Indeed, the initial appeal of KAWB for many was the Black and Asian multiracial family it revolves around, but the Oak family is nothing more than an assemblage of racist and misogynistic tropes caught in an esperpentic, apocalyptic play. As is the aesthetic of the *esperpento*, the glass through which one gazes contorts the spectacle to show the grotesque in its racist critique of society. For the audience, the Oak family represents a horror with a laissez-faire amorality. Thus, one must look to the defeated villain to find the puppeteer's true heroine and the hidden message of KAWB.

In KAWB it is ultimately not Hugo/Scarlemagne with his mind-raping hormones nor the Oak parents with their unrepentant human experimentation and subsequent embracing of the occult that are the true enemies of Kipo's unification dream. It is Dr. Emilia: an extremely intelligent, White, female geneticist and leader of seemingly the last human burrow-village on earth. She has dedicated her life to furthering the goal of her scientist father to save human civilization at all costs by finding a cure to the catastrophe that caused the unnatural mutation of the animals and devastated humanity. Blonde, thin, blue-eyed, determined, and single-minded, her scientific knowledge and leadership is unchallenged by all (perhaps in intelligence only matched by Song) until the very end of the three-part series. She is feared by the Oak parents as the voice of human reason and serves as the enforcer of human and scientific morality and ethics in the surviving human enclave. They know she will kill their mandrill son, Hugo, if he is found, and denounce their work, so they hide him. They know she would kill or try to reverse the hybridity of Kipo if it becomes known, so Lio hides her hybridity internally with the help of the goat witches. Dr. Emilia also stands in stark contrast to Lio and Song Oak in her concepts of citizen and social responsibility. The Oaks consistently choose the individual over the community in their actions, eventually destroying humanity's last hope of survival and a rebalance of the natural world. Dr. Emilia, on the other hand, consistently chooses the human community over her individual connections and emotional needs in her quest to rectify the human wrong which caused the apocalyptic catastrophe and save human civilization.

In the esperpentic lens, she appears unjust and inhumane. She is shown murdering her dim-witted brother when his opinion evolves toward an alliance to the mutated animal world in an effort to protect the human burrow. Wholly rejecting any alliance with the titular Wonderbeasts and the known simianized characters, Dr. Emilia instead steals the sexual, mind-raping hormones of Hugo/Scarlemagne to carve a path back to the surface by using it on mega-mutes like Song. At the series' end, a simple and liberalized remnant of humanity turns its back on her and joins Kipo. When she is forcibly contaminated by Kipo's (and thus Lio's) DNA, turning into a mega-mute, two-headed crustacean-like creature, she refuses to submit and accept her hybridity. In this metaphoric rape of Dr. Emilia by the hybrid mutes, she chooses to refuse the intoxicating help of Kipo as she plunges into oblivion. She chooses to allow her human mind to be erased by the overwhelming animal consciousness of the mega-mute she has become and disappears from the story's universe forever. Her last act is to preserve, even in the face of death, the morals and ethics of her human community, its consciousness and civilization. She decides to reject the decayed and crippled, mimicked copy of her world inhabited by the Wonderbeasts. As the antithesis of Kipo, Dr. Emilia's character is the other side of the visual, racial dialogue that creates the counter-narrative of the series. She is the true hero of this author's tale. The invisible puppeteers of KAWB spin a tale about Dr. Emilia's (and by extension the Western world's) unjust demise by the likes of the Kipos of the world in this contorted critique of contemporary society.

In the post-apocalyptic world of KAWB, there is no indication that race or race-consciousness exists. The audience is peering into the future through an esperpentic lens to experience a glimpse of this possible world. Race and racism are communicated visually as the main topics of discourse to an audience still infused with its reality. Through use of conceits based in racist tropes, the themes of race and power guide the entire narrative. KAWB only seems to reward the efforts and decisions of the Oak family at its conclusion. It only appears to condemn Dr. Emilia who disappears into an oblivion within the mega-mute she transforms into at the end. Being a modern *esperpento*, KAWB does just the opposite, cleverly and silently communicating its warning in visually racist animal hybridity. The *esperpento*, by design, is a fascist and racist form used to critique society, "helping" humanity to see the deformity of hybridity that lies hidden in their midst and that is destroying them. KAWB indeed found appeal to a wide, global demographic on Netflix. One is hard pressed to find even *one* critique of it. It is and will likely remain successful whether or not the entirety of its audience consciously recognizes its true stance on diversity and inclusion. Indeed, that fact alone makes KAWB a series that does untold harm to the very populations it is purportedly holding up as heroes.

Approaching the topic of how one should live while providing a moral critique of society is no light topic for any fiction. The use of animal hybrids complicates such a discussion as outside of newly imagined, fantastical creatures with no reference to actual animals, almost all carry with them some cultural reference. In KAWB, it is obvious that the animals chosen align with the perpetuation of racist and misogynistic beliefs, but this failure is not inherent in the anime form. Rather it is part of the fabric of the message of the writers. The use of the anthropomorphic animals and hybrids is part of the innovation of anime. KAWB highlights the importance of the provenance of those chosen and how they function to imbue meaning into a work.

NOTES

1. Heyden Smith, Betty, "Some Contemporary Aspects of the Esperpento of Ramón del Valle-Inclán," (Master Thesis, Texas State University, 1971): 1–3. The *esperpento* is a theatrical genre "whose style is characterized by the dehumanization and degradation of man, distortion and animalization... The distortions of time, setting and character lead to a world of the grotesque, and therefore the tragicomic." The critiqued aspects of the targeted culture in Inclán's work often revolved around the need to remove Semitic influences in Spanish culture. Works such as *Los Cuernos de Don Friolera* were extremely antisemitic in nature though widely acclaimed. 'Esperpento' is a word in Spanish that means an ugly person or thing or something that is absurd.

2. Heyden, "Some Contemporary," 5. Three main ways dehumanization is achieved in Esperpentos are: physical distortion, animalization and mechanization. It also includes surreal aspects of the setting and time which is seen in the KAWB in

the fantastic setting and undefined location in a timeline as well as the span of time in the series.

3. Caviness, Madeline, "From the Self-Invention of the Whiteman in the Thirteenth Century to the Good, the Bad and The Ugly," *Different Visions: A Journal of New Perspectives on Medieval Art* 1 (September 2008): 13–22. https://differentvisions.org/wp-content/uploads/sites/1356/2020/03/Issue-1-Caviness-2.pdf. Through a careful study of the evolution of the European as an actual White person in medieval art, the author traces the link between light and goodness in Christian art to the eventual removal of skin tones to make saints and other figures actually white themselves, embodying what was holy light in their actual biology. Contrasting to this evolved representation of whiteness was a complementary darkness of representatives of vice and Othered groups who were not Christian or European. Caviness concludes that the definition of 'human' as 'white, Christian European' was solidified during this time period causing all Others to be automatically dehumanized and/or ranked according to their similarity to the actual and only 'human.'

4. Lledó, Pilar Bravo and Miguel Fernando Gómez Vozmediano, "El Alboryaque: Un Impreso Planfletario Contra los Conversos Fingidos de la Castilla Tardomedieval," *Historia, Instituciones, Documentos* 26 (1999): 57–84. Depictions of the hybridized Jew in medieval marginalia were based on a long history of antisemitism in the region. The rumors spread to dehumanize the Jewish people and thus make them ineligible for equal status and treatment in European society were the basis of the antisemitic images that proliferated the margins of many medieval religious texts. What will be gleaned here is how the composition of the animal-hybridized Jewish caricature reinvigorates antisemitic and racist tropes while guiding the reader/audience in how the subject should be interpreted as a villain and threat to society without writing a single word about them.

5. Lledó, "El Alboryaque," 57–84. Lee, Debbie, "Johnson, Stedman, Blake and the Monkeys," *The Wordsworth Circle* 33, no. 3 (Summer 2002): 116–118. https://www.jstor.org/stable/24044845

6. Hund, Wulf D., "Racist King Kong Fantasies: From Shakespeare's Monster to Stalin's Ape Man," in *Simianization: Apes, Gender, Class and Race*, ed. Wulf D. und, Charles W. Mills and Silvia Sebastiani, 19–42 (Zurich: Lit Verlag, 2016).

7. Walker Vadillo, Mónica A, "Apes in Medieval Art," Medieval Animal Data Network (Blog on Hypothesis.org), Octobe 28th 2013. [Online] https://mad.hypothesis.org/172

8. Walker, "Apes," [Online].
9. Hund, "Racist," 46.
10. Hund, "Simianization," 9.
11. Belhouse, "Candide," 745.
12. Walker, "apes," [Online].
13. Hund, "Simianization", 7.
14. Hund, "Simianization," 8.

15. "hot-housed" children are those who are aggressively guided to academic learning that is usually not appropriate for or linked to the child's cognitive age.

16. Bellhouse, "Candide," 745.

17. Mills, "Bestial," 38.
18. Hund, "Racist," 46.
19. Hund, "Racist," 45–46.
20. Hund, "Racist," 48.

It is to be noted that mandrills specifically figure into the woman-mated-with-ape stories as supposedly confirmed to have been able to mate with human women.

21. Macaque monkeys are native to many East Asian countries and macaque also was a widely-used, racist term (*macaca* in some languages) coined by European colonists to refer to indigenous and North African populations.

BIBLIOGRAPHY

Bellhouse, Mary L. "Candide Shoots the Monkey Lovers: Representing Black Men in the Eighteenth Century French Visual Culture." *Political Theory* 34, no. 6 (December 2006): 741–784. https://www.jstor.org/stable/20452508.

Caviness, Madeline. "From the Self-Invention of the Whiteman in the 13th Century to the Good, the Bad and the Ugly." *Different Visions: A Journal of New Perspectives on Medieval Art* 1 (September 2008): 13–22. https://differentvisions.org/wp-content/uploads/sites/1356/2020/03/Issue-1-Caviness-2.pdf.

Connors, Catherine. "Monkey Business: Imitation, Authenticity and Identity From Pithekoussai to Plautus." *Classical Antiquity* 33, no. 2 (October 2004): 179–207. https://www.jstor.org/stable/10.1525/ca.2004.23.2179.

Hernández-Pérez, María Beatriz. "Human/Nonhuman: Gender Dynamics and the Female/Animal Condition in Medieval Culture." In *Masculinity/Femininity: Re-Framing a Fragmented Debate*, edited by Jon Ross and Ambrogia Cereda, 47–57. Leiden: Brill, 2012.

Heyden Smith, Betty. "Some Contemporary Aspects of the Esperpento of Ramón del Valle Inclán." Master Thesis, Texas State University, 1971.

Hund, Wulf D. "Racist King Kong Fantasies: From Shakespeare's Monster to Stalin's Ape Man." In *Simianization: Apes, Gender, Class and Race*, edited by Wulf D. Hund, Charles W. Mills, and Silvia Sebastiani, 43–75. Zurich: Lit Verlag, 2016.

Hund, Wulf D., Charles W. Mills, and Silvia Sebastiani, eds. *Simianization: Apes, Gender, Class and Race*. Zurich: Lit Verlag, 2016.

Lee, Debbie. "Johnson, Stedman, Blake and the Monkeys." *The Wordsworth Circle* 33, no. 3 (Summer 2002): 116–118. https://jstor.org/stable/24044845.

Lledó, Pilar Bravo, and Miguel Fernando Gómez Vozmediano. "El Alboryaque: un Impreso Panfletario Contra los Conversos Fingidos de la Castilla Tardomedieval." *Historia, Instituciones, Documentos* 26 (1999): 57–84.

Mills, Charles W. "Bestial Inferiority: Locating Simianization within Racism." In *Simianization: Apes, Gender, Class and Race*, edited by Wulf D. Hund, Charles W. Mills, and Silvia Sebastiani, 19–42. Zurich: Lit Verlag, 2016.

Patterson, Serena. "Reading the Medieval in Early Modern Monster Culture." *Studies in Philology* 111, no. 2 (Spring 2014): 282–311. https://www.jstor.org/stable/24392086.

Sechrist, Radford, creator. *Kipo and the Age of Wonderbeasts*. Directed by Young Ki Yoon, featuring Karen Fukuhara, Sydney Mikayla, Coy Stewart, Deon Cole, Dee Bradley Baker, Sterling K. Brown, Dan Stevens, Jee Young Han, and Amy Landecker. Aired 2019. https://www.netflix.com/title/80221553.

Smith, David Livingstone, and Ioana Panaitiv. "Aping the Human Essence: Simianization as Dehumanization." In *Simianization Apes, Gender, Class and Race*, edited by Wulf D. Hund, Charles W. Mills, and Silvia Sebastiani, 77–104. Zurich: Lit Verlag, 2016.

Thimann, Heidi. "Marginal Beings: Hybrids as the Other in Late Medieval Manuscripts." *Hortulus: The Online Graduate Journal of Medieval Studies* 5, no. 1 (2009). https://hortulus-journal/volume-5-number-1-2009/thimann/.

Walker Vadillo, Mónica A. "Apes in Medieval Art." *Medieval Animal Data Network* (Blog on Hypothesis.org), October 28, 2013. https://mad.hypothesis.org/172.

Chapter 11

(Un)learning with "Monsters"

Animals, Patriarchal Oppression, and Ethics of Care in Guillermo del Toro's **The Shape of Water**

Monica Sousa

In film, animal or animalistic characters are often represented as heroic, anti-heroic, or villainous. These representations have the potential to reflect societal mindsets toward animals as informed by the intersectionality of many social markers, including gender, race, sexuality, class, or disability. Based on societal perspectives and treatments, animals and women—groups that are victims of patriarchal oppression—have much in common. Feminist scholarship discusses the male gaze, which serves to objectify and essentialize women, where they are forced into a dichotomy of "good" and "bad." Since Western culture often objectifies and essentializes animals as well, animals, too, are often treated as such in film representations.[1] Although heroic animal characters are still, somehow, closely associated with humans, the villains are separated from humanity; instead, they are seen as monstrous. With the easy potential for animals to be placed into the category of "bad" animals too, much like women, they can easily be considered monstrous.

There are notable similarities between the cultural representation/treatment of women and animals as well as discussions within the literary fields of feminist theory, animal studies, and monster studies. Pramod Nayar argues that animal studies and monster studies are similar in how they engage with the figure of the Other. These Others are beings who "do not fit the norms of the 'human' [and] are deemed monstrous and consigned to the categories of 'freaks,' non-humans, or the inhuman."[2] Animal studies highlights how "the animal as a life form is the constant other to the human."[3] Similarly, Margrit Shildrick and other feminist scholars have noted that female bodies are often Othered and culturally seen as "monstrous." Shildrick notes that society often tightly associates women/women's bodies with nature in the nature/culture dichotomy, and states, "when set against culture as that which is managed and regulated, nature is at best base and unruly—that which must be controlled—and at worst that which is deeply disruptive and uncontrollable."[4] Animals, too, are often associated with nature. While some feminist scholars may be inclined to reject the connection between women and animals in an attempt to disengage from their associations with animality and corporeality, Carol J. Adams argues that feminist theory must engage itself with the treatment of animals; it must offer an analysis of oppression and "a vision of liberation that extends well beyond the liberal equation, incorporating within it other life-forms besides human beings."[5]

In considering how women and animals are Othered and treated like "monsters," this chapter examines Guillermo del Toro's romantic fantasy film *The Shape of Water* (2017). *The Shape of Water* follows Elisa Esposito, a mute White woman working as a cleaner in a secret government laboratory in Baltimore during the Cold War in the 1960s. Elisa has been mute since she was a baby, when she was found by a river with slash scars on her neck. Elisa forms a bond with a humanoid amphibian, named the Asset, that was captured by the laboratory. While del Toro has explained that the Asset is a "river god,"[6] and not necessarily an animal, the Asset certainly displays animalistic qualities (specifically, aquatic amphibian) that cannot be dismissed. As her relationship with and love for the Asset develops, Elisa soon becomes determined to rescue him from the laboratory.

By examining this film, I argue that ethics of care approaches can allow people to learn and unlearn with "monsters"—animalized/dehumanized beings that are treated as monstrous. In other words, one can unlearn oppressive anthropocentric attitudes, and learn how to view these beings as subjects worthy of care. When considering moral decisions, ethics of care emphasizes care and benevolence as virtues and focuses on interpersonal relationships, rather than only focusing on the question of what is just. It is important to note as well that ethics of care originated as a branch of feminist thought. Gilligan's ethics of care was established because she believed women had different emotional responses compared to men, which called for a different ethical system directed toward women. It is also significant that contemporary scholars have demonstrated how ethics of care can also be applied to other beings (human or nonhuman) who are sidelined within a given system. Certain scholars in animal ethics, such as Josephine Donovan and Daniel Engster, approach animal welfare by connecting ethics of care with animal ethics to form an animal ethics of care. Their goal is to try to focus on the personal relationships that humans have with animals and recognize how those relationships call for proper care approaches. Joan Tronto argues, for example, that one ethical element of care (that can be applied to both humans and nonhumans) is competency, which requires a willingness to learn more/ be attentive to the care recipient and their needs.[7]

Similarly, learning with monsters means choosing to not see them as frightening "freaks," but instead as worthy care recipients. Unlearning with monsters means rejecting patriarchal/anthropocentric ideas of what constitutes a monster by instead considering how the oppressiveness of humans is itself a monstrous quality. Edward Chamberlain argues that del Toro's film suggests that some U.S. institutions and figures associated with them are more appropriate examples embodying monstrosity. As he further notes, "Del Toro's film encourages viewers to re-envision what counts as monstrous and thus reconsider what happens when people engage in simplistic, unthinking ideology that often pits humans against monsters from beyond their local realm."[8] Indeed, this ideology also applies to "monsters" that are from our local realm: animals, women, and other human victims of patriarchal oppression. This chapter, then, aims to highlight the ways in which patriarchal human oppressors are themselves monstrous, and to outline the intersectional oppression between animals and Othered humans, and how care approaches can allow people to fight against this oppression. When examining del Toro's film, this chapter will first outline the need for care as demonstrated in the lack of it in the callous and exploitive way that the government and the character of Strickland treats the Asset and the film's female characters, the cooperation from Elisa's non-patriarchal allies that help her save the Asset from the laboratory (such as Giles, her homosexual male neighbor, and Zelda, her Black female coworker), and the compassion and vulnerability in the relationship between Elisa and the Asset.

A NEED FOR CARE

In film, it is more common to present the monstrous animal figure as a true antagonist, a one-dimensional villain figure. For example, this pattern is exemplified in the shark in the films *Jaws* (1975) and *The Meg* (2018), the *Godzilla* franchise, and many kaiju (giant monster on the loose) films. Yet, the storyline in *The Shape of Water* challenges this generic convention; rather than presenting viewers with an uncaring and dangerous nonhuman creature, they are instead given uncaring and dangerous humans. As viewers learn early in the film, the film's main antagonist, Colonel Richard Strickland, and other U.S. agents capture a mysterious creature—which audience members later learn is an Amazonian River god called "the Asset"—from a South American river and bring the Asset to a secret government laboratory facility in Baltimore for further study. While the origin of its name is never explored in the film, the word "asset" suggests property, and a resource with economic value. This meaning of the word emphasizes the lack of care and cruel treatment given to the creature. Since the implication is that the creature is to only be seen in terms of use-value and not as a subject, Strickland can try and justify the way he oppresses him. This oppression imitates the real oppression of many animals, where they are seen as an object and not as a sentient individual. Strickland and the U.S. authorities subject the creature to cruel and violent treatment. In a torturous scene, Strickland wields a cattle prod to electrocute the Asset while it has a chain over its neck. This image of a cattle prod being used on the Asset immediately animalizes it, since we can imagine this painful shock being inflicted on animals. While the Asset's physical traits already help paint him as an animal, I use the term "animalizes," here, to indicate that the cattle prod is making him into an animal that humans think they are allowed to exercise control over—even if that form of control is oppressive and uncaring. As the Asset cries out in evident pain, Strickland offers no sympathy: "There you go again. Making that god-awful sound. Is that you crying? Is that you hurting? Huh? Or maybe you're angry? Yeah. Maybe you'd like to get another bite at me."[9] While viewers watching this scene can easily tell that while the Asset may be feeling anger, his cries are also clear cries of pain. It is safe then to assume that it is not that Strickland does not know if the Asset is in pain, it is that he does not *care*. When he asks the Asset if he wants to get "another bite" out of him, he is referring to when the Asset, understandably, bit off two of his fingers when he caught him. Strickland cares more about his pride and his own bodily autonomy than the well-being of the Asset. His pride and sense of governance over his own body are key reasons why he can justify treating the Asset as an Other. As Nayar notes, "Humanity survives by constructing modes of exclusion, and the monster's ontological liminality enables domination, persecution, incarceration/containment, exhibition/display, genocide, displacement and elimination of certain forms of life."[10] Strickland's anger and violence toward the Asset adopts an "us versus them" (or humans versus monsters) mindset that enables him to dominate the Asset and not let himself feel any remorse. Instead of remorse, Strickland exhibits entitlement.

Strickland's behavior, especially when compared to the way he treats the female characters in the film, is not only anthropocentric, but also patriarchal. Indeed, human superiority can easily slip into patriarchal mindsets as well; both belief structures (anthropocentrism and patriarchy) condone domination over women and animals. In a scene where Strickland discusses the Asset with Elisa and Zelda, he speaks to them in a rather patronizing tone: "You may think that thing looks human, stands on two legs, you don't think that's what the Lord looks like, do you?"[11] He then adds that while the Asset may resemble a human like Elisa and Zelda, while looking at Zelda he quickly reconsiders that thought and clarifies it by saying "maybe a little more like me."[12] This statement is not only sexist in how it excludes women from some sort of higher state of being, but it also carries White supremacist beliefs, as he "distanc[es] Zelda from his belief system due to her gender and skin colour."[13] This is only an early example in the film where Strickland is clearly hinting at his personal justifications for mistreatment that are based around ideas of human, male, and White privilege. Chamberlain observes, for example, that toward the midpoint of the film Strickland makes a crude comment toward Eliza that is sexual harassment. Elisa is ordered to clean up a spill in Strickland's office at the laboratory, and Strickland, at this point feeling like Elisa cannot be trusted (because he suspects her relationship with the Asset), tells her "I bet I can make you squawk a little"[14]; this comment "reduces her to the level of an animalized sex object."[15] There is a compelling irony to this statement, especially when considering his expressed disgust toward the cries of the Asset. While Strickland generally prefers the women in the film to remain silent (as exemplified, for example, in a sex scene with his wife at home where he covers her mouth and tells her to keep quiet), he would welcome Elisa's "squawking" if he was the one not only permitting it, but causing it. Elisa runs away from the office before Strickland can do anything to her, but his comment is enough to make her feel unsafe. Strickland's sense of masculinity, then, is one where women are encouraged to only "make noise" if it is in validation of patriarchal desires. The Asset is not encouraged to make noise because it disrupts Strickland's certainly that he is allowed to cause the Asset harm.

What Strickland's treatment of the Asset, Elisa, and Zelda demonstrates is a lack of responsibility. Tronto outlines that responsibility is another ethical element of care; one needs a sense of responsibility in order to care for an individual or care for a situation at hand.[16] Ethically, Strickland should be feeling a sense of responsibility. He captured the Asset and brought it to the government facility, so he should recognize his responsibility to take proper care of it. He also should be attentive to the ways in which he has some responsibility to Elisa and Zelda. Since he is in a higher and more privileged position in that government laboratory (and Elisa and Zelda are women and janitors), he should feel a sense of responsibility to at least ensure that they feel safe in their workplace; these women should not have to worry about misogyny and racism. Yet, as implied before, Strickland does not want to take responsibility. He cannot provide the competency that also comes with being in a position of giving care, because we do not see any willingness on his part to learn about these Othered beings whom he should be treating as care recipients or individuals worthy of care. Instead, Strickland seems to believe that he already knows all there is to know about these two women. As for the Asset, he seeks to exploit him for U.S. advantage in the Space Race competition against the Soviet Union. This is demonstrated when he tries to persuade General Frank Hoyt to vivisect the creature.

Strickland's attempts to have the Asset vivisected are in striking contrast with the reaction of Dr. Robert Hoffstetler—a scientist and secret Russian spy—who pleads to keep the Asset alive. After hearing Strickland suggest vivisecting it to Hoyt, Hoffstetler immediately objects, and upon seeing the Asset faint (from being kept out of water for too long) pleads with the General to hurry and put the Asset back in the tank. This first act alone already helps paint Hoffstetler as possessing more of a caring mindset toward the Asset. His willingness to show care is further exemplified later in the film in a scene where he is arguing with Strickland over the effectiveness of vivisecting the Asset. Hoffstetler explains to Strickland, "I don't want an intricate, beautiful thing destroyed."[17] While the word "thing" could easily objectify the Asset, it is worth also looking past this flawed word choice and considering what Hoffstetler's sentiments mean. For example, how is one to interpret his choice of the word "beautiful"? While the word "beautiful" may suggest a worthiness based on aesthetics or attractiveness, I would argue that by beautiful, Hoffstetler means *wondrous*—especially when paired with the word "intricate." This feeling of wonder that the Asset stirs in people should promote care, not fear or violence. Here, Hoffstetler understands the importance of care by outlining to Strickland the futility of destruction when trying to learn more about others. Care relations cannot be established if the Asset is killed, and thus, one cannot learn more about him. After these tensions and disagreements with Strickland and rest of the authority figures, Hoffstetler further solidifies his role as a caring figure in the film when he aligns himself with Elisa, Zelda, and Giles. In recognizing the monstrosities being inflicted upon the Asset by Strickland and the rest of the authorities, Hoffstetler decides to help Elisa, Zelda, and Giles when they come together to try and save the Asset from being vivisected.

While it may be hard to fully argue that Hoffstetler is a non-patriarchal ally for Elisa, since he is not made an Other by gender, race, or sexuality, it is still important to note that he rejects the common attitudes of the cold and detached male scientist. In her discussion of laboratory animals and scientists, Lynda Birke explains that "objective detachment" is associated with masculinity and, to no surprise, sentimentality and compassion are associated with femininity. While Birke does not imply that only women are capable of empathizing with laboratory animals, she does explain that caring and feelings of connectiveness are stereotypically associated with femininity, and thus regularly devalued in the pursuit of scientific discovery and outweighed by scientific objectivity and detachment.[18] In his insistence on keeping the Asset alive, Hoffstetler willingly demonstrates an effeminized mindset and challenges the film's key patriarchal figures. Because of the Asset's presence,

Hoffstetler unlearns what it means to be a true scientist, and instead argues for the value of care and relationality. Later in the film, as Strickland is torturing him for information (after realizing that he is a spy), Hoffstetler reveals/implies that Elisa and Zelda were the ones to steal the Asset from the lab. However, Hoffstetler's actions until this point allow Elisa, with the aid of Zelda and Giles, to escape with the Asset in a getaway van and bring him to her home to take care of him. It is his conscious choice to be a scientist who cares that ultimately leads to more care being given to the Asset.

NON-PATRIARCHAL ALLIES

One of the characters in the film who comes around to Elisa's side and assists her attempts in trying to save the Asset is Zelda. Zelda first becomes suspicious of Elisa when she catches her coming out of the laboratory, realizing that she was hiding in there while Strickland and the other authority figures were in there with the Asset. At first, Zelda is angry with Elisa, and panics, telling her not to carry out her plan. Zelda, here, is clearly aware of the lack of power she and Elisa have and the trouble they will be in if they are caught. Yet, when Elisa conducts a plan to take the Asset away from the laboratory and hide him, Zelda's initial reluctance turns into assistance. She exercises agency by distributing care instead, even though—as is subtly suggested throughout the film—she is told that she is not allowed to have true agency because she is Black. Zelda helps Elisa (along with the assistance from Hoffstetler and Giles) load the Asset into their getaway van. While the film does not necessarily suggest that Zelda cares about the Asset, she still provides care for him.

In her discussion of ethics of care, Noddings notes that there is a difference between what it means to care for and what it means to care-about. As she explains, "Caring-for describes an encounter or set of encounters characterized by direct attention and response. It requires the establishment of a caring relation, person-to-person contact of some sort. Caring-about expresses some concern but does not guarantee a response to one who needs care."[19] Noddings also recognizes that it is impossible for people to provide care for everyone in the world. Even if someone cares about animals, for example, they may not be in the position to care for them because we are limited by time, resources, and space. Viewers are not necessarily told that Zelda actually cares about the Asset or feels much concern regarding his well-being. However, she still provides care for him. It cannot be overlooked, after all, that some people in standard, paid caregiver positions do not necessarily actually care about their care recipient. Yet, Zelda certainly cares about Elisa; throughout the film, they are presented not only as coworkers, but friends. Zelda clearly knows that Elisa cares about the Asset.

Another one of Elisa's allies who goes through a similar journey is Giles, Elisa's homosexual male neighbor, who does the film's occasional voiceovers. Before viewers meet the Asset, they are first introduced to the friendship between Elisa and Giles, who often enjoy each other's company at Giles house, watching old films. Since Giles is her neighbor and one of the few friends she has, it makes sense that Elisa would go to Giles and ask for his help with freeing the Asset. However, Giles does not initially respond favorably, refusing to agree to her plan since it is breaking the law. He even asks Elisa, "Does this mean when we go to a Chinese restaurant, you want to save every fish in the tank?"[20] Giles's question to Elisa is certainly a valid one; as I previously mentioned, Noddings acknowledges that it is impossible for someone to provide care for everyone. However, in this scenario, Elisa wants to provide care for one being. While some people are not even able to care for one being, Elisa still wants to try, and likely feels that she has an advantage since she works in the facility where the Asset is being kept. Nonetheless, eventually, Giles shuts down the conversation: "There's nothing we can do. What are we, Elisa? You and I? Nothing. What can we do? Nothing."[21] Since Elisa is disabled and Giles is homosexual, they are portrayed as "solitary outsiders" and are both "marked as different by the dominant U.S. culture and society."[22] Much like Zelda, Giles is aware of where they fall on the social hierarchy and seems to accept powerlessness. Much like how the Asset is considered an outsider because of his animality and separation from the human realm, Giles and Zelda are treated as "less than human" because of heteronormative and racial prejudice.

After shutting down the conversation, Giles adds, "And—I am sorry, but it is not even human."[23] With this confession of his true feelings, Giles reveals the ways in which he, too, is conditioned by anthropocentrism. What this statement means is that since the Asset is not human, he is not worthy of all this effort to try and save his life. Elisa, however, does not stand for this excuse. She signs back to him, with the subtitles reading "If we don't do something. . . Neither are we."[24] To Elisa, the idea of being human is closely associated with acting humane—to act this way means to show compassion, benevolence, and/or care. Elisa may feel that if they carry on with apathy, they are instead just condoning the violence toward the Asset.

Ironically, while Giles tells Elisa that the Asset is "not even human," very soon after this scene he meets a human being who does not, in fact, act with humane qualities. When eating at a diner that he frequently goes to, Giles observes racial discrimination and experiences homophobic discrimination from the server with whom he is chatting. Giles misinterprets the server's act of giving him free pie and his statement that part of his job is getting to know people. When Giles puts his hand on the server's and tells him "I would like—to know you. Better,"[25] the once friendly server quickly turns hostile and tells him he got the wrong idea. Immediately after, a Black family enters the diner, and the server becomes angrier and denies them entry. The server then turns to Giles and tells him, "You should leave too. And don't come back. This is a family restaurant."[26] With Giles's shocked and hurt facial reaction, it is clear that this statement makes him remember that he is low on the social hierarchy that prioritizes heteronormativity—and, essentially, excluded from care.

Noddings's explanation of "caring-about" aligns with Adams and Donovan's assertion that animal care ethics requires attention: "Attention to the individual suffering animal but also . . . attention to the political and economic systems that cause the suffering."[27] Giles may not have the same level of concern (or perhaps any) toward the suffering of the Asset as compared to Elisa, but he certainly gives attention to the political and economic systems that cause the suffering because she, too, is oppressed by these systems. Even though Giles was initially reluctant to help Elisa and go against the U.S. law, his experience in the diner motivates him to look closely at the political systems that cause suffering and strive to fight against injustice and oppression. In the following scene, he returns to Elisa and tells her "I have . . . no one else. You are the only person that I can talk to."[28] While in the previous scene in the diner Giles tells the server that his neighbor (Elisa) is "not much of a conversationalist,"[29] here, Giles recognizes that human speech is not an absolute criterion for proper or desirable communication. The server, after all, used human language to exercise hateful and discriminatory thoughts. Even though Elisa can only communicate through sign language, their relationship is still valid because they care for each other and try to listen to each other's needs. He tells Elisa, "Whatever this thing is . . . you need it. So, just tell me what to do."[30] Giles then becomes a key assistant in helping Elisa with her getaway van plan. He enters the facility in a van, posing as a driver for a laundry service, and helps Elisa drive the Asset away to safety.

ELISA AND THE ASSET'S RELATIONSHIP

From as early as the opening scene, as Giles introduces Elisa's story, viewers already get an idea that *The Shape of Water* is going to be a film advocating for interconnectedness and multispecies relationality. In this opening scene, a watery world with fish swimming by is placed within Elisa's apartment, an image that "links the underwater world with that of humanity."[31] As Chamberlain observes, the mixing of the underwater world with the human world highlights "the relational nature and togetherness that arises [sic] between ostensibly distinct cultural identities."[32]

Indeed, viewers get a glimpse of this relational nature and togetherness in one of the earliest scenes between Elisa and the Asset. In this scene, Elisa lets the Asset know, in the only way she can in that moment, that she does not mean to bring it harm. As she eats her lunch beside the pool in the laboratory, the Asset slowly swims up and approaches her. After staring at each other for a while, Elisa offers him an egg. In fear, the Asset hisses, expanding his gills. Realizing that the considerate move is to act slowly, Elisa carefully places the egg on the edge of the pool, offering it to him and signing "egg." This moment foreshadows the progression of their relationship. After this encounter, Elisa makes a habit of sneaking into the laboratory, bringing the Asset eggs, and even begins to teach him sign language. The Asset's interest in Elisa's gift of eggs draws further attention to his lizard-like and reptilian characteristics. Furthermore, eggs can be seen as a symbol for reproduction/ fertility. Since the gifting of eggs clearly helps to establish a bond between Elisa and the Asset, the eggs help reveal the intimacy and care that shapes their bond. On the one hand, the eggs can be seen as a symbol that foreshadows their later sexual—and consensual—intimacy, as depicted when Elisa and the Asset are in the bathroom while it is filling up with water, a harmonious scene that starkly contrasts with Strickland's aggressive sex with his wife. On the other hand, the eggs can also symbolize Elisa's acceptance of the Asset. While literal reproduction never occurs in the film, the egg can symbolize Elisa's acceptance of a world where more creatures, like him, are allowed to exist and flourish, because she does not restrict her actions of care and love only to humans.

One important component that contributes to Elisa's ability to easily bond with the Asset is her recognition of the ways in which they are the same. In the conversation with Giles when she tries to convince him to help her free the Asset, Elisa signs her frustration when Giles calls the Asset a "thing" and a "freak": as she signs, "What am I? I move my mouth—like him—and I make no sound—like him. What does that make me?"[33] Elisa's recognition that she and the Asset are both social outsiders, devalued and/or dehumanized, allows her to feel empathy for the Asset and want to help him. Furthermore, she appreciates the fact that the Asset accepts her for who she is: as she signs, "The way he looks at me. He doesn't know what I lack . . . Or how I am incomplete. He just sees me for what I am. As I am. And he is happy to see me, every time."[34] Likewise, even though Elisa draws attention to the ways in which they are the same, she also pays close attention to the ways in which they are different.

As the film progresses, the relationship between Elisa and the Asset becomes romantic. Depictions of romance between women and nonhuman Others, or monsters, is often a motif in fairy tales and the fantasy genre. The premise of *Beauty and the Beast*, for example (including the original eighteenth-century fairy tale, the 1991 animated Disney film, and 2017 musical film) includes this type of romance. Yet, each version of the story remains consistent; Belle may be attracted to the Beast's personality, but she cannot fully love him without physical attraction—which would be much easier if he were human. Belle only gets her happy ending (true love) when she kisses the beast out of fear of him dying, and he turns into a handsome prince. *The Shape of Water*, however, subverts this trope. Elisa never tries to deny her bond or attraction to the Asset. Even though neither of them can speak, they bond over sign language, food, music, and sexual intimacy. Rather than trying to change the "monster," Elisa tries to preserve and protect him. On a smaller scale, viewers see her attempts when she brings him to her apartment and immediately places him in a bathtub full of water and salt, considering his physical welfare and the fact that both their needs will differ in some respects. On a grander scale, she continuously tries to prevent him from being killed.

As Elisa hides the Asset in her apartment, she aims to live with him in "respectful co-existence," a term that Raymond Corby and Annette Lanjouw use to refer to "the ability to share resources and space, as well as to respect each other's needs and self."[35] They also explain that *respectful coexistence* refers to co-flourishing in shared environments. To flourish means to prosper, to develop, or to live out one's natural capabilities. Even though Elisa treats the Asset with care while he is in her home, the ethical question over whether this wild animal can sufficiently flourish while indoors is a difficult one. Elisa seems aware of this too, since she plans to release the Asset into a nearby canal which will provide access to the ocean. Even though Elisa will surely miss the Asset, she knows that taking proper care of the Asset means allowing him to live his best life.

Near the film's end, Elisa is forced to release the Asset when Zelda warns her that Strickland found out that she has him. At the canal, as Elisa and Giles are saying goodbye to the Asset, Strickland arrives and shoots both the Asset and Elisa. The Asset (who has been shown throughout the film possessing healing abilities) heals himself and kills Strickland by slashing his throat. The Asset then jumps into the canal with Elisa in his arms. Chamberlain notes that in the opening voiceover when Giles refers to Elisa as a "princess without voice,"[36] she is a princess who is different but "still resembles the archetype of 'damsel in distress,' who often is scripted as needing a heterosexual white man to save her from a villain or peril."[37] As he further notes, del Toro challenges this common trope by making Elisa the heroine and having her save not a White male hero, but a nonhuman amphibian male creature. Yet, more than this, it is important to also note that the Asset saves her too. Once they are underwater, the Asset applies his healing ability to the scars on Elisa's neck. As they open to reveal gills like his, Elisa jolts back to life. While one may argue that Elisa had to change in order to live, this argument also comes close to suggesting that turning animal-like is a degradation. Moreover, viewers should remember that Elisa was found by a river as a baby. While we do not know the specifics as to what happened to Elisa, this connection with the water can suggest that she has always encompassed a world that is more than human. Nonetheless, more important is the fact that the Asset saves her life. This action indicates that care can be a mutual activity and is not necessarily exclusively a human ability. Ultimately, Elisa and the Asset care about and care for each other.

TOWARD A CONCLUSION: CAREFUL STORYTELLING, CAREFUL LEARNING

It is perhaps ironic, but still fitting, that in this conclusion we begin by looking at a line Giles delivers as a voiceover at the film's beginning: he tells the viewers that he is going to deliver the truth of "the tale of love and loss and the monster that tried to destroy it all."[38] Viewers who start watching *The Shape of Water* already knowing the film's premise can assume that the "monster" is not the Asset. From the onset, the film's storytelling wants to rethink the idea of "monsters." As the film progresses, it consistently tries to distance the Asset from the antagonist/monster role. For example, an important cinematography decision is not directly showing the viewers the Asset biting off two of Strickland's fingers. While we learn about this happening to Strickland early in the film, this event happens off-camera. By denying viewers this violent image, the storytelling takes care of the Asset's character. By the end of the film, when the Asset slices Strickland's throat, Strickland has already been established as the antagonist and the film's rightful monster figure because of his discriminatory mindset. In fact, his monstrous nature is continually established not only by Strickland's inhumane actions, but by the constant reminders and images throughout the film of his rotting fingers and his bloodied bandages. While Strickland sees himself as a figure of superiority throughout the film and epitomizes human exceptionalism, the film puts in an extra effort to challenge this human exceptionalism by suggesting that the Asset, this animalized figure, may actually be a god. Despite Strickland suggesting that the Asset is lesser than humans and unworthy of the same level of care and respect because he was not "created in the lord's image," he also reveals to Hoyt some details regarding the backstory of the Asset: he explains that "the natives in the Amazon worshipped it like a god."[39] Alluding to the Judeo-Christian religious tradition, the Asset performs little miracles throughout the film, such as touching Giles's balding head, resulting in Giles having new hair the next day; he also, as we know, performs bigger miracles, like healing himself and healing Elisa at the film's end. These acts portray the Asset as a caring figure, who exercises a desire to help the people who also help him. Even though he has great capacities that Strickland does not have, the Asset is never portrayed as a character like Strickland who asserts his own self-entitlement and self-importance.

Nonetheless, the Asset helps convey important messages throughout the film. The human characters, as well as the film's viewers, can learn from the Asset. They learn how harmful discriminatory practices can be and become, and their attention is drawn to a need for caring relations instead. His bond with Elisa and his relationality with Elisa's allies allow viewers to understand how oppression is intersectional in a patriarchal society, and how care can allow people to fight against oppression. The senselessness of animal cruelty is certainly a theme in del Toro's film, and it is coupled with the theme of unjust and harmful discrimination against women and other human beings whom the patriarchy sees as "others" and the need to challenge these forms of discrimination. As we recall, Zelda and Giles were initially reluctant to help Elisa free the Asset from the laboratory. It would have been understandable if Elisa, being in a similar low position as Zelda and Giles, was also initially hesitant. Yet, the loving bond between her and the Asset makes her realize that she must do something to save him, and that there is a version of herself that is not silenced and overpowered by oppression.

As Shildrick notes, "Monsters signify . . . the otherness of possible worlds, or possible versions of ourselves, not yet realized."[40] I would argue that this outlook can also apply to animals. Mary Midgley writes, "'Our animal nature' exists already as a Trojan horse within the human gates."[41] It may be up to an individual, however, to determine how they view and/or exhibit their animality. On the one hand, if the term "animal" is to be understood as applicable to humans if they act inhumanely and without any moral or ethical sensibilities, then Strickland only offers that version of himself. On the other hand, if we use the term to mean something "benign and inclusive of humanity,"[42] and perhaps something bodily/emotional versus the male tradition of rationale and intellect, Elisa offers this version of herself. The film's end, which reveals Elisa's gills (aligning her with the animal world) and the moment when she and the Asset embrace and kiss, serves as a reminder of the importance of care in shaping our relations with others, and in shaping the type of world we want and the version of ourselves that we want to be.

NOTES

1. Randy Malamud, "Animals on Film: The Ethics of the Human Gaze." *Georgia State University,* https://english.gsu.edu/files/2015/06/Spring.pdf, 2015. 7.

2. Pramod Nayar. *Posthumanism* (Cambridge: Polity Press, 2014), 111.

3. Nayar, *Posthumanism,* 111.

4. Margarit Shildrick. *Embodying the Monster: Encounters with the Vulnerable Self* (Thousand Oaks: SAGE Publications Ltd., 2002), 11.

5. Carol J. Adams. *Animals and Women: Feminist Theoretical Explorations* (North Carolina: Duke University Press, 1995), 3.

6. Sam Briger. "Director Guillermo Del Toro Says 'Shape of Water' Centers on 'Love Beyond Words.'" *NPR* (5 Dec. 2017).

7. Joan Tronto. *Moral Boundaries: A Political Argument for an Ethic of Care* (Oxfordshire: Routledge, 1993), 134.

8. Edward Chamberlain. "Rethinking the Monstrous: Gender, Otherness, and Space in the Cinematic Storytelling of *Arrival* and *The Shape of Water*." *CLCWeb: Comparative Literature and Culture* 21, no. 7 (2019): 3.

9. del Toro, *The Shape of Water*, 00:40:22.

10. Nayar, *Posthumanism*, 116.

11. del Toro, *The Shape of Water*, 00:28:48.

12. del Toro, *The Shape of Water*, 00:29:11.

13. Chamberlain, 7.

14. del Toro, *The Shape of Water*, 00:58:46.

15. del Toro, *The Shape of Water*, 00:58:46.

16. Tronto, *Moral Boundaries*, 134.

17. del Toro, *The Shape of Water*, 01:00:31.

18. Lynda Birke. "Into the Laboratory." In *The Animals Reader: The Essential Classic and Contemporary Writings*, ed. Linda Kalof and Amy Fitzgerald (Oxford: Berg Publishers, 2007). 326.

19. Nel Noddings. *Caring: A Relational Approach to Ethics and Moral Education* (Berkeley: University of California Press, 1986), xiv.

20. del Toro, *The Shape of Water*, 00:45:25.

21. del Toro, *The Shape of Water*, 00:47:54.

22. Chamberlain, 2.

23. del Toro, *The Shape of Water*, 00:48:04.

24. del Toro, *The Shape of Water*, 00:48:13.

25. del Toro, *The Shape of Water*, 00:50:13.

26. del Toro, *The Shape of Water*, 00:50:37.

27. Carol J. Adams, and Josephine Donovan. "Introduction." In *The Feminist Care Tradition in Animal Ethics*, ed. Carol J. Adams and Josephine Donovan (New York City: Columbia University Press, 2007), 3.

28. del Toro, *The Shape of Water*, 00:51:06.

29. del Toro, *The Shape of Water*, 00:49:59.

30. del Toro, *The Shape of Water*, 00:51:10.

31. del Toro, *The Shape of Water*, 00:51:10.

32. del Toro, *The Shape of Water*, 00:51:10.

33. del Toro, *The Shape of Water*, 00:45:45.

34. del Toro, *The Shape of Water*, 00:46:42.

35. Raymond Corbey and Annette Lanjouw. *The Politics of Species* (Cambridge: Cambridge University Press, 2013), 2.

36. del Toro, *The Shape of Water*, 00:02:32.

37. Chamberlain, 4.
38. del Toro, *The Shape of Water*, 00:02:40.
39. del Toro, *The Shape of Water*, 00:41:47.
40. Shildrick, *Embodying the Monster*, 8.
41. Mary Midgley. "Beasts, Brutes, and Monsters." In *What is an Animal?* ed. Tim Ingold (Oxfordshire: Routledge, 1994), 35.
42. Tim Ingold. "Introduction." In *What is an Animal?* (Oxfordshire: Routledge, 1994), 4.

BIBLIOGRAPHY

Adams, Carol J. *Animals and Women: Feminist Theoretical Explorations.* Durham, NC: Duke University Press, 1995.
Adams, Carol J., and Josephine Donovan. "Introduction." In *The Feminist Care Tradition in Animal Ethics*, edited by Carol J. Adams and Josephine Donovan. New York City: Columbia University Press, 2007, 1–20.
Birke, Lynda. "Into the Laboratory." In *The Animals Reader: The Essential Classic and Contemporary Writings*, edited by Linda Kalof and Amy Fitzgerald. Oxford: Berg Publishers, 2007, 323–335.
Briger, Sam. "Director Guillermo Del Toro Says 'Shape Of Water' Centers on 'Love Beyond Words'." *NPR*, 5 December 2017. https://www.npr.org/2017/12/05/568561089/director-guillermo-del-toro-says-shape-of-water-centers-on-love-beyond-words.
Chamberlain, Edward. "Rethinking the Monstrous: Gender, Otherness, and Space in the Cinematic Storytelling of *Arrival* and *The Shape of Water*." *CLCWeb: Comparative Literature and Culture* 21, no. 7 (2019): 1–11.
Corbey, Raymond, and Annette Lanjouw. *The Politics of Species.* Cambridge: Cambridge University Press, 2013.
del Toro, Guillermo, dir. *The Shape of Water.* Fox Searchlight Pictures. Disney Plus, 2017.
Ingold, Tim. "Introduction." In *What is an Animal?* Oxfordshire: Routledge, 1994, 1–16.
Malamud, Randy. "Animals on Film: The Ethics of the Human Gaze." *Georgia State University.* https://english.gsu.edu/files/2015/06/Spring.pdf, 2015, 1–26.
Midgley, Mary. "Beasts, Brutes, and Monsters." In *What is an Animal?*, edited by Tim Ingold. Oxfordshire: Routledge, 1994, 35–46.
Nayar, Pramod. *Posthumanism.* Cambridge: Polity Press, 2014.
Noddings, Nel. *Caring: A Relational Approach to Ethics and Moral Education.* Berkeley, CA: University of California Press, 1986.
Shildrick, Margarit. *Embodying the Monster: Encounters With the Vulnerable Self.* Thousand Oaks: SAGE Publications Ltd., 2002.
Tronto, Joan. *Moral Boundaries: A Political Argument for an Ethic of Care.* Oxfordshire: Routledge, 1993.

Index

21st Century Fox, 64
101 Dalmations, 40

Adams, Douglas, 17
Adams, Richard, 119, 124
Adlon, Pamela, 160
The Adventures of Rin Tin Tin, 73–74
Aitaki, Georgia, 155–72
Aladdin, 64
Alien, 106
aliens, 4, 7, 21, 36, 42–43, 106, 110, 135–52
Amazon Prime, 64
Amelie, 40
animation, 2, 5–8, 33–69, 119, 128, 136, 141, 155, 158–61, 163–64, 168, 173–74, 177, 180, 187, 212
anime, 2, 7–8, 174, 192, 198
anthropomorphism, 1–2, 4, 7–8, 14–15, 23, 38, 43–44, 49, 61–62, 74, 98, 104–5, 123–24, 129, 155, 158–60, 164, 187–88, 191–92, 198, 204, 210
antisemitic/semitism, 8, 187–88, 191–92, 198, 204–6, 210
Anubis, 99
Aphrodite (goddess), 128
Aristocats, 64
Aristotle, 157, 187
Avatar: The Last Airbender, 187
The Avengers, 39, 145–47

Babylon 5, 13
BAFTA awards, 49
Ballard, Bob, 14
Bambi, 59
Bamford, Maria, 160, 165
Barker, Ronnie, 38
Batman, 36
Bats, 39, 43. *See also* vampires
Bay, Jessica, 135–52
BBC, 23, 43–44, 49, 99
Beacham, Stephanie, 18–20
bears, 2, 37, 146, 173, 179
A Beautiful Mind, 40
Beauty and the Beast, 212
Bedford, John, 14
Beeler, Karin, 1–9, 73–92
Beeler, Stan, 1–9
Beethoven, 74
Belle, 174
Benji, 74
Betty, 168
Big Mouth, 7, 155–72
The Bionic Woman, 102
birds, 1, 34, 39–47, 49, 62, 66, 123, 125, 184
The Birds, 123, 125
bisexual, 158, 163
Black Widow, 64
Blade: Trinity, 99
Blanc, Mel, 44

Bodin, Jean, Cardinal, 193
The Boy and the Beast, 3, 173–84
Bram Stoker's Dracula, 34, 99
Brandis, Jonathan, 14
The Breed, 101, 103
Brer Rabbit, 129
Brolin, Josh, 141
Browning, Todd, 60
Buddhism, 178–79, 182, 192
Buffy the Vampire Slayer, 41
bugs, 160
Bugs Bunny, 44, 128
Bunny the Killer Thing, 120, 125–30
Burger, Alissa, 13–29
Burton, Tim, 63, 65–66

Campbell, Joseph, 138–39
Canal, Studio, 159
cats, felines, kitties, ix, 7, 38, 64, 156, 160, 164–65, 189, 194
Cerberus, 99
Chaosium, 37
Chaplin, Charlie, 60
Charlemagne, 192
A Christmas Carol, 46
The Circus, 60
cisheteronormative, 163
Cleese, John, 43
Colossal Pictures/MTV, 40–41
comedy, 2, 5, 13–53, 159–60
Cooper, Bradley, 135
Cosgrove, Brian, 38
Cosgrove Hall Films, 33, 38–40
Count Duckula, 33–53
coyotes, 35, 121–22
Crow, Jim, 62
crows, 34, 46, 61–64
Cruella, 64
Cumberbatch, Benedict, 140

Daffy Duck, 36, 43–44
Damian, Peter, 193
Danger Man, 38–39
Danger Mouse, 38–41, 44, 46
Darwinism, 126

Dawn of the Dead, 107
del Toro, Guillermo, 7–8, 203–17
demons, demonic, 105, 139, 178, 188, 190, 194
Depp, Johnny, 35
Desperate Dan, 48
devils, 20, 128, 163, 188–89, 191
DeVito, Danny, 65
Diesel, Vin, 135
disability, disabled, 2–6, 8, 57–69, 110, 203
Disney. *See Aladdin*; *Aristocats*; *Bambi*; *Beauty and the Beast*; *Black Widow*; *Cruella*; *Donald Duck*; *Dumbo*; *Fantasia*; *Frozen*; *Guardians of the Galaxy*; *The Hunchback of Notre Dame*; *The Jungle Book*; *Jungle Cruise*; *The Lady and the Tramp*; *The Lion King*; *Maleficent*; *Mistress of Evil*; *Mulan*; *Old Yeller*; *Peter Pan*; *Pinocchio*; *Raya and the Last Dragon*; *Swiss Family Robinson*
Disney, Walt, 59, 64
dogs, ix, 2, 6, 73–92, 97–115, 129, 184, 187, 190
A Dog's Purpose, 74
Dog Soldiers, 104, 106–7
dolphins, 5, 13–29
Don't Breathe, 2, 103, 108–9
Donald Duck, 36–37, 43
Donnie Darko, 6, 120, 126–29
Downey, Robert Jr., 140
Doyle, John, 40
Dr. Strange, 140
Dr. Van Goosewing, 40, 42–43, 46–49
Dracula, 34, 40, 99
Dracula's Dog/Zoltan, 99
Dragon Pass, 37
dragons, 37, 64
Dreamcatcher, 102
ducks, 33–53
Dumbo, 6, 37–69

East Los High, 168
ecocriticism, 119–20, 130

eco-horror, 103, 107, 120–21
ecology/ecosystems, 6–7, 13, 18, 47–48, 119–22, 125, 128
ecophobia, 121
ecoterrorists, 21
Edebiri, Ayo, 158
elephants. *See* Dumbo
Engels, Robert, 24
Eon Flux, 40–41
esperpento (theatrical genre), 187–200
eudaimonic entertainment, 156–60, 167
Euphoria, 168
Eyes Without a Face, 106

fairy tales, 49, 99, 107, 139, 144, 212
Fantasia, 59
fantasy, 2–8, 37, 39, 48, 120, 139, 147, 160, 204, 212
Farrell, Colin, 65
Fawlty Towers, 43
Flacket, Jennifer, 155
fleas, 147
Fleming, Ian, 38
Flipper, 16–17
folklore, 98–100, 128
Footloose, 137
foxes, 38, 121
FR3, 159
Franklin, Don, 28
Freaks, 60
Freud, Sigmund, 24, 103
frogs/toads, 38, 40, 156, 160, 166
Frozen, 67
Frye, Northrop, 135, 138–40, 143–44
Fuller, Samuel, 6, 73, 75–76, 78–81, 88

Galifianakis, Zach, 160, 166
Game of Thrones, 97, 101, 106
Gary, Romain, 73
geese, 34, 40, 42–43, 46–49
Genera+ion, 168
genocide, 141, 206
Gerber, Steve, 36
ghosts, 98–99, 160, 178
Gibson, Jessica, 57–69

Ginger Snaps, 106
goats, 194–95, 197
goblins, 128, 178
Godzilla, 205
Goethe, 48
Gojyō shusse, 173, 177–79, 182
Goldberg, Andrew, 155
Goodman, Brandon Kyle, 160
The Good Place, 187
Gothic/ecoGothic, 46, 98, 120–21, 123, 128
Greyfriars Bobby, 98
Groening, Matt, 35
Guardians of the Galaxy, 3, 7, 135–52; Avengers, 137, 140, 142–43, 145–47
Gunn, James, 147
Gunn, Sean, 142

Hachiko, 74, 98
Halloween, 102
Hamlet, in *Count Duckula*, 41
Happy Tree Friends, 162
HBO, 168
Hel (Norse), 99
heterogeneous, 105, 136, 163, 211
The Hills Have Eyes, 97, 102, 107
Hipple, David, 33–53
Hitchcock, Alfred, 123
Hitchhiker's Guiide to the Galaxy, 17
Hobbes, Thomas, 103
Holland, Tom, 140
homosexual, 105, 158, 205, 210
horror, 2–7, 76, 80, 84, 97–115, 119–21, 123, 125, 129–30, 155–72, 196
Hosada, Mamoru, 7, 173–86
Hound of Dracula, 99
Howard, a New Breed of Hero, 37
Howard the Duck, 35–38, 43
Hugo, Victor, 191
Hulu, 168
The Hunchback of Notre Dame, 67
Huyck, Willard, 37

I am Legend, 97, 102, 108
Il était une fois... la vie, 159

Inland Empire, 129–30
insects. *See* bugs; fleas; mosquitoes
Iron Man, 140
Izumi, Katsuya, 2, 7, 173–86

James Bond, 38
Jason, David, 38, 44
Jaws, 205
Jeunet, Pierre, 40
Jews/Jewish, 188, 190. *See also* antisemitic/semitism
Journey to the West, 2, 177–79, 182
Judge Dredd, 36–37
The Jungle Book, 64
Jungle Cruise, 64

Keaton, Michael, 66
King, Stephen, 75
King Arthur, 119
Kipo and the Age of Wonderbeasts, 2, 8, 187–200
Klein, Jesse, 158
Klementieff, Pom, 147
Kroll, Nick, 155, 158–59
Kyenge, Cecile, 190

The Lady and the Tramp, 64
Lassie, Lassie Come Home, 73–74, 102
The Last of Us, 109
Laybourne, Geraldine, 38–39, 42
leopards, 2, 188, 194, 196
Levin, Mark, 155
Life, 159
The Lion King, 64
lions, 64, 175, 189
Lord of the Rings, 142–43
Lost Boys, 102
Love at First Bite, 40
The Lovebugs, 160
Lynch, David, 6, 120, 129–30

Maleficent, 64
Man's Best Friend, 103
mandrills, 101, 191–93, 197
Mantzoukas, Jason, 158

Marley and Me, 74
Marvel comics, Marvel Cinematic Universe, 36–37, 64, 146
McGoohan, Patrick, 38
The Meg, 205
Melville, Herman, 173–75, 177, 180
Meyerik, Val, 36
mice. *See Danger Mouse*; *Timothy Q. Mouse*
Miller, Christopher Jones, 24
minority groups, 83–86, 89
Mistress of Evil, 64
Miyazaki, Hayao, 173, 180
Mizoguchi, Kenji, 176
Moby-Dick, The Whale, 173–75, 177
monkeys/apes, 8, 178–79, 189–94, 196
Monomyth, 138–39
monsters, 6–8, 61, 75, 77, 79–80, 87, 89, 97–155, 158–72, 178, 182–83, 193, 199, 203–17
Monsters, Inc., 7, 162
Monty Python and the Holy Grail, 119
Mork and Mindy, 42
mosquitoes, 2, 7, 156, 160, 164–66
Mulan, 64
Mulaney, John, 158
Mundruczó, Kornél, 6, 73, 81–83, 85–89
My Dog Skip, 74
mythology/myths, 37, 77, 98–99, 110–11, 124, 135, 138–44, 146–47, 187–88, 194

Nakajima, Atsushi, 173, 177
National Geographic, 64
Netflix, 7, 155, 160, 167–68, 198
Nickelodean, 33, 38–39
Night of the Lepus, 119–23, 125
Night of the Living Dead, 125

Obama, Barack and Michelle, 190
Old Yeller, 74–75, 80
Once Upon a Time, 159
Open All Hours, 38
orangutan, 23

Osborn, Jonathan, 135–52
owls, 130
Ozu, Yasujirō, 176

Pace, Lee, 141
The Pack, 103
Palmer, Keke, 160
Paramount Pictures, 75
Paranormal Activity, 2, 102
penguins, 34, 44, 47
PETA: People for the Ethical Treatment of Animals, 63, 66
Peter Pan, 64, 140–41
phantoms, 47, 99, 103, 110, 178
pigs, 2, 38, 44, 178–79
Pinder, M.K., 119–34
Pinocchio, 59
Pixar, 64
platypus, 43, 48
Poltergeist, 106–7
Popeye, 48
Porky Pig, 38, 44
Pratt, Chris, 135
Pugh, Catherine, 97–115

Rabbits, 5, 120, 129–30
rabbits, bunnies, 28, 41, 43–44, 77, 119–30, 184
raccoons, 3, 135–36, 141–43
race/racism, 3–6, 8, 62, 73–81, 83, 85, 88–89, 110, 121, 187–98, 203, 207–8, 210
Raimi, Ted, 24
Rannells, Andrew, 158
Raya and the Last Dragon, 64
Rear Window, 106
Resident Evil, 97, 101, 103
Rin Tin Tin, 73–74
Rolufs, Heather, 73–92
Romance Mythos, 135, 138–40, 143, 146
Rooker, Michael, 142
Rudolph, Maya, 159
Run, Joe, Run, 102
Runequest, 37
Russell, Kurt, 142

Sanchez, Marco, 24
Scheider, Roy, 14
science fiction, 2–7, 13–14, 17–18, 26, 38, 44–45, 120, 122, 138
seaQuest DSV, 13–29
Secret Window, 106
semitic. *See* antisemitic/semitism
sex. *See* bisexual; cisheteronormative; heterogeneous; homosexual; *Sex Education*; sexism; sexuality/gender; transgender
Sex Education, 168
sexism, 75
sexuality/gender, 7, 62, 105, 110, 155–56, 158–63, 168, 190–94, 196–97, 200, 203, 207–8, 212–13
The Shape of Water, 3, 7–8, 203–17
Shatner, William, 14
Sheppard, Sumor Ziva, 187–200
Signs, 102
The Silence of the Lambs, 105
The Simpsons, 35
Slate, Jenny, 158
Smart, Jean, 160
Sousa, Monica, 203–17
Spider-Man, 140
Spielberg, Steven, 14
Spirited Away, 173, 180
Stafford, Greg, 37
Stargate, 13
Star Trek, 13
Star Wars, 64
Stevens, Cat, 146
Stoker, Bram, 99
Storks, 59
Swiss Family Robinson, 64

Tarzan, 43, 46
Thames Television, ITV, 33
Thunderbirds, 45
Timothy Q. Mouse, 61–62
Torquemada, 189, 191, 193
transgender, 158, 165
turkeys, 44
Twin Peaks, 130

vampires. *See Buffy the Vampire Slayer*; *Count Duckula*; *Dracula*; *Dracula's Dog/Zoltan*; *I am Legend*; *Love at first bite*; *Vampire Vacation*
Vampire Vacation, 45
Vietnam War, 24
vultures, 43–44, 47

Wacky Races, 42
The Walking Dead, 97, 108
Warner Brothers, 36
Watership Down, 119–21, 123–25, 127, 129
Wells, H.G., 126
werewolves, 103–4, 107
whales, 173–75, 177, 185

Where the North Begins, 74
White Bear and Red Moon, 37
White Dog, 73–92, 103
White God, 6, 73–92
Wilderness, 97, 102–3
Wile E. Coyote, 35
Willo of the Wisp, 49
witches, 49, 128, 194–95, 197
Wolf Children, 7, 173–74, 176, 181, 183–85
wolves, 7, 99, 102–4, 107, 109, 173–74, 176, 181, 183–85, 188, 195
worms, 160
Wu, Cheng'en, 173, 177

zombies, 98, 104, 108, 125
Zoo, 101, 103

About the Contributors

Georgia Aitaki is senior lecturer in Media and Communication Studies and member of the Centre of Geomedia Studies at Karlstad University, Sweden. Her current research interests focus on critical approaches to television and popular culture and, specifically, questions of inclusions/exclusions, (un) ethical spectatorship, and compassion culture. Her work has appeared in journals such as *VIEW: Journal of European Television History and Culture, Media, Culture and Society, Social Semiotics, Screen,* and in a number of anthologies.

Jessica Bay is a PhD candidate in the Joint Communication & Culture program at York and Toronto Metropolitan Universities. She has previously completed an MA thesis in Popular Culture at Brock University on blockbuster sequels and an MA thesis in English at the University of Lethbridge on fanfiction and the genre of urban fantasy. Jessica was recently published in *The Journal of Fandom Studies*: "Corporate Fandom: Recreating Media Fans as a Public," and her work can also be found in *Flow, On Access,* and the *National Post*. Her dissertation research examines the use of fan practices in marketing strategies for the screen industries with a particular focus on American franchises.

Karin Beeler is a professor in the English Department at the University of Northern British Columbia, Canada. Her research focuses on film and television studies, comparative literary studies and animal studies, particularly representations of animals in literature, film, and television. She is the author of *Seers, Witches and Psychics on Screen: An Analysis of Women Visionary Characters in Recent Television and Film* (2008) and *Tattoos, Desire and Violence: Marks of Resistance in Literature, Film and Television* (2006), and co-editor of *Children's Film in the Digital Age* (2014) and co-editor of *Investigating Charmed: The Magic Power of TV* (2007). She has recently co-authored (with Stan Beeler) and published "Going Digital in a Small City Hub: Community Theater and Dog Performance Events During Lockdown" in *Creative Resilience and Covid-19* (eds. Irene Gammel and Jason Wang, 2022). She has participated with her dogs in a variety of canine sports such as scentwork, rally obedience, parkour, draft work, water rescue work, and conformation.

Stan Beeler is professor emeritus of English at the University of Northern British Columbia, Canada. His research focuses on popular culture, film, and television studies, and the application of technology to research and teaching in the humanities. He is the author of *Dance, Drugs and Escape: The Club Scene in Literature, Film and Television Since the Late 1980s* (2007) and co-editor of *Children's Film in the Digital Age* (2014), *Investigating Charmed: The Magic Power of TV* (2007), and *Reading Stargate SG-1* (2006). He recently co-authored (with Karin Beeler) and published "Going Digital in a Small City Hub: Community Theater and Dog Performance Events During Lockdown" in *Creative Resilience and Covid-19* (eds. Irene Gammel and Jason Wang, 2022).

Alissa Burger is an associate professor of English and director of Student Success at Culver-Stockton College. She teaches courses in research, writing, and literature, specializing in gender, horror, and the Gothic. She is the author of *The Quest for the Dark Tower: Genre and Interconnection in the Stephen King Series* (2021), *Teaching Stephen King: Horror, The Supernatural, and New Approaches to Literature* (2016), and *The Wizard of Oz as American Myth: A Critical Study of Six Versions of the Story, 1900–2007* (2012).

Jessica Gibson is a PhD student at the Centre for Research on Education and Social Justice in the Department of Education at the University of York in England. Her research looks at at the representation of disability in Disney animated films, and she is currently writing up her thesis. Her research interests include Disney, popular culture, theme parks, disability studies, representation, equality, education, and higher education studies. Alongside her PhD, she has worked as a research assistant evaluating students' learning gain in University volunteering projects.

David Hipple is a freelance researcher and author. Following a first degree in English, then MAs in Education and History, he earned a PhD studying the history and criticism of "fantastic narratives." More recent studies also led to a BSc in Systems, Philosophy, and other analytical methods. David publishes on a range of topics mainly concerning the cultural uses of unreal worlds to explore real human experience. A recent article discussed perceptions through the twentieth century of artificial intelligence, and its potential impact on the numinous aspect of traditional religious thinking. David resides in Milton Keynes, UK, and is the proprietor of magicspacetime.com

Katsuya Izumi received his PhD in English from the University at Albany. He is currently the head of Japanese section in Language and Culture Studies at Trinity College. He has taught Japanese language at all levels, Japanese literature and films, as well as American literature and English Writing. He has published essays on Japanese American literature, nineteenth-century American literature, and Japanese anime.

Jonathan Osborn is a Toronto-based educator, researcher, and artist. He holds degrees in English, Dance, and Dance Studies (PhD, York University). Jonathan's SSHRC-funded dissertation, *Between Species: Choreographing Human and Animal Bodies*, focused on kinaesthetic human–animal relations in a variety of quotidian and artistic contexts, and his research on zoological gardens and virtual bodies appears in the collections *Zoo Studies: A New Humanities* (2019) and *Narrative in Performance* (2018). Jonathan focuses specifically on the solo form, and his choreographic works have received support from municipal-, provincial-, and national-funding bodies. His most recent creations—ARK (2017), ARCHE (2018), GARDEN (2018), and FOSSIL (2019)—are based upon the movements, rhythms, and forms of diverse nonhuman bodies staged within different urban cultural forums including zoos, gardens, and museums. Jonathan currently serves as adjunct faculty at York University in Toronto, Canada.

MK Pinder is a secondary school tutor and PhD candidate at Deakin University, Australia studying ecoGothic representation in video games. She has a Master of Arts in Writing and Literature and a Master of Communications in Digital Media. Her research interests are in the intersection of genre, transmedia narratives, and ecocriticism. She writes about nature, Gothic texts, and literary adaptation.

Catherine Pugh completed her PhD at the University of Essex and is now a writer and independent scholar. Primarily writing about horror and science fiction across cinema, television, theater, and video games, she is particularly fascinated by ideas of monstrosity and mental illness versus literary madness. Her research interests concern disability, mental illness/"madness," metamorphic monsters, and horror landscapes. She has contributed to various collections including "At Home in the Whedonverse: Essays on Domestic Space, Place and Life; Politics of Race, Gender, and Sexuality" in *The Walking Dead*, "Essays on the Television Series and

Comics; Vying for the Iron Throne: Essays on Power, Gender, Death and Performance" in HBO's *Game of Thrones* as well as online journals including *Studies in Gothic Fiction* and *Aeternum: The Journal of Contemporary Gothic Studies*. She is also a volunteer puppy raiser for Guide Dogs for the Blind (UK).

Heather Rolufs has an MA in English literature from the University of Northern British Columbia, a BA in English Literature, and a BEd in high school education. She has published articles on science fiction and fantasy, including *Battlestar Galactica* and Tim Burton's *Alice in Wonderland*. While finishing her graduate degree, she also worked at the BCSPCA as an Animal Care Attendant where she worked extensively with dogs and other domestic animals. Currently, she is teaching high school English at Southridge Senior School, a university preparatory school, in South Surrey B.C.

Monica Sousa received her BA (Honors) in English and her MA in English from Brock University in St. Catharines, Ontario. She is currently a PhD candidate in English at York University in Toronto, Ontario. Monica specializes in contemporary literature, and her research focuses on animal studies, posthumanism, and biotechnology in contemporary science fiction. Her research explores human and nonhuman animal relations in contemporary science fiction, with a focus on biotech animals (genetically modified animals or animals with cybernetic/robotic enhancements). She is interested in the ethics regarding how we treat, engage with, and ethically practice care toward these animals, and how literature allows us to understand these scenarios and imagine new possibilities. Monica has contributed chapters to a few book publications: *Posthumanist Perspectives on Literary and Cultural Animals* (2021); *Transhumanism and Posthumanism in Twenty-First Century Narrative* (2021); and *Critical Insights: Life of Pi* (2020). She has also presented at many conferences; some of these conferences include WorldCon, the European Association for Critical Animal Studies, the Academic Conference on Canadian Science Fiction and Fantasy, the Science Fiction Research Association, and the Association of Canadian College and University Teachers of English (ACCUTE).

Sumor Ziva Sheppard is an assistant professor of Spanish at Prairie View A & M University. She has published on peninsular theater's role in Spanish nation-building and its representations of hegemonic masculinity, religion, and antisemitism. Dr. Sheppard has published on various aspects of the esperpentos of Vasconcelos. She is currently completing a book project on the presence of fascism in Spain's Generation of 1898 and is a fall 2022 NYU-FRN scholar in residence in connection with that research.

www.ingramcontent.com/pod-product-compliance
Lightning Source LLC
Chambersburg PA
CBHW020117010526
44115CB00008B/858